Eisenhower Public Library

4613 N. Oketo Avenue

Harwood Heights, IL. 60706

708-867-7828

Wounds to Bind

Wounds to Bind

A Memoir of the
Folk-Rock Revolution

Jerry Burgan
with Alan Rifkin

Foreword by Sylvia Tyson

ROWMAN & LITTLEFIELD
Lanham • Boulder • New York • Toronto • Plymouth, UK

Published by Rowman & Littlefield
4501 Forbes Boulevard, Suite 200, Lanham, Maryland 20706
www.rowman.com

10 Thornbury Road, Plymouth PL6 7PP, United Kingdom

British Library Cataloguing in Publication Information Available

Library of Congress Cataloging-in-Publication Data

Burgan, Jerry, author.
  Wounds to bind : a memoir of the folk-rock revolution / Jerry Burgan with Alan Rifkin ; foreword by Sylvia Tyson.
        pages cm
  Includes index.
  ISBN 978-0-8108-8861-6 (cloth : alk. paper) — ISBN 978-0-8108-8862-3 (ebook)
  1. Burgan, Jerry. 2. Folk musicians—United States—Biography. 3. Rock musicians—United States—Biography. 4. Folk-rock music—History and criticism. I. Rifkin, Alan. II. Title.
  ML420.B8835A3 2014
  782.42166092—dc23
  [B]   2013043825

∞™ The paper used in this publication meets the minimum requirements of American National Standard for Information Sciences—Permanence of Paper for Printed Library Materials, ANSI/NISO Z39.48-1992.

Printed in the United States of America

When I woke up this morning
You were on my mind
And—you were on my mind
I've got troubles
I've got worries
I've got wounds to bind

So I went to the corner
Just to ease my pain
Said, just to ease my pain
I've got troubles
I've got worries
I came home again

But I woke up this morning
You were on my mind
And—you were on my mind

I've got troubles
I've got worries
I've got wounds to bind
And I've got a feeling
Down in my shoes
Said, way down in my shoes
That I've got to ramble
I've got to move on
I've got to walk away my blues

When I woke up this morning
You were on my mind
And—you were on my mind

I've got troubles
I've got worries
I've got wounds to bind

"You Were On My Mind," words and music
by Sylvia Fricker, adapted by We Five

Contents

17   Wounds Not Bound   185
18   Funeral for a Friend   195
19   Folk Songs and Stories   206

     Notes   211
     Acknowledgments   217
     Index   221
     About the Authors   231

Foreword

Sylvia Tyson

$\mathcal{I}$n the second week of August 1965, Ian and I had just finished playing four nights at the Golden Bear in Huntington Beach, California, and a night at the Hollywood Bowl with Judy Collins, and were driving north to Portland, Oregon, on Highway 101. We were cruising through Big Sur and had the car radio tuned to a pop station but weren't paying much attention. Suddenly we realized we were hearing my song "You Were On My Mind," but definitely not our version of it, and the DJ was predicting this was going to be a huge hit for a group called We Five. If I'd been driving, we'd have gone off the road.

Those were the bad old days when publishers took 100 percent of publishing royalties and often didn't bother to tell songwriters when a song had been covered. I believe someone in the office of our manager, Albert Grossman, had mentioned to me that the song had been recorded, but not who by, and I had no idea it was going to be a single, let alone a hit. What followed was one of those happy situations that songwriters pray for, but that seldom materialize.

A little background here. In 1962, the two of us were hanging out in Greenwich Village with a bunch of folkies including this kid from Minnesota called Bob Dylan, who'd impressed everyone by starting to write his own songs. I guess we all figured if he could do it, we could do it, and so we did. Ian started writing his first song, "Four Strong Winds," in Albert's apartment sometime early in 1962. Not to be outdone, I wrote my first song, "You Were On My Mind," a few months later. We immediately sent demos to Witmark and Sons, our publisher, but apparently they didn't see any urgency, because the songs weren't officially registered until the spring of '64 when our second Vanguard album came out with Ian's composition as the title song. In September of '64, we then recorded "You Were On My Mind" for our third album, *Northern Journey*. How We Five came to do the song is described in Jerry's book, so I'll leave the rest of the story to him.

Many songs remain very personal to the writer, but certain ones take on a life of their own. That was definitely the case with "You Were On My Mind." From the moment the We Five single took off, I felt as if the song had totally left my hands. The singer/songwriter phenomenon was just beginning back in the early '60s, and unlike the Cole Porters and George Gershwins of the '30s and '40s, the writers of hit songs in the '50s and '60s were seldom if ever recognized by the public. When I perform the song, I consistently meet people who are surprised to learn that I wrote it. In fact, at times it's been a drawback. When Ian and I toured England in '66 with Gordon Lightfoot and the Ian Campbell folk group, we were opening our segment of the show with "You Were On My Mind" and getting hisses and boos from the audience, because it had been a big copycat pop hit there for the singer Crispian St. Peters. The hardcore British folkies, having no idea I'd written it, weren't shy about letting us know what they thought of a folk group doing a pop song. To add insult to injury, St. Peters had naively put his name on it as writer, a misstep that Witmark and Sons swiftly rectified. This was only one of many covers by artists as diverse as Barry McGuire and Paul Anka, the most recent by Canadian singer/songwriter Serena Rider. There were successful French and Italian versions, and Italy is still one of the major royalty sources to this day (I get occasional plaintive calls from my accountant asking if I could write another one of those). It's been used several times as a theme for commercials.

As strange as it may seem, I don't recall ever meeting any of the members of We Five. For some reason, our paths never crossed, although it might have had something to do with the great east/west divide in the musical approach at the time. When Jerry initially contacted me a couple of years ago, he seemed a bit nervous. He had heard, way back when, that I was unhappy with the changes the group had made to the lyrics. It's true that I wasn't pleased with the changes, but I was well aware of the cold, hard facts of AM radio at the time and that the words "drunk and sick" wouldn't pass muster. In retrospect, I can hardly say I regret it. In the twenty-first-century world of Google and Twitter, I've read many comments from fans of the song saying how much it meant to them, including a lengthy analysis by some college professor who claimed (in the absence of the fatal words "drunk and sick") that the line "Went to the corner just to ease my pain" pertained to shooting heroin, and that the "whoa, whoa" parts were actually "woe, oh woe." I would suggest to him that the song was written in the very early '60s and that, other than a little grass, booze was the drug of choice for most of us. Heroin and coke didn't rear their ugly heads until a lot more money was being earned.

And it's the moment when big dollars entered the equation that this book deals with: the beginnings of a lucrative merger between folk and pop/rock, when that east/west divide started to narrow and the rough-edged lyrics and melodies of the hardcore folkies gained broader appeal (and even some Hollywood glamour). Although We Five provides the context, this is much more than the simple biography of a band. Jerry Burgan, along with Alan Rifkin, has provided an entertaining and informative look into a transformative scene that later added country music to the mix and blossomed into groups like the Byrds, the Flying Burrito Brothers, and Creedence Clearwater Revival.

In closing, although I've written other successful songs, it's been an extraordinarily wild and eventful ride for this one. A couple of years back I was chatting with an old friend who's written many iconic songs. He was criticizing me for allowing "You Were On My Mind" to be used for commercials. "Easy for you to say," I replied, adding, "for Christ's sake, love, it's not *War and Peace*; it's a pop song!" Easy for me to say, too, but it's been much more than that. It has seen me through being a single mom, paying off an 18 percent mortgage, and establishing a solo career, among other trials. All I can say to We Five is "Thanks a million, guys."

Permissions

We are grateful for permission to quote from previously published material:

"You Were On My Mind," words and music by Sylvia Tyson, Warner-Chappell, used by permission.

"Rifleman's Song at Bennington," traditional, arranged by John Stewart, used by permission.

"With Their Eyes on the Stars," words and music by John Stewart, used by permission.

"Lonely Afternoon," words and music by Jerry Burgan, Burgansongs, used by permission.

"What's Going On," words and music by Mike Stewart, used by permission.

"I Can Never Go Home Again," words and music by John Stewart, used by permission.

"Hallowed Ground," traditional, arranged by John Stewart, used by permission.

"For Old Times," words and music by Jerry and Debbie Burgan, Burgansongs, used by permission.

"Tattered Hand Me Downs," words and music by Jerry and Debbie Burgan, Burgansongs, used by permission.

"Sing Out," words and music by Mike Stewart, Alfred, used by permission.

PART ONE

· *1* ·

Foreshocks

I am drawn to the sound of an acoustic stringed instrument like metal to a magnet—and I was aware of that almost before I became aware of who I was. But not just one person strumming. It was, first, the richness of guitar sounds—wooden, earth-toned—and then the complexity of two slightly different rhythms played at once, one on top of the other, a unity that in some ways couldn't hope to last, and so every minute that it did was like the uplift that the Wright Brothers must have felt at Kitty Hawk: transcendent. Fleeting. You could feel it in the calypso-folk guitar layerings of the Tarriers,[1] in the rich, island pickings and strummings that accompanied Harry Belafonte, in the rockabilly of the Everly Brothers: the thrill of "Bye, Bye Love," that *jump*, the thing that crawled up your back and left you smiling like a dope, came from two guitars doing not exactly the same thing—you might get close with one person, but you wouldn't arrive there alone, any more than you'd find harmony in one voice singing.

And who harmonized better than the Everlys? For me, an eleven-year-old California kid in 1957, that song had it all—a sad, sweet melody masked in sunny rhythm, driven by two brothers playing off each other—way more appealing to me than the harder, trudging, snare-drum cadence of their later and bigger hit, "Cathy's Clown."

So I would look for it. I'd look for the song late at night on a crystal set that I'd brought into the room I shared with my father, who slept apart from my mother—this was Catholic birth control. We lived in Pomona, about thirty miles inland from L.A., in a two-story farmhouse with a full basement, a barn, chicken coops, and a stable, around which once existed walnut groves and pastures, and the closets were so huge they had windows. But there were only three bedrooms: three sisters in one, mom nursing the

3

baby in another, and my dad and me in the third as the simplest way to deal, however awkward. Music was a rare common ground between the two of us. He'd even brought home a ukulele once, which I immediately began to play, so he brought home a four-string tenor guitar, too, with the same result. If it strummed, I liked it. So the magic of hearing the Everlys strum and sing in that room was partly that music connected me to my father—and him to me. The fact that the crystal set needed no power source, that you just stuck in an earbud and heard sounds vibrating free in space, was part of the magic too.

Then my parents bought a hi-fi, with twelve-inch speaker and a tweeter, and for the first time I heard the high percussive sounds that a rhythm guitarist had to make on records in order to mix with whatever the drummer was doing on the high hat. Michael Stewart—my boyhood buddy and rival, We Five's creative genius—would later teach me how that worked. If these accents mixed, if they struck against one another on that percussive edge, they produced what to me is the spark of life. Motown founder Berry Gordy made sure that at his studios pipes and xylophones were always on hand, anything tonal that was also bright, to make the rhythms dance as they combined. It's why Latin music stirs you, the complexity and sparkle, the thing that makes it snap. If you close your eyes, listening, the layers can overwhelm you, but see it live and you're surprised that it's often just separate people doing simple things.

Michael and I caught some of that feeling the first time we played together in eighth grade. He was on banjo[2] and I was on my tenor guitar, two white suburban kids singing, with all clueless conviction, the escape song of runaway slaves: "Follow the Drinking Gourd." (It would be six years before Martin Luther King Jr. led the first freedom marchers from Selma to Montgomery.) Mike played an E minor chord, and I followed. We switched to A minor. And then back. Switching back and forth—together—we started to strum in time. Tentatively at first, but then with more conviction. As we got more comfortable with the basic up-and-down strokes, we began to add individual accents and emphasis—still never departing from the basic rhythm we were both playing. It was like two kids on a teeter-totter. You could get into a groove and play for hours.

I also remember wondering how far you could take embellishment till complexity brought it down. Once, in 1963, the two of us worked with John Stewart of the Kingston Trio (a God to me, if I didn't know him already as Michael's older brother) on a short subject called "With Their Eyes on the Stars." It was a NASA film that connected pioneer history to Kennedy's call for a space race, all through images and song. Today, when there are as many ways to pick a fight musically as there are personal playlists, the swell of inspiration and unity that folk music used to raise in the average man's heart can seem impossibly long ago. But when we listened on playback to "The Riflemen's Song at Bennington," with the whole spirit of a nation foretold in the dare of an earlier generation,

> Why come ye hither, Redcoats,
> Your minds what madness fills?
> In our valleys there is danger,
> And there's danger in our hills.
> Oh hear ye not the ringing
> Of the bugle wild and free?
> Full soon you'll know the singing
> Of the rifle from the tree

something odd stuck out, a freaky flourish that I'd thrown into the rhythm.

John Stewart called out, "Hey! Who did *that?*"

I gathered myself, and confessed. . . and that was when John congratulated me for the energy of what I'd brought to the track. Yet my first impulse had been to deny it.

Both feelings were doing battle within me. Sometimes music was daring me, pulling me outward to a world of new ideas. But I also wanted to be grounded, held in place. Music and radio in our home meant stability, goodness, and right—we'd had no TV at all till third grade. (My mother to the end of her life, even with Alzheimer's, could still harmonize on cue.) Maybe other kids were getting screamed at when they played their records at home, but music was never about rebellion for me. Instead of "Rock Around the Clock" or "Hound Dog," I liked "Love Me Tender" and (for something up, but not edgy) "Don't Be Cruel." There was a softness I always craved, with whatever is the opposite of an aversion.

Ears were made for sound, eyes for light. Some colors agreed with your eyes and others shocked them. The same was true for sound. I wanted harmony. I wanted synergy, not just brute strength. I wanted all sorts of things to agree.

★ ★ ★

They were hard things to name, looking back. But they could be summed up, maybe, by a series of records.

"Mockingbird Hill" was sweet lyricism. Les Paul played guitar, and Mary Ford was on vocal, each doing harmony with themselves. Even more than Paul's revolutionary guitar work, I remember the eerie timber of that one voice split in two registers, like siblings whose voices vibrate unnaturally the same. The science of multi-track recording had made this effect possible. I didn't know why, but it left chills.

"Dark Moon" by Gale Storm (1957) stood for mystery. Much like "You Were On My Mind," it both implied and kept shrouded its lost-lover melodrama. What turned my head was the acoustic guitar, the minor key, ethereal, the way that it wafted along.

"Party Doll" was an early rock hit my dad told me not to play. It targeted the same pre-teen longing as Buddy Holly and Marty Robbins, but the real reason it got air time (I myself wasn't drawn by the rock element) was that it made the get-me-laid language of black R&B acceptable to white radio. Here, I could rebel without seeming to rebel . . . so what if the guy liked to party? I sang it to a pair of girls two years older and growing boobs, and got to watch the way it made them giggle—my back foot behind the line of innocence, because nothing in the words *make love* was technically illicit.

Belafonte's "Jamaica Farewell," in which the singer left his girl in Kingston Town, was the organic, acoustic, textured approach to calypso, as versus the steel-drum and electric edge of today's reggae. Even the sadness in the arrangement was smooth—it was sadness that slid past you like a kayak. How bad, then, could sadness be?

The gallows song "Tom Dooley"[3] (a condemned man having taken his lover's life) was earth-bound sorrow, an eternal lover's triangle with weeping choruses—while the vocal to "All in the Game" ("Many a tear . . .") had so similar a whisky-and-smoke quality that, as a kid, I actually thought the two singers were the same. The embrace of fate seemed similar too . . . that strange, almost brimming release that comes from a sorrow owned and shared.

One day, for what it's worth, "You Were On My Mind" would combine every one of these elements.

But what I couldn't have put into words in 1957 was the cultural earthquake about to hit. One moment, music was in a strange lull. Folky-novelty songs had begun to scrape bottom— "How Much Is That Doggy in the Window?"—and pop meant, almost exclusively, big bands and Sinatra. In 1957, as if overnight, the Kingston Trio took simple earthy music into the educated mainstream, inventing the college tour along the way, while black music desegregated the pop charts, or began to. I could not have read the signs of this socio-musical shift very precisely, but some people did. They could tell there was something completely new going on—one part Elvis Presley, one part Drifters—in music, in the culture, in the demographics of millions of postwar kids coming of age all at once.

Independent producers stepped in, not just because they'd tapped into the sound of a new generation but because new, accessible equipment, some of it built on Les Paul's multi-track technology,[4] meant that soon anyone could make a good-sounding record beneath the radar of the commercial giants. That freedom fed the music, and the music fed the freedom, the sort of thing that happens in every generation—but no generation of Americans was ever seventy million strong before. And every generation is sure that no older generation ever really knew what it was like to be young. Change itself was speeding up, which seems like a cliché nowadays, but if anyone was talking about the fact back then, it was not with any sense of being used to it. By 1965, Fred Astaire, a man standing for two or three decades all at once, wearing a black tuxedo that would seem dated by the end of the hour, would introduce We Five on television's "Hollywood Palace" with a Houdini snap of the fingers. "Just like that!" he said with his gaunt twinkle, snapping fingers for the camera. (You can watch the whole clip today on YouTube.) "I think the biggest change that's taken place within the entertainment business is the speed with which stars are born. A couple of weeks ago, five youngsters from San Francisco made a recording, and *just like that* [snap!], it became one of the top musical hits in the country." We were thrown on stage the way a dream throws you out of your house with no clothes. Overnight, recalls my bandmate Pete Fullerton, "John Sebastian of the Lovin' Spoonful was flinging his new hit 45 to me from a driver's side window on Columbus Avenue." Within a matter of days, you could come up with a song, work out an arrangement, and place it before the world. And you didn't have to book an orchestra into Capitol's Studio A anymore to do so. You could record it in a basement in San Francisco.

1965

When Folk Met Rock

$\mathcal{O}$ur recording of "You Were On My Mind" was a fusion of what had been mutually exclusive musical forms—acoustic folk and electric rock—that exploded into the world in June 1965 to top the charts in what came to be called folk-rock. I've never been comfortable saying it was the first folk-rock hit, because the Byrds' cover of "Mr. Tambourine Man" broke in April, the same month we were recording, and the Beau Brummels, the Searchers, Jackie DeShannon, and even the Kingston Trio had all been coming close. But it would be late July before Dylan caused a storm by plugging in an electric guitar at the Newport Folk Festival. Which tells you that the waters were still pretty uncharted. I don't know that my personal contribution was anything that history will call significant, but I've certainly been witness to a lot that was. This whole memoir is largely about where that revolution in music and culture took some really young people, especially my childhood buddy, Mike Stewart, and me—how we grew up and got there, and how new it all was, and what it all briefly seemed to promise. And later, what it cost us. At the time, it was just this very special, very timely song.

We recorded it in a studio that was a bunch of alcoves built within a triangle, because Columbus Tower was a triangle too, a seven-story flatiron across from City Lights Books on the wedge formed by Columbus, Kearny, and Jackson Streets. Dim lights and padded burlap were supposed to turn the shape into easy intimacy and creative focus—the kind of nook where a trio of vocalists could sing facing each other half in darkness—which is how Frank Werber, the Holocaust survivor who managed the Kingston Trio since they were frat boys at nearby Menlo College, had it built. His production offices were six floors above, and every inch of that basement seemed to serve double purposes: if you turned right after leaving the elevator you would hit the restrooms that were shared with Zim's Burgers, whose kitchen was one floor up a back stairwell.

We were standing around, Mike Stewart and Beverly Bivens and Pete Fullerton and Bob Jones and me, chatting and explaining things to the drummer, Jerry Granelli, a jazz percussionist on loan from Vince Guaraldi. It was Vince Guaraldi whose piano cadences would give the soundtrack to "A Charlie Brown Christmas" both its holiday bustle ("The Peanuts Theme") and its melancholy snowfall ("Christmas Time Is Here"), and the brushes that slid ever so sleepily off the cymbal in the background were Granelli's.

At the risk of stereotyping: a few drummers like Buddy Miles and Ronnie Tutt (Elvis's drummer in the post-movie era) have the mass to play with a lot of power. But playing takes such kinetic stamina that while drummers may be strong—even muscular—they are just as often thin, even wiry. Jerry Granelli was that way. He had a scrappy look not unlike George Carlin's: slight with thinning hair and a Zen twinkle in his eye. Aged thirty or so, a good ten years older than the rest of us, he had a tremendous amount of drive, but the energy was more that of an overwound music box than a Humvee. He was a perfect match to the outrageous peaks and valleys of "You Were On My Mind," because he understood finesse. Yet there was nothing passive about him. Even when playing subtler sections of the song, he never lost intensity. I often visualize drummers as stationary dancers with their feet, arms, hands—even their heads—all moving in different directions, but still in perfect synchronicity with the groove; Jerry in action looked like a Greg Hines or Sammy Davis Jr. marionette, tap-dancing while strapped to a drum throne.

"What's next?" Werber called from the smoke-tinted booth.

We had just finished recording "Cast Your Fate to the Wind," a Guaraldi jazz melody that traced big atmospheric major seventh chords, giving it a searching, Charlie Brown quality of its own.

"A rock tune," Michael Stewart explained. He leaned in toward Granelli, forelock drooping over mad-scientist glasses. Much the way women can dress down to mousey, I often thought Mike dressed down to waifish. Maybe it was to minimize comparisons to his tall, good-looking, erstwhile Elvis-imitator brother in the Kingston Trio.

"This one's a rock song," he told Granelli again. On his guitar, he showed the drummer how all the emphasis in the rhythm was just before the downbeat, instead of on it.

Granelli—virtuoso that he was—began calling out the rhythm that Michael and I had laid down on guitar: "AND-ONE. . . ." And he began to play what seemed like a succession of nonstop fills and rolls on the high hat and snare, all of this over a Phil Spector kick-drum pattern, but with the ANDs out front, drawing the beat forward—

JUST LIKE THAT.

"When I woke up this morning . . ."

JUST LIKE THAT, as Fred Astaire might have said, snapping his fingers, we were no longer a folk band. We went from being a late-fifties folk music ensemble (albeit with electrified acoustic twelve-string) to something new entirely.

Folk musicians, rhythmically speaking, are more used to following a singer. This was different—practically a drum solo within our structured vocals, forcing us to get in flow and stay there: it was like grabbing hold of a moving train. For a split second, I caught bassist Pete Fullerton's eyes—we were fascinated and apprehensive. Did we even know how to hang on from here?

The funny thing is, we'd almost had that drum track in our heads before we added drums. It was suggested in the guitars and bass, or in the gap between them—that was the rhythm that Jerry Granelli was now driving, relentlessly. All of this synergy has a certain inevitability about it when you hear the song now. It's impossible to imagine it not happening.

At some point, Werber exclaimed, "This is getting good!" Then we all stepped up to face our microphones, ready to try Take One. But the record should show that where "You Were On My Mind" really entered the physical world, the crowning at the end of the canal, was that moment when Mike Stewart leaned in beside Jerry Granelli to show a rock rhythm to a drummer who'd been versed in classical jazz.

Recently, I came across a picture of the aging Granelli, seated alone in what looks like an upscale, exposed-brick pub. He has a white mustache, bracelets and rings, a red corduroy shirt, and a velvet serpent of a paisley scarf, with a kind of stricken humanity and warmth about his eyes. I've read that he not only toured with Ornette Coleman and Charlie Haden, but also performed in studio with acts as hilariously disconnected as Sly Stone and Glen Campbell. (Not to mention opening for Lenny Bruce and a stripper in the lean San Francisco years.) Lately, he's been collaborating with the rap DJ Stinkin' Rich. It's interesting to consider how these far-flung elements might once have been compressed into one place, one time.

But for all that Jerry Granelli added to the dawn of folk-rock, he was just the culmination to a months-long obsession taking place in the mind of Mike Stewart.

★ ★ ★

Until this recording, Mike's creativity had never gone farther than the usual re-harmonizing of all the spirituals and folk tunes we'd been picking up in our journey as a band. For "My Favorite Things," he'd arranged voices as though they were strings in a Bach quartet.

Yet producers kept telling us (so often it made Mike wince), "You guys are good, but you need a rock song." Mike was trying to work out exactly what that meant. We'd added Bob Jones's electric guitar. But still we needed the right composition.

"You Were On My Mind" was the first time I can think of that Mike Stewart flat-out reinvented a song.

It was more country than rock when Canadian folksinger Sylvia Fricker composed it for the astonishing 1964 Ian and Sylvia album *Northern Journey*— a folk lament over the purity of a moving bass line and three chords that sounded as plain and deliberate as if she were summoning courage to play them. ("Got up this morning/You were on my mind") A sudden reiteration ("And—you were on my mind"), sung as vulnerably as a bird who fell from a nest, lent the song an air of almost heartsick acceptance. "Got some aches and/Got some pains and" hinted of a possibly more disturbing back story. It also had words about going down to the corner (for what?), which, combined with an uncensored nod to vengeance drinking ("I got drunk and/I got sick and"), added the kind of realism that critics who look for roots and bridges to the later 1960s still revere. That was one claim to the era.

The other claim, even two years before the Summer of Love, was more eclectic, choral, floral, and warm. It was Kingston Trio folk, combined with driving rhythm and electric twelve-string jangle, combined further with Brian Wilson's Beach Boy experiments with melody and harmony. For the better part of a year, Mike had been listening to equal parts Wilson and the Beatles.

"You Were On My Mind," if it succeeded, would fuse together all these elements. It would be a rock song. And a pop song. And a folk song. And a jazz song. And a blues song. All blended into the emerging youth spirit of the time (and with an amazing chick singing it). It would be the Seekers, but with balls, a "whining song," but with release. It would be twelve-string folk, but with an electrified razor-edge. It had this amazing dynamic ascension, which Mike referred to in cartographic terms: "He wanted to start real quiet," says Bob Jones, "then for the song to get really big, then go back down to nothing, and then come back in the last thirty-five seconds all the way to where we'd been—he had this whole vision of the emotional map of the song."

On top of all that, it would be an *anthem*—with enough power in the hands-whanging-on-dashboard finale to answer whatever yearning was in Michael's spirit and in the spirit of millions of Americans who still find magic in the song. That was part of it too. There was a mood this song tapped, and a pain that Mike wanted to transcend, which, frankly, I was too shallow to grasp at the time. I'd known Mike since we were eleven years old, and over the years I know that I hurt him myself, numerous times—Michael simply had a need to go beyond pain that in those days I could never have understood.

• 3 •

1956

Kids with Guitars

When I met him in Catholic school, he was a bookworm. He had horn-rimmed glasses and inhalers and stayed indoors if the weather was smoggy. I was a thick-haired kid destined to go bald; Mike's hair managed to look thinning even in childhood, and he never lost a lock of it. I went out for track—he went out for equipment manager.

A few years later, maybe in honor of the Kennedys, he started playing touch football on the lawn. And in the 1970s, when producing the *Piano Man* album for Billy Joel, he entered a yuppie-shark kind of phase that included garage handball with a volleyball. I think he liked that he could beat you by playing the angles, by preventing you from making a return—it didn't require power as much as cunning. At his house, while my wife got to stay comfortably indoors with his wife, I'd have to go outside and be subjected to his prowess. They lived in Studio City then, where the heat and smog could get merciless. Chasing a volleyball on burning-hot cement was never my idea of fun, but Mike took great delight in it. Being beaten was the price I paid for friendship, and I came to accept my time on the driveway as penance for some of the pain I'd brought on him in the past.

But when he transferred from public school to St. Joseph's, there were plenty of reasons for the jocks to make fun of him. He arrived on a cloud of privilege, stepping out of the new air-conditioned Lincoln that his mother drove, and what his father called a job was training trotters. Even his jokes had an unfamiliar cleverness. There was one about an American Indian installing lights in an outhouse—"the first person to wire a head for a reservation."

Later his jokes became elaborate, staged things. Plenty of kids thought about placing a dollop of peanut butter in a boys' room stall to fool passersby, but Mike went through with it, arranging the scene to the point of pushing through a crowd of spectators to taste a sample. ("Looks like shit, smells like shit . . . no, it's peanut butter.")

I might never have become friends with Mike Stewart at all except for sixth-grade boys choir. Our director was Gil Robbins, father of the future actor Tim Robbins, and in class Mr. Robbins liked to blow our minds with dusty exotica, things like foot-driven pump organs and biographies of Beethoven. (Gil recognized there was a creative payoff to showing us a world outside St. Joseph's, whether the artifacts came from the cathedrals of Vienna or a cabin in Virginia.) When Gil landed in the Cumberland Three alongside Mike's older brother John, not yet in the Kingston Trio, Mike got John's old banjo. He showed up at my door a couple of days after eighth-grade graduation with the banjo and a copy of *Folksing*, the folksinger's pocketbook, with knobby-jointed cartoons on the cover by *Mad Magazine*'s Kelly Freas.

The banjo was a longneck with a capo at the third fret, and when we tried a few of the songs, anything I may have learned before about guitar chords simply vanished. The only solution I could come up with was to tune my four-string tenor guitar like a banjo, and play the same chord fingerings as Michael. But it worked.

I don't remember how long we played that first day. I do know that our fingertips cracked, and our voices were hoarse, and my parents rejoiced: I'd been avoiding the guitar for two full years to protest the teacher my parents got me—a guy who kept wanting me to play electrified boogie. When my mom saw that Michael and I weren't just going to strum for a few minutes and then go ride bikes, she knew something important had happened. Each time she came in to offer us cookies or something to drink, the look of pride on her face was over the top. "You could be on Lawrence Welk!" she beamed.

That was high praise from her, even if it was the furthest thing from our goal.

★ ★ ★

Mike was a better student at St. Joseph's—he had the third highest IQ in our class, upwards of 150—and, I later realized, a shakier believer. I was religious, and not just for show. By the time of my first communion at age six or seven, I was contemplating how my evil works displeased God. I felt wrong about lying, or stealing gum from the supermarket, and most of what the nuns taught only seemed consistent with how I felt. Baptized as an infant, I had never had a chance to accept or reject.

But I could recite the catechism questions. I served as an altar boy and sang in the choir. I knew that we all fall short of perfection, but I was able to push back guilt and just enjoy whatever life sent my way. Without nuns or priests to remind me I was a sinner, what was out of sight could be also out of mind. Yet faith, as a word, had always been there, unquestioned, like heaven, or hell—or France, for that matter.

My most profound sense of what salvation meant came once a year on Good Friday, which concluded with a three-hour service. It felt like an eternity, though it only ran till 3 p.m., most of it spent on our knees as we joined in the Stations of the Cross. "It hurts me to prick my finger with a pin," we would read out loud. "How much more must those nails have hurt as they were driven through Your hands?"

Not that I embraced the nuns' view of pop culture. In fifth grade, one of them caught me singing Tennessee Ernie Ford's "Sixteen Tons." A slight blonde girl named Penny and I had been serenading about fifty students before class began (postwar classrooms were getting as clogged as bus stations on a holiday weekend). "Here she comes!" someone cried, and we stopped mid-verse. But the room was still abuzz, and in stepped Sister Septemia, demanding to know what was happening.

"Penny and Jerry were singing," came the reply.

There are women who look good even in a nun's habit. Sister Septemia wasn't one of them. She was one of those knuckle-busters who would call you to the front of the class for any meager violation. So I was surprised when she didn't erupt. Instead, she inquired what song we were singing.

Sheepishly, we told her the title.

"Okay, singers. Let's hear it. Maybe we can all sing."

Ridiculously, we took her curiosity at face value. After all, she liked to sing. We knew that. She liked "Sidewalks of New York."

It was when we got to the line about not being able to come to heaven because the company store owns your soul that Septemia cut us off.

"You can't tell St. Peter when to call you!" she reprimanded us, adding, "And if he called you today, *you wouldn't get in.*"

I still don't know if she meant it. But many of us heard her words as a Church pronouncement. Penny and I protested that the lyric was more like dialogue in a drama, not a statement of belief, but Sister Septemia wouldn't hear it.

It was the first time I recall even being tempted to doubt a church representative. And plenty of classmates were happy to tell me how stupid they considered her stance.

It took me another ten years before I openly agreed with them. For the time being, I began pulling D's. I didn't quite join the school heretics, but I didn't care to do the work the teachers expected me to do when they expected me to do it.

Mike was more adaptable. And he had the Joycean gift of knowing how to taunt religious believers without seeming to be taunting. As we entered high school, he would tease our friend Tom Finsterbach, a brilliant future Jesuit and Stanford researcher, about his claims to purity: "C'mon, Tom— you've never done it even *once?*"

★ ★ ★

Of course, he had his own gospel—our whole generation did. It was a loose-knit idealism that looked for hypocrisy to reject and a banner of conviction to march under. In music, it combined the authenticity of folk with the borrowed soul of the Negro spiritual, whose rhythms made it a form of R&B. On one thing Mike and I could always agree: a good song was a good song. The first one he ever wrote for his brother John and the Kingston Trio was a spiritual with a hot gospel clap:

> You gotta [clap!] Sing out! If you wanna get to heaven, gotta [clap!]
> Sing Out! Join in and pray!

He didn't care if the line was about prayer or tiptoeing through the tulips. Those were days when Elvis Presley could sing "How Great Thou Art" to a popular audience. It's almost impossible to find such crossovers today.

As for Catholic music, it meant a Latin mass: designed not to wake up anything carnal. Or Gregorian chants, an exercise of pure, almost mathematical devotion.

Yet the same priest who taught us those forms also encouraged Mike and me to play at school assemblies. So we did. We made our way through high-school forming bands, singing things like "Oleana"—a folk song with nonsense rhymes that none of our peers cared about. All its energy was squandered, because you couldn't dance to it.

So while our audiences knew we were technically good, we didn't register with our age group the way the Kingston Trio, five years older, registered with theirs. It was rock bands who began to get attention—not us.

I tried to push the boundaries in other small ways. Canvas tennis shoes were my notion of a rebellion, along with white or tan jeans. Leather only was their rule. Since the Kingston Trio had begun wearing Italian pull-on boots, well before the Beatles reached America, I went and bought a pair myself, as a *gotcha* to the faculty . . . but the football players harassed me: they called the shoes cockroach killers (a slur against Mexicans) or simply queer.

Outside, we heard clues and whispers of all the grownup things we didn't know. One of the sounds that called to me in 1961 was "Angel on My Shoulder" by Shelby Flint, a wishing-well song that dreamed about love from the too-young side of sexual knowledge. I was aching for the same powerful thing the singer was, with no knowledge of what that meant. I just loved her wispy voice and her deft accompaniment on guitar, and when DJ Bill Ballance announced that she'd written the song herself as a teenager (she recorded it at twenty-one, innocence and mastery revolving in one tossed coin), the best I could do was to learn to play it. Ballance also chuckled about what other secrets besides pennies might be found in that girl's pocket.

What I yearned for was to be hip.

But I had little sense of hip beyond the Kingston Trio. Hip was still whatever Mike's brother, John Stewart, did. Playing banjo in the world's most famous touring band. Being a freedom marcher. Managing to answer Kennedy's call to national service in a way that was more than firing off guns with a flag in one hand. And then, in the summer of '61, before my junior year, when Mike and I flew to Northern California, I got to see for the first time the way the Kingston Trio actually lived, although that wasn't my purpose for the trip.

I was setting off to Japan as a sea cadet.

★ ★ ★

If I was going to follow in the footsteps of my Navy uncle, this made total sense. In fact, I had done similar things before, cool things, helping on a schooner, and even a minesweeper, though never for long enough to know what it was to live the life. This time, I was going on a one-month trip from Treasure Island, in San Francisco Bay, to Japan and back on a troop transport—

But first: the magic prelude. The glimpse of an alternative life.

Here was John Stewart, picking us up at the airport on the eve of my *bon voyage*, and driving us north to Marin, to the top of the top of a hill, to the home of Bob Shane, the Kingston Trio's heart and soul and hushed boom of a voice, that voice I'd heard on "Tom Dooley" years before, now an actual human with sports cars in his driveway and guitars hanging from his living room walls. The view looked down upon, and beyond, all the bridges of the San Francisco Bay. Here we listened to the Trio practice three hours straight, preparing for John's September debut with them at the Hollywood Bowl. Was I blown away? I got to see the difference between "singing" and singing like you meant it. I got to see *conviction*, got to feel and hear the un-miked power and energy of world-class performers holding nothing back. These were crucial rehearsals for the group, undertaken as if that living room were the Hollywood Bowl itself. And at the same time, for all their intensity, they were doing it funny, doing it light. It was their life.

Then—being forced to pull myself away. Saying goodbye to John and Mike. My Sea Cadet friend Michael Higdon and I rode with his mother to the Navy base, and I changed into my uniform, stepped aboard, and entered, I think, a time machine. With a head full of music, I stepped into a world of bowling alleys with manual pin spotters. Sweaty engine rooms, swabbing decks, soldiers puking while waiting in mess lines. No one on board had a clue where I had been the night before, what I'd seen on that hilltop in Marin, and we headed toward Japan, and the emptiness set in.

It unfolded that we were on an Army ship, not a Navy ship, which struck me as sloppy planning, and no one offered us a taste of any activity more romantic than working in the engine room, which strikes me as deceptive recruiting. A few days' bad weather pushed me to a breaking point before I asked a chaplain if he had a guitar. He didn't, but he knew someone in the troop band who did. It was a cheap electric Silvertone, virtually the same instrument I'd rebelled against when taking lessons. Definitely not meant for folk, but it was better than nothing. Then one of the lieutenants—a would-be Vic Damon condemned to a military life by a family with six generations from West Point—knew some Kingston Trio songs, so instead of waiting on tables, Mike Higdon and I got to play in a vocal group that gave breaks to the soldiers' band. It was a reminder of the mainland, only faded, like a wrinkled love letter you unfold in a foxhole.

When the soldiers played, we got to dance with a variety of girls in evening gowns, which seemed to magnify the sense of unreality: there was plenty of delusional, B-movie talk among the guys waiting tables about their plans to meet up with the officers' daughters. (The possibility that officers brought their wives and kids with them to foreign shores hadn't occurred to me, but it made perfect sense: they'd be in Korea for two years.) This ballroom had wood paneling and soft lighting like a night club, trying to contrast with the gray bulkheads and watertight hatches everywhere else. Military people bring their own world with them.

The closest thing I've ever felt to being lost in outer space occurred in the moments we were allowed on deck at night. If the sky was moonless, with only blackness in all directions and the enormity of the universe over my head, the fragility of life, and of my place in it, would hit me like a bomb—hardest on the night we watched the movie *On the Beach* beneath the stars. Here were two thousand soldiers who'd left everything and everyone to cross the ocean in a ship. When the movie's submarine crew resolved to make the most of the time left before the nuclear fallout reached them, I thought: *What if we got back to San Francisco and all of it was gone?* I wish I could say that my faith gave me strength, but I don't even remember it as a factor. I just felt unimportant and alone.

In Yokosuka, on the south end of Tokyo Bay, I went to Thieves' Alley. It was the first time I ever drank, the first time I'd gone a month without church (and I noticed I didn't die or go to Hell), the first time I'd seen a condom, let alone been issued one, but I chose deliberately not to follow any barmaids into back rooms—I was the straight-arrow kid. Strolling outside in Thieves' Alley, I saw some nylon-stringed guitars, forerunner of all the glossy instruments to come that were copies of Martins and Goyas, but an ocean removed from the source.

I was not a sailor who came to life at sea. I knew that I'd had an adventure, but there was nothing endearing about it. On our last night out, I picked up San Francisco's pop station, KSFO, and the DJs were talking about the Kingston Trio. I decided that when I got back to Pomona, I would resign the Sea Cadets. My dad and my uncle would be disappointed, but I did not see Annapolis or a life at sea in my future.

Mike Stewart came with my mom to LAX and brought my guitar, and we sang together all the way home.

· 4 ·

The First Time Ever

*W*e'd been performing a couple of years by then—at women's clubs, music stores, and talent shows. We'd added a third player, Mike Strub, who had a good Martin 00028, basically his qualification for joining. We'd been learning at the feet of John Stewart, who would come to town and show us things he was working on; John brought me my first D'Angelico guitar strings, and he taught me to finger-pick, that gallop of fingers like five soloists at once. "He's going too fast—what chords are those?" Mike whispered to me one time, scrambling to transcribe the chords to "Molly Malone," and John laughed because they weren't chords at all; they were passing notes bridging one chord to the next. The simplest composition could get richer and richer like that. We were learning that music could be both rootsy and gorgeous, a lush garden, and all this seemed very new to our generation.

We learned how to sustain driving power in the spaces between notes. Folkies were big on using the guitar body like a bongo to tap out rhythms; the chords in the soundtrack for *High Noon* came from hitting the bridge with an open palm, fusing drum and guitar into a single, dreadful sound that pushed the story along like a heartbeat. That snare-like *snap* on Kingston Trio records eluded me till John showed me how to relax the left hand while letting my right palm meet the strings at the same time, and I'd unlocked the secret of the sound that distinguished the Trio, pulsing but not yet rock, from the softer Brothers Four.

Mike brought a portable stereo record player to one rehearsal and set it on the floor, the speakers barely a foot apart and, incomprehensibly, *facing each other.* "You're not gonna believe this!" he promised, as I lay suspiciously in the designated spot. It was typical for Mike to fly in ecstatic about some new universe of knowledge he'd plundered—you'd think he just discovered gravity. Then he dropped the needle and I could feel a huge smile spread across

19

my face as Bob Shane *and* his guitar, with John and Nick on my left and right, appeared just as clearly as though the three were kneeling around me—or with us back at Shane's house. Virtually every folksinger my age made a similar discovery, and note by note we learned to copy what we heard.

Through each new development, you could see Mike planning, exploring, taking notes . . . singing with anyone willing to try a new part that had just burst into his brain . . . branching out.

Also he had inklings of the girl-singer sound that was trying to be born. Or maybe it was just hormones. Acting goofy one night after a contest at Claremont High School (with our future bassist Pete Fullerton watching from the audience), Mike wanted a volunteer to be a standup microphone to show how three people stood around one. Being Mike, he seized the available arm of a large-breasted girl with long blonde hair. Her name was Sue Ellen Davies, and it turned out she could sing.

The meeting looked accidental, but I don't think Mike had failed to calculate: she had talent; she had a vocal range that could swing from soprano to high alto to another, deeper, *ballsier* tenor range that was something else entirely. And she made us look great. A year later, when Peter, Paul and Mary—beating us to fame—had their first hit with "Lemon Tree," Mike sarcastically referred to them as Winkin', Blinkin', & Knobs.

In a short time, Strub was gone—for him, music had been only one more obligation in a schedule that always had him setting his watch—and Susie projected herself into the life of the Ridgerunners. We started playing in Upland at a coffee house called the Meeting Place, literally the multipurpose room for the Sierra Swim Club.

We also hung around the Folk Music Centre in Claremont—although the owner, Charles Chase, branded us as commercial, because we emulated the Kingston Trio instead of someone like coal-miner's daughter Hedy West, whom he considered pure. A Merlin-like figure at eighty-nine, with steely tangles of shoulder-length hair, Chase was still making regular appearances at the store until he died in 2004. He influenced two generations of noted musicians, including David Lindley, Chris Darrow, and his own grandson, Ben Harper, and was the source of John Stewart's first banjo—helping prolong, despite his own distaste, the Trio's monstrous success.

Mike and I started dropping in on the L.A. scene, first in clubs, then visiting friends and musicians who lived off Sunset in Hollywood. We spent Sunday afternoons watching "College Bowl" and eating peanuts with future Rock and Roll Hall of Fame photographer Henry Dilts, who then played banjo with the Modern Folk Quartet.

I still hadn't knocked enough options off the table to be as committed as Mike was. I was simply going to ride the moment as far as it took me, with no vision of how far that might be. I wasn't even thinking of independence or an apartment in Hollywood. Life was coming fast enough that I felt no need to go out and make things happen. We were just getting better and better as performers, stretching the boundaries of what we wanted to do—that was enough.

★ ★ ★

John Stewart, whose visibility was white hot now, was getting word of hit songs as they were being written. The Ewan MacColl ballad "The First Time Ever I Saw Your Face" had been conceived a capella for MacColl's lover, the folksinger Peggy Seeger, and the legend was that MacColl sang it to her that way over a phone line. But John couldn't help hearing the emotion embodied by subtle root chords. He began softly finger-picking it for us, and we caught hold of the sweetness of the melody, the honesty of the chord progression, and the rich potential for a group vocal to search out the hidden layers. Mike worked up an arrangement that wove Susie's pristine soprano amid countermelodies from me and Mike, all bound together perfectly with the lyrics. There was magic here, and John knew it—something to do with what our young, mixed voices could draw out of just the right material—so he dug up another song, a traditional, and called it "Big River Rising," a "wait for me, I'll be back in the spring" story embellished with images of rebirth and low-flying rain crows down by the watch road. Then he got in touch with producer Nik Venet, the head of A&R at Capitol Records, who'd earlier signed the Beach Boys and the Lettermen—and incredibly, Michael, Susie, and I were booked for a demo audition at Capitol Records.

Mike was the one with all the swagger when it came to not falling over at the sight of the Capitol building, but only because he'd tagged along with John in the past. To me it had always been this mystic tower: the stacked-records landmark with visored windows, topped by that aerodynamic spindle scratching the clouds. I'd passed by it on the way to Clifton's Cafeteria or Music City, ever wondering what happened inside, while Mike bragged about taking breaks from John's sessions and eating hot dogs at the stand across the street.

We arrived after hours, and rather than use the front door like tourists, we went through the guard house out back and were directed past parking places marked for the likes of Sinatra and Nat King Cole. Passing through heavy glass doors, we descended to a tunnel-like hallway that felt more like a bomb shelter than a place for making music. At the end of that labyrinth, above insulated double doors, we saw the first evidence of our destination—flashing red lights and a sign that read, "Do Not Enter During Recording."

The enormity of the room overwhelmed me at a glance. It must have had a twenty-five-foot ceiling. It was designed for an orchestra, but this night it was empty, except for three microphones suspended from towering mic stands a few feet apart from each other. John waved his hand around the room like he was about to bow before the king, and said, "This is where the hits are made."

Capitol's first studio had been a former KHJ radio theater on Melrose Avenue, famous for the natural echo chambers built into the roof. In 1955, when the Vine Street tower was constructed, the old chambers were modified by Les Paul and isolated in concrete thirty feet beneath the ground. During tours, Capitol used to put listeners in a dark room while a variety of sounds were played in stereo, creating the illusion of sitting in front of a full-sized orchestra—or, in one case, on a railroad track while a train rolled straight through the room. It was here that the Kingston Trio recorded "Tom Dooley."

I was still staring in badly disguised wonder when a young, dark-haired guy who introduced himself as Nik Venet asked if we could do their engineer a favor: Could we let him get some levels on our instruments and voices? Just tune up and play through our first song. "See Pete in there?" Venet said. "Give him a wave."

So Mike and I began "The First Time Ever I Saw Your Face" while an audio engineer positioned the mics near the front of our guitars in a way that must have made sense to him. Susie started to sing along, and they did the same thing for her voice—placing the microphone just so behind a screen positioned in front of her mouth. As she sang, he gently moved her body to the exact spot he had in mind. We delivered the song a couple more times, really listening to each other, concentrating on our parts, getting more and more familiar with the sound of our voices blending from our outposts, as the sound dissolved into the darkness of the huge room, floating up into the unknown, like Dorothy's house bound for Oz. It felt both comfortable and intense, singing what might be the most haunting song ever written about first times, standing for the first time ever in Capitol Records while singing about "the first time ever." I looked at Mike and Susie. We would never be like this again.

Old hands now, we switched to "Big River Rising," and we had run through that a couple times when the door opened and Nik appeared in the studio. I wondered what was wrong.

"Okay, I want you to listen to something."

The enormous speakers hissed. The sound of "The First Time Ever I Saw Your Face" exploded from the speakers, two guitars, larger than life and soaked in reverb, like a Kingston Trio record but somehow better. And it was us. Mike, Susie, and I were already grinning ear to ear when the voices began, perfectly blended and in tune. I shivered, smiled, and even teared up a bit as Susie caught my eye and winked at the line "the first time ever I held you near." Then the moment was gone as I realized what had happened. We'd been tricked by a professional record producer. He'd recorded our "practice" to eliminate beginners' nerves.

No longer fearful of doing an actual recording, we took our positions and jumped in with full force to do the overdubs. The sound of my original voice was so strong through that big speaker, I had to sing really strong and well to even tell what I was doing. I really missed that process in later years when headphones took the place of playback speakers.[1]

When John and Nik returned for playback, I was overwhelmed listening to three people sound like six. . . . This was why people made records. Mike had ditched his jaded pose, shouting, "Wow! Yes!" At the first chorus of "Big River Rising," Nik and John were laughing and slapping hands, and Nik was declaring, "It's going to be the folk hit of the year."

My high lasted for weeks. The demo copy they gave us never sounded quite as good at home, but any time it was played, I could go back to Capitol in my mind.

Unfortunately, "Big River Rising" was stillborn—John had followed the model of using traditional songs as a basis for new copyrights, but this one was not in the public domain. While that legality was being untangled, Nik left Capitol, and the project lost its champion. But the unresolved potential of the young folk trio seemed to stick. When he later returned to Capitol, Nik signed a group called the Stone Poneys with Linda Ronstadt that had a lot in common, looking back, with the Ridgerunners.

★ ★ ★

A couple years after the Capitol experience, we started college, at the University of San Francisco, and Mike would go out and explore the whole San Francisco scene, to which I was indifferent. I didn't read Kerouac's *On the Road*; I wasn't a beatnik or a seeker; I wasn't looking for the meaning of life.

Whereas for Michael, I think music became a kind of substitute religion. All those Catholic-school questions I used to ask—about why you couldn't wear tennis shoes with your uniform, about whether the things we'd been taught were based on substance or only an Oz-like authority —would soon obsess our whole generation. And that spirit of inquiry would begin to touch on ultimate questions about what was right and wrong, and why. If people didn't have a traditional understanding of God, they simply reinvented faith from whatever felt magical, loving, and timeless—just so long as it was esoteric enough that it couldn't finally be proven or not.

For me, music seemed a way to make a living out of life—not sense out of life. I wasn't driven, at least not yet.

Michael was. He started hanging out at the Purple Onion, trying to pick up chicks with his surrogate big brother: an Irish-Mexican folksinger and ukulele virtuoso named Fred Thompson, his guide to the carnival of obscure North Beach bistros and clubs that were a showcase for the near-famous. If they couldn't find girls, they'd go to Tad's on Powell, which looked like a 1920s San Francisco whorehouse and offered a bone-in steak, baked potato, and salad for $1.19. Then they'd be charged up to play music all night. But the music they played was changing. Even the Kingston Trio was becoming passé. Nearly ridiculous success (to the point of having seven albums in the top ten in 1959) had seemingly turned against them. They'd represented the last wave of pre–Baby Boomers—but the first wave of collegiate hip—and now they were about to give way to a more radical groundswell of rebellion.

I had typically mixed feelings about all this. Even in Elvis Presley, from the start, I'd sensed an unrealistic, life-denying foolishness. In the '70s, when Elvis made his comeback, his audience was no longer interested in rebelling just to rebel. They'd grown up, but he hadn't, and I think it killed him. The Kingston Trio, while they reigned, had made possible a different sort of hipness. They'd been earthy but *intelligent*, as well as funny, and they sang proficiently enough to be pleasing while simply enough that a host of followers thought, "We can do that." They spawned Lindsey Buckingham (who has said he picked up his guitar style from watching the Trio play banjo), the early Beach Boys[2] (in both harmony and striped-shirted look)—and the dabblings of young Michael Stewart.

★ ★ ★

Only *dabbling* isn't the word. He was too competitive for that. He might goof off from time to time—the same way you'd get up to stretch if you sat too long at a desk—but even fun, for Mike, was a little fanatical. When I was in Tokyo, I'm sure he spent the whole month intellectually sparring, pondering John's life in the Trio, and thinking of new material for us to play. He identified early on with Woody Allen: outwardly frail and insecure, but totally possessed in his area of expertise. Girls were not drawn to this monomania quite yet. That fact, possibly, formed a scar. But he was only getting started.

Magnifying the normal teenage boy's insecurity was a horrible ordeal with acne. Between freshman and sophomore years in high school, he came back literally looking like someone else. "You look like someone threw pink shit at you through a screen," said one of the more heartless jocks.

No one failed to notice Mike's complexion. Few girls at school paid attention to him. And all too often, the ones he liked, liked me.

It started with Susie—proximity led to a bond. She both teased and encouraged me, although she ultimately picked another guy. But while Sue was in the group, Michael wanted her. I sometimes wonder if she didn't choose the new guy just to keep our triangle from hurting Mike. For she cared about Mike and about the group. Life was easier for all concerned when Sue and I were not together.

We had a series of extremely emotional incidents in cars. One night, driving back from Hollywood, when I made a left turn at a corner that made clear I would be dropping Mike off before Sue, he opened the car door and ran—a full mile away from his house—shrieking, "I can't take it! I'm going to kill myself!" But the next time we saw him, it was as if nothing had ever happened.

Sometimes John Stewart would be in the driver's seat, trading one-liners with his pal George Yanok (who later wrote for the Smothers Brothers and produced "Welcome Back, Kotter")—their comic timing was so polished, so radio-worthy, that when we shot beneath an overpass Mike said he expected to hear the sound of their voices fade. Heading to Warner Bros. to record songs for that NASA film, "With Their Eyes on the Stars," Mike was riding shotgun, and I was nestled in the backseat between Sue (now married, pregnant, and officially leaving the group) and Eileen Duffy, Sue's rival for vocal parts. Both girls, as I saw it, were coming on to me—competing, maybe, in advance of their vocal competition in the studio. Michael must have been thinking: *Well, this sucks.* Sue's attention, of course, struck me as outrageously inappropriate, but I half wanted it—she was a type not shy about taking what she wanted, though our relationship was over—and when Eileen got into the act, I wanted to draw the line—but also not. Mike cared about both of these women, and we were in a working relationship with them. In music-world legend, that kind of conflict either kills creativity or kindles it. Certainly the Mamas and the Papas and Fleetwood Mac made great music out of romantic complication. But the bottom line was, a big night for everyone was rendered awkward, even painful, for Mike. And, in retrospect, for me.

There would be one more misadventure with Michael in a car, this one involving Debbie, my wife to be. We'd gone to a rehearsal with Debbie's group, the Legendaires, as well as actor Jon Provost of "Timmy and Lassie," because a woman who managed both acts saw some potential synergy in bringing us all together. Since Mike's Falcon wagon was loaded with instruments and equipment, plus our bass player Pete Fullerton, and Pete's stand-up bass, I rode with Debbie in the back of the manager's '59 Cadillac, which was leading the caravan with the manager's son at the wheel. We went through the first of two linked yellow lights, and Mike, following us, sped to keep up. But then we stopped for the second light, causing Mike to brake hard. His Falcon slipped on the rain-slick street—slamming into the tail fins of the Cadillac.

On impact, the hinged front seatback tipped forward, creating a gap—which is where Debbie happened to plant her foot as she braced herself. The seat snapped back to upright, breaking her foot.

Ultimately, the manager sued Michael (arguing that he was following too close), and she even subpoenaed my testimony, pitting friend against friend. She wore a neck brace for months, one of those kinds of people—I didn't believe her. But I bet the whole thing felt to Mike like one more situation where luck, love, and loyalty were lined up against him.

★ ★ ★

At Warner Bros. we walked through a soundstage door to an unlighted hangar the size of a football field, stepping through old sets and props draped in canvas. Before my eyes could adjust to the dark I heard the strum of a clean-spun guitar, alongside the gorgeous floating mystery of Scott McKenzie's voice—his later hit was "San Francisco (Be Sure to Wear Flowers in Your Hair)." It brought its own echo; it seemed to issue without air. He was seated across the room beneath a bare bulb in an area set up for some folkies to sing and play. John Phillips, then of the Journeymen, future founder of the Mamas and the Papas, would also be participating. The same cool wind that carried the sound of Scott McKenzie brought a sudden fear there'd be no use for me.

Moreover, we'd all be directed by the great John Stewart in the music arranged by Mike, eighteen, suddenly not just a kid brother. The clumsiness about Susie and Eileen gave way, I guess, to a sense of pure awe.

A number of things really got to me at this session—not least the simplic-ity, beauty, and timeless energy of the folk-ensemble form. If you combine rich, earnest voices with songs that have sweetness and depth, plus power and drive—not to mention a message that I can relate to—you will have captured my mind and my heart. The project went miraculously well—so well that, looking back, we got the best of all worlds. Susie wound up getting most of the female leads, on account of her pure fluidity, and since Eileen Duffy had been classically trained (she'd been voted top soprano in California under the age of seventeen, or some such thing), the precision of her harmonies made Susie's voice better grounded, while Susie humanized the operatic correctness of Eileen.

Along with this technical success, we felt the forward-looking energy of the moment. Kennedy would still be alive for another three months, and his vision of a New Frontier—that an American could gaze upward and vow to reach the moon—had unlocked some vital quadrant of the brain, of *What If?* I was truly moved by the northern and southern folk tunes that John Stewart had dug up: the inseparability of history and the music of a people. Throw in Scott McKenzie, throw in the stratospheric female harmonies on "Santianno," throw in the girl in "The Cruel War" saying, *I'll tie down my bosom and cut my hair and go with you*, and this was no empty public-service exercise.

Nor was the music nostalgic. John Stewart was adapting an old musical form to modern events, something that, frankly, had never been tried before. He wasn't writing about old West Virginia or Grenada or the Gypsy Rover— in "With Their Eyes on the Stars," he was writing a kind of traditional music for our time.

> And I said to myself
> As I sat 'neath that tree
> Look you out yonder
> Just as far as you can see
> That's a big harvest moon
> And it's calling to me

And later:

> 'Cause there's so much to see
> O let it be me!
> Or at least a man who is free
>
> Up there we must go
> No goal is too high
> No road is too far
> Not for those with their eyes on the stars

It's a song you can push to the heights, and the minor chords will surge with real emotion, but you can also play it with a softness and subtlety that's simply profound.

I've been singing it both ways ever since. There are songs I call front-porch songs, which I'll play sitting on my porch swing after dark: this is one. But for years I never performed it publicly. It's almost as if the joy was too personal.

Back then, it was simply a product of John asking himself: *What is our time about, right now? How can I fit in and make our own era better?* He'd written a song of hope that addressed the unknown future, exactly the kind of song that folk music was heading toward, though we saw only a hint of it then. In a couple of years, with power chords, drums, and 4/4 rhythm, people started calling it Americana.[3] All this promise was contained in the Warner Bros. session.

In the car afterward, as the performance pressure dissolved into celebration, the backseat flirtation renewed. One moment we were exulting about all the cool things that just took place, and then, in the silliness, Eileen's arms threw themselves around me, and I had to tell her this wasn't the time. I carried the awkwardness of Mike's discomfort all the way home.

It might explain Mike a little to remember that his older brother undoubtedly had his pick of groupies. Whatever I imagined I saw from the fringes, Mike saw more. Earlier that night—unzipping in the Warner Bros. urinal, and with me as his only audience—John Stewart half-sportingly showed me a sore that must have meant an STD. What struck me as odd was that I'd been chosen for this confidence. I wondered if some sibling unease made it more natural for him to pass that torch of initiation above Mike's head. I was probably seventeen. For all I know, John Stewart was genuinely scared about the sore.

★ ★ ★

I'm not saying that Mike didn't enjoy any fruits of success with girls. He was witty, he was intimidatingly smart, he had a band, he was the brother of a world-famous brother—he was attractive, at least to girls who shunned jocks. There'd been girls in Claremont who knew about Mike and who even pursued him. But I do know, after Susie, that he began concealing that life from *me*. Possibly that spared him the pain of competing with a lifelong friend and bandmate. Not to mention the possibility of losing.

One further development followed the Warner Bros. session: Eileen Duffy, Susie's presumed successor, left the group. Her classical vocal coach took a stand: you work with them, or you work with me—you can't do both. Her departure opened the door to an unofficial talent search. We were in need, now, of the yet-unknown Beverly Bivens.

★ ★ ★

Looking back—looking far and wide, from the Ferris Wheel apex of the mid-1960s—what made Mike's and our creative experimenting possible, what really incubated it, was an uncanny, probably lost-forever, suspended note of musical coexistence. Our generation's time was the time when AM Hit Radio might play, in the course of half an hour, everything from the Rolling Stones to Al Hirt, from Lady Soul to Tex-Mex, from Johnny Cash to Peter, Paul and Mary, from Bob Dylan to Henry Mancini. Our dreams of love and justice were at the front end of their unbroken-pond moment—not the back.

Whereas now it's so easy to see the potential for things to fly apart—how, for instance, our version of "There's a Place for Us," from *West Side Story*, would appeal to only a fraction of the audience that liked "You Were On My Mind." (John Chambers, the drummer we toured with, is dead, so we can't ask him, but I'm sure some nights he must have sat at his drums and waited for it to be over.) Or how Cream's blues-rock distortion would appeal to one half of the band and not the other. To me, the magic of our group was how we could bring the audience down to a whisper just like an actor could—quiet intensity is so much harder to achieve than arena rock. But quiet intensity lacked the unifying power of a dance tune, and at times this put me at odds with Chambers, or with lead guitarist Bob Jones. Pete Fullerton, with his string bass, was cut from cloth similar to mine—so John Stewart called us "The Bobbsey Twins."

It would one day seem like a lot for all of us, and Mike as our leader, to straddle.

★ ★ ★

My wife, Debbie, has a favorite picture of Mike playing. His tongue is out like the basketball legend Michael Jordan's, and he's comparably in a zone, into his folk-gospel straight-four glide. Near the end of his life in 2002, battling emphysema, Mike had come full circle. "You and Debbie have a studio, right?" he asked me on the phone, laboring for air. "And you've written a lot of spiritual songs? If I can get my oxygen tanks to your house, can I stay with you and record those? I'd really like to do a spiritual album." He never made the trip, and he died literally a couple of days after. Yet I felt the touch of God, because Mike's first step into professional music had been rewriting a spiritual song, and he wrote to the heights not always being spiritual himself, but in the end he was brought back to those two things at the core: His spirit and the need to convert it to music.

After he died, for several years there were certain songs I couldn't sing on stage without crying—"You Were On My Mind," for one. That song and We Five were Mike Stewart's baby.

• 5 •

If You're Going to San Francisco

$\mathcal{E}$ileen Duffy's departure from the Ridgerunners in 1963 created a vacuum. It left the group in need of a multi-capable, multi-talented, pretty, soprano/alto, animated, do-it-all . . . "chick singer," as we'd have said back then. And without the one we found, Mike Stewart's premonition—of folk meeting pop and rock in a vocal group that had places for both rough edges and smooth-sanded harmonies—could easily have remained just a dream. Beverly Bivens, in plenty of ways, symbolized everything Mike foresaw. She was mystery, hypnotic enough to fuel his dream, but also a beautiful person real as day. She was the future you didn't know you were waiting for until it shook your hand.

At that San Francisco session where we would eventually record "You Were On My Mind," a lot of the activity was happening near the edges of the photo. Mike was explaining the rhythm; drummer Jerry Granelli was giving that rhythm a name and a manic, downhill momentum; Pete Fullerton and I were picking and strumming to keep pace; Bob Jones was overlaying his electric twelve-string jangle. And any onlooker might have eventually noticed all those things. But not when they first walked in the room. What everyone notices is the girl.

They remember her performing the song on Hullabaloo, or on Hollywood Palace (and if not, they can watch it on YouTube today), making the most of her teensy cubit of space—deftly ponying, winking at her lines, a cheeky tomboy spirit in a V-neck velour, her energy flung upward in starts.

In the studio, she was like that too, but with a different sort of serious-ness—a craftsman-like intensity to match Bob Jones's as he held the neck of the guitar for an oncoming solo like a soldier ready for battle. Her focus mattered especially to a perfectionist like Mike. Untroubled and carefree as she appeared, Beverly was always consciously in control of her instrument. If she

30

held any kind of drink at all, it was probably tea, to keep her voice easy and loose. And the speaking voice was just as hickory-smooth as the singing voice: a nonspecific Southern-esque drawl, which is even more California than knowing where anyone came from. Back then, no one in L.A. was from L.A.

Her stage look was calculated to an extent. On airplanes she'd read *Vogue* and *Mademoiselle*, mentally tearing out photos of Capri pants or chiffon dresses to suit her not-quite-pageboy flip. (A surprising number of people today, when they see videos of the band, actually confuse Beverly with Barbara Feldon: Agent 99 of "Get Smart.")

But honestly, she was totally comfortable in her own skin and never seemed to give fashion a moment's thought outside the imperatives of the job.

In the history of female vocalists, she combined the technical mastery of Barbra Streisand and Nancy Wilson (both of whom I consider "vocal actresses," and not at all in a bad way) with a pre-hippie sexual equality that went way past how Mary Travers used to balance a folk revue in a knee-length dress. Beverly was a newer kind of woman, always, at some level, one of the guys. Even while she drove guys' dreams.

That was going to be her job on stage: to be the visual center, to sing like crazy, and to project herself in a way that made the guys in the room want her, and the women want to *be* her. And the effort succeeded with almost every man I saw. Probably the only reason I didn't fall for Beverly myself was that I was already head-over-heels for my future wife, Debbie, who has a similar power. But God help Mike.

★ ★ ★

We'd met her during Christmas break in December '63 when she was seventeen, a senior at Santa Ana High School. Mike had dropped by that coffee house in Upland, the multipurpose lounge of the Sierra Swim Club where Terry Kirkman (who later wrote "Cherish" for the Association) was serving hamburgers and beer. "I gotta find a girl singer," Mike said.

"My girlfriend's kid sister sings," Terry said.

A couple of days later, the four of them gathered at Terry's mom's house in Chino, where Mike and Bev sang together, but I don't know what. It was only when Mike asked, "Can you sing down in *this* voice?"—that smoky sound that Nancy Wilson, like most girls, sang at the low end of a soft soprano, but that Susie Davies had opened up into a ballsier alto—that they were off to the races. It turned out Beverly thrilled to that sound too, and she could slide seamlessly back to the upper register after dipping down low.

It had been almost an axiom till then that female vocalists who could sing soprano didn't have pop hits in the power-alto range. But once the door

opened, some unforgettable examples started walking through it. Linda Ronstadt, Joni Mitchell. Almost every hit by Aretha Franklin.

My own first glimpse of Beverly, a few nights later, was that of her silhouette being kissed by Mike's as they sat in a parked car behind a Montclair
coffee shop. Mike had arranged for me to meet them there, and there's no
doubt in my mind he staged the scene, in order to warn me off his romantic
turf. And I didn't miss the point.

He had repeatedly advised her, she later told me, to "watch out for
Jerry," who was certain to hit on her.

★ ★ ★

It's not boasting to point out how historic the girl-singer-in-a-guy-group
idea was in 1964. When Sue Davies opened Mike's ears to the sound, it had
never, to our knowledge, been tried in contemporary pop—and in folk, Peter,
Paul and Mary didn't even exist yet. Joan Baez and Judy Collins were solo
acts. The Fleetwoods had girl singers, but not girl leads. Dusty Springfield, the
irresolvably sensual soul prodigy, didn't hit the mainstream until she broke
out of the Springfields folk trio to release a 1963 solo album that was more
Phil Spector-ish, ranging from upbeat to hard-knocked and timeless. Her epic
bluesiness, fully explored in drink, drugs, and lifestyle, was something only
another woman—only a Beverly—might really grasp.

There was also the white-girl stereotype to overcome. The idea of a
pretty white woman singing the blues, Dusty aside, was still too odd for lots
of audiences to decode. I remember telling Michael about one of my guitar
students, a girl maybe 90 pounds, with red hair and freckles, who'd confided
that she wanted to learn blues. (Young Bonnie Raitt could certainly identify.)
Michael half-joked, "Did you tell her to chop off her hand and go through
three bad marriages first?"

On the other hand, everything odd about seeing a girl like Beverly in
front of a group of guys at this moment in history was what helped make
it work. When Frank Werber became our manager, he caught on to that
intrigue and ran with it. Mike would be the leader, mouthpiece, and comedian, in an intellectual Mort Sahl style; I'd fill in a few words when Mike was
changing instruments. And Bev, well. Frank didn't want any just-folks approachability in that equation. "She'll be as cute as can be, and she'll sing her
ass off, and she'll be *in* on the jokes, but she won't talk," he'd visualize aloud.
"They won't know who she is until she sings."

★ ★ ★

The band was spread all over Southern California. Lead guitarist Bob
Jones was living in Palmer Canyon, fifteen miles north of Mike's and Pete's

houses in Claremont. Beverly lived in the heart of Orange County, while I lived about forty-five miles north of her in the Pomona valley. To get to her folks' place, we carpooled, taking the 71 south, a two-lane road through ranch land in what's now Chino Hills, then the 91 west from the Prado Dam, then the 55 South to Chapman Avenue . . . then east to the foot of the Anaheim Hills. This was early Orange County, mostly orange groves, no sidewalks, untamed: on breaks from practicing, we used to swim in her pool or ride her folks' Honda 50 motorcycles up into the undeveloped hills. Then Beverly's dad traded her classic black '57 Chevy for a 1964 Mustang—a six-cylinder notchback in classic red—and she began driving in style to where the rest of us were. She was seriously California.

She was equally sensitive. I remember riding in her Mustang back from Palmer Canyon one afternoon and coming to a sharp right turn in the middle of nowhere. The car spun out—harmlessly—but she was so shaken she had to give me the keys, and I drove her the rest of the way home.

Another time, very late at night, we hit an animal. Beverly was in the driver's seat, pushing eighty or more, speeding to L.A. from San Francisco. Between King City and Atascadero back then was totally undeveloped, nothing along the side of the road but fields. I remember passing the sign for Mission San Miguel, which burned in my mind because I was a Southern California kid fascinated by the appeal of points north. The Kingston Trio had done a song about the place, "Down by the Mission San Miguel," filled with romantic impossibility between a ranch hand and the Don's beautiful wife. In the darkness those ghosts of early California seemed to mingle with another Kingston Trio song, "South Coast," in which a young bride falls to her death from a horse that is frightened by the scream of a mountain lion in the moonlit barranca. . . .

I couldn't make out the breed of animal at first. It was too small for a deer and too slow for a possum or a raccoon, but it might have been a large rabbit. It froze in the headlights—in a stomach-wrenching flash you could tell: a bobcat—then disappeared under the car with a single thump.

We rolled to a stop on the shoulder.

Beverly was beside herself. "Should we go back and look?" she wailed.

But when we stepped outside the car, we found a tuft of tan-colored fur on one of the A-frames inside the front wheel.

It was a moonless, pitch black night. I knew that there was no one around—and had no desire to start searching for a vet miles from anywhere. It was so late it was practically early, and we had been probably only semi-conscious, possibly high.

"We were going way too fast for it to have survived," I said. "And what would we do if we found it? We'd have to go find a town, the police—where would we find a vet out here?"

"You're probably right. But I feel so bad," she said.

The whole thing affected her in a personal way—how she'd been driving too fast, how the bobcat would have made it if only he hadn't hesitated.

The idea of going back to find the misery we might have left in our wake was too much for Beverly.

"It's probably dead, or will be," was my best answer.

★ ★ ★

Not that she spent much time in that vulnerable zone. Especially around the band. It was partly that we were guys, several of whom were frankly in love with her, and her best hope of keeping things in hand was not to go deep.

But there was another reason, an instinctive caution innate either to Beverly or to young women generally in the middle of a decade whose ties to social tradition were all about to unravel.

An example was when Bob Jones started talking about smoking grass (he was raised in Hawaii, where it grew by the side of the road). Beverly had been curious enough to try it—only not with him, and certainly not alone. "I'm going to need someone else there," she said to me and my artsy-surfer high school friend Bill Crutchfield.

Bill offered to stick around. Out of character, so did I. We wound up in my grandmother's house in Pomona, Beverly asking no one in particular: "Like *this*? Kind of take it in and *hold* it?"

It was the first-timer's cliché: five minutes in, none of us felt a thing, but we were hungry. We walked to DiCarlo's Liquor Store and came away with bags and bags of munchies and a bottle of hard cider, that staple of the folk era. We'd at least get a buzz off of that.

We got used to how Beverly's magnetism warped the space-time-sex continuum. When Fred Marshall, the hip jazz bassist with renegade good looks who'd ultimately sweep Beverly away from the group, eyed her at a recording session, manager Werber was aghast he didn't see it coming.

"Let's go to a movie," she said one night—and instead of seeing whatever was playing at the drive-in, I found myself in the more artsy stretches of North Orange County watching *The Pink Panther* and being instantly infatuated with Italian starlet Claudia Cardinale. Whose mystique, of course, Beverly shared— that Swiss-army-knife femininity—something about being dark, small, and mysterious; continental yet unspoiled; and competent to deliver on whatever role was required, whether to sing or be a clown, hostess, lover, pal.

After a performance at the Rouge et Noir in Seal Beach, she fell and twisted her ankle, and you could have sold tickets to the queue of chivalrous men. That time I think the victor was David Somerville, the golden-haired, open-shirted former lead singer of the Diamonds (as close as doo-wop had to a matinee idol), and he carried her to the car, a scene Beverly handled with just-right embarrassment and charm.

Undoubtedly Mike fell hardest. Returning to the University of San Francisco (USF) for spring semester, with his studies growing pale beside his love of music, he took to playing guitar with Bob Jones in the tile shower rooms, for the echo. He'd been pinning his hopes on a relationship with Beverly. He would call and talk for hours, says Beverly, staging emergency breakthroughs on her phone line—even threatening to kill himself when she made clear she didn't share his seriousness. It went on for months. By the middle of spring, his sense of dislocation went over the top. The school had only recently gone co-ed, and there were virtually no unclaimed girls upon whom to transfer his passions. At one apparently desperate moment, he checked himself into a psych center through the College of Nursing. The diagnosis was, and is, unclear to me. *Nervous breakdown* was a popular term in those times.

I must have been in the dormitory, Phelan Hall, and someone handed me a message to call Mike at an unfamiliar number.

"I'm in St. Mary's," said the voice on the other end of the line. He sounded matter-of-fact yet also tentative, like he knew this was going to require a bit more explanation.

"What's this about, Mike?"

I couldn't tell if he laughed or sighed. All he'd say was that he was struggling with a whole lot of stuff, and that finally it led him into some sort of counseling. "In any case, I'm gonna be spending a couple of days down here, and I can't leave. Can you bring me my guitar? We can talk more when you get here." That's probably when he mentioned *nervous breakdown*. "*Bring the guitar.*"

"How do I find you?"

"Go to the psych ward at St. Mary's and give my name. They'll have to get you to the elevator, because there's some kind of controlled access."

I knew Mike was good at grandstanding. The jumping from the car stunt over Sue Davies came to mind. So I couldn't be sure this wasn't just melodrama. Still, the fact he'd called his oldest friend, rather than his roommate, for the guitar made me feel like I ought to take it seriously. If all he wanted was the guitar, why drag me in? We'd been leading such separate lives in school. I'd been hanging around with the folk geeks, whom Mike and Bob Jones had pretty much rejected. He'd been exploring the town with Fred Thompson, never inviting me—except one time at Tad's, where he pocketed all the free food he could and told me how Fred lived on packets of crackers, ketchup, and mustard for days at a time.

Now I had to find Mike's roommate—which involved not letting on why I wanted to pick up the guitar—then walk the block and a half to the hospital psych ward. A uniformed control person checked me in to an eerie gray sector, throwing me back to the time when our boys choir had visited the state prison at Chino with Mahalia Jackson, and we'd had to sign away our right to leave without permission. You're aware of cages, keys, doors, chains, locks. It hits you like a sledgehammer—you're in a different world, and you don't get out without a pass.

When the elevator reached his floor, I stepped into a hallway: brighter, lots of windows, although totally covered with bars. Mike was waiting for me in the common area, same smile, same droopy forelock, and he opened with something charming, like, "Welcome to the loony bin."

Around us people were playing board games, or staring off with blank looks; others looked confusingly normal. Mike gave me a pleasant little walk-through, told me he'd been playing way too much checkers, and said without his guitar, he'd been going crazy (ha-ha), and that he sincerely appreciated my bringing it.

It was Bob who would fill me in, years later, about Mike's romantic loneliness at USF. That isn't something he would have shared with me. By this point, we'd developed safe zones of interface. He talked about school and his slipping grades. If I got wind of his emotional life, it was usually from being with him in a group setting where plenty of subjects were on the table. Music notwithstanding, we even went through a period toward the end of high school where we simply didn't talk—all because of the trouble with Sue Davies.

Yet we could always play music. And now, as we camped ourselves in his room—a small square with a bed and a dresser—he opened the guitar case. Next thing I knew, we were singing, and drawing a crowd, and I remember one nurse exclaiming, like a fan: "You really *can* play that thing!"

Mike had status again. The star of the psych ward.

The whole episode would formalize an observation I'd already had: that certain artists feel compelled to go straight to the edge, a la Brian Wilson. It's almost as if they need to fall overboard to confirm that they're brilliant. Mike was willing, and able, to push past a limit of convention, and now he had the badge. He'd been to the nut house.

But I never voiced that opinion or tried to shame him. I never said, "Oh, this was just Michael being Michael."

Which says a lot about me too—my shallowness—my willingness, back then, to accept almost anything in life without digging for understanding. I lacked the curiosity to get to the bottom of it.

★ ★ ★

When the hospital released him too late to prepare for finals, Mike realized that his days as a straight-A student would be over. That is when he decided to leave USF early. Bob had the same dread about finals plus an aversion to USF overall, so with only two weeks left in the term they packed Mike's Falcon wagon and headed back to Southern California to try and make a go of it in music. And they asked me to join them back in L.A. if I could.

I could—but not before passing my finals, with scores barely in the middle of the pack. That modest effort enabled me to convince my folks I wasn't through with school, just USF. In retrospect, the calculation looked smart. I needed every one of my USF credits twenty-five years later when I got readmitted in the College of Professional Studies.

Whereas Mike and Bob had made the leap, it would take me two more months to jump in after them.

★ ★ ★

Alongside all this chaos were the musical recombinations within the band that Beverly's presence had only compounded. We had Mike trying to make rock songs out of Disney ("Zip a Dee Doo Dah") and Ira Gershwin ("I've Got Plenty of Nothin'"); we had Pete Fullerton on bass, weaving in his love of classical and bluegrass; we had Bob Jones pushing us toward more aggressive electric guitar licks and toward dance. Now we began blending in Beverly's torchy loyalties. If you brought together in a room all the people we looked up to—Ray Brown, Nancy Wilson, Chuck Berry, John Phillips, Brian Wilson, Scott McKenzie, the Dillards, the Beatles—their shadows on the wall would have made something cool and hydra-headed but unclassifiable, like: *folk-rock-pop-Broadway-jazz*. Indeed, a year or so later, in their *Rubber Soul* period, the Beatles started smushing together folk, cabaret, and Indian raga. It was the beginning of Anything's Fair.

You could see a similar chaos in fashion. The Beatles went from Nehru jackets to torn jeans. Mike and I went from horrific pastels and wavy vertical stripes (Kingston Trio shirts, but with the vertical hold gone awry) to plaid jackets like Soupy Sales would wear, to velours and British herringbones like the early Monkees. At the Troubadour in West Hollywood you saw both eras at once: folk bands still wore sport coats and ties but they started to play raw kinds of singer-songwriter material from Dylan, Leonard Cohen, Phil Ochs, and Gordon Lightfoot. L.A. was teeming with folksingers and pop singers trying to reinvent themselves in the face of the British Invasion.

On every front, I was being assaulted with a sense of *Have You Tried This?* It could be as predictable as a passed joint or as unexpected as a homosexual pass. When a guy who'd shared billing with us at a club hit on me in the car going home, it was so unprecedented I had to run it through the Burgan linear flow chart, having never been trained in what women were so used to doing: saying no. He had a beautiful singing voice, but too sweetly sensitive even for my taste. "So what kinds of things make you happy?" he said. "Have you ever had a really strong attraction to someone that comes from within?" He reached for my hand, sliding himself across the seat in my direction. My mind flashed to hundreds of films of men wooing women—not to mention a few front car seats—but now the tables were turned, and I didn't like it.

"You're a fine singer and I'm sure you're a very nice person," I heard myself more or less recite. "But I've got to go." The trunk wasn't locked, so I opened it, grabbed my guitar, and headed through the gate without a look back.

He was black besides, and it dawned on me that the racial stereotypes that used to trip silent alarms among white folk in my Pomona childhood had suddenly morphed into a new question: Did black guys do that too?

★ ★ ★

Not every kind of experimentation freaked me out. At Beverly's house, I opened myself up to her jazzy influences, learned to count out the Bossa Nova beat to "Girl from Ipanema." I started to get the difference between a waltzy 3/4 and the more powerful flow of 12/8 time, and to mess around with 5/4—the time signature of Dave Brubeck's "Take Five." Bob was showing us how it swung, three beats in one direction, two beats back to start.

As we strummed, Mike launched into the song "Small World" ("Funny/ You're a stranger who's come here"), and Bob yelled: "Whoa! You're singing in five-four time! It's almost like they wrote it that way!"[1] We'd somehow synthesized Dave Brubeck with Johnny Mathis.

That kind of interplay was happening all the time now.

Mike's creative envelope just kept getting larger, shaping itself into a repertoire. By fall, he had a new, theater-arts-major girlfriend, and the two flew off to see New York—a pivotal trip, because it was there Mike saw *West Side Story* on Broadway. (Bernstein's traditional yet experimental urban-epic folk opera opened yet another direction for Mike—one that would take him from being just a singer in a band to being a world-class arranger and producer for years to come.)

Arrangements began oozing out of us as we learned our roles and how they meshed. One day, just fooling around after rehearsal in Beverly's living room, our non-musician surfer friend Bill Crutchfield offhandedly sang a gospel bass line,

O when the saints,
O when the saints . . .

The moment could have been awkward, but Beverly said something gracious and bright about having never heard Bill sing before. That made him glow and get more outsized in his delivery of each low note—grinning like a Cheshire cat—and without even thinking, we all joined in, the guys blending three-part harmony, Beverly lofting a gospel solo over the top.

Whenever I hear the harmonies in Olivia Newton-John's "Let Me Be There," from 1976, it still takes me back farther, to that day in Bev's living room. We were a group of teenagers coming into our own, having fun while discovering all that we could do and how easily it came.

That was our life from the summer of '64 until June '65. It was a year of We Five becoming We Five. What was going to happen next depended only on the addition of this haunting Sylvia Fricker song that Mike had begun to fool around with—reworking it toward an anthem all his own—and a manager who, having already brought folk music to the mainstream, had the vision to grasp that a new thing was about to be born in San Francisco and wanted to be the one to put his mark on it.

"You know, we could do something with this," Mike said at a party one night, playing the track from Ian and Sylvia's *Northern Journey* album.

I wasn't sure yet. I liked the moving twelve-string lines. I didn't like that it lacked a chorus, because what would be the part that audiences couldn't get out of their heads? What would they whistle when they walked away?

Meanwhile the culture neared critical mass.

· 6 ·

Convergence

 $\mathcal{T}$he feeling of a new day dawning—the folk spirit that Mike had been chan-
neling into vocal harmony driven by an amplified twelve-string jangle—was
starting to cast its dayglo on the landscape of politics too. Folk music had done
an end run around McCarthyism in the person of Pete Seeger, who simply
began playing in venues where the witch hunts would leave him alone—first
in schools, eventually on PBS. Without anyone realizing the impact, he
wound up teaching the largest generation in history how to express themselves
in song. Switching channels from Howdy Doody's peanut gallery (where
kids screamed, "Watch out for Clarabell!") to the integration of Little Rock
schools, we saw people our own age uniting in a cause. They joined first with
the folk movement, then added the power of electric guitars, amplification,
and transistor technology. Folk-rock was merely a transition to this mass phenomenon, but a few producers like John Hammond, Tom Wilson, and Lou
Adler saw it coming, and their foresight shaped history.

Frank Werber was with them. In late summer '63, he'd hosted a
fundraiser for a San Francisco mayoral candidate named Jack Shelley, with the
Kingston Trio headlining. It was still months before JFK's assassination, and
the Democratic Party seemed to represent all the youthful luck and glamour
of Kennedy's coronation. A new era of college-educated, Hugh Hefner en-
lightenment was on the horizon, and it was going to thaw out all the Cold
War darkness of the past. Maybe it was going to start in San Francisco. John
Stewart wrote a jingle for the campaign: "There'll be sunshine/Everywhere/
When Jack Shelley is our mayor." (Shelley would govern from 1964 until
1968, straight through the Summer of Love, the first Democrat in fifty years
elected as SF's mayor—this was the page that was ready to turn.) Mike told
me he was going to be hanging backstage, and he said I ought to be there too.

My then-girlfriend, Donna, a freshman at Santa Clara, had been dating some other guy since starting school there, which bugged me. She had been an infatuation since sixth grade. So I played my close-personal-friend-of-the–Kingston Trio card, hoping to win the battle for her heart. She was a Kennedy Democrat besides, but I didn't know that. I was as unawakened to politics as I was to everything else.

I borrowed a car and picked her up at Santa Clara in my high school graduation suit with black shoes and white socks, which I suppose I thought looked grown up (the Kingston Trio wore white socks too, but not with *suits*), and we arrived at the Masonic Auditorium just before dark with the crowd outside dressed way too well for me, in gowns and tuxes. Right away my white socks didn't look so good. By no means was I sure that I could swim in this pool. Things got even more awkward at the front of the line when Donna and I asked for the backstage entrance.

"There *is* no backstage," the ticket girl said, bewildered. "The stage is just built out into the room."

A sinking moment, until suddenly, in the preliminary foot traffic, I saw a familiar figure walk past in a tuxedo. "There's Frank Werber!" I said, loud enough to stop him.

I'd seen him a couple of times before. The first was at John's debut with the Trio at the Hollywood Bowl, where I'd sat with the Stewart family. The second was at the Hollywood Sands Sunset Motor Hotel, a slightly seedy place even back then, but it was where the Kingston Trio always stayed in L.A. (not to mention Tommy Smothers, whom I'd met there, and Mason Williams). That was where Werber had tried talking a background singer we knew into getting an abortion. Motherhood, he felt, would be the death of a perfectly promising career.

Now he came toward me and Donna by the ticket booth, suppressing a smile—maybe about my white socks, or maybe at the spectacle of two teenagers on a date. When I told him about my ticketless situation, he had no idea what "backstage area" Mike had been talking about.

"Isn't there at least someplace we could stand?" I asked.

He steered us inside and positioned us in the lobby. "Wait here," Werber said, and I took that to mean there might be hope.

Pretty soon he came back holding up two tickets, and he extended them to me with a humble flourish. Seeing how embarrassed I was about how to repay him, he couldn't resist whispering in my ear: "Don't worry about the money—*but make sure that pretty girl sees how much they're worth.*"

I looked down at the tickets: One hundred dollars each. This was 1963, when a bottle of Coke still cost a dime.

Werber had been robbed of his own boyhood as a Jew in Hitler's Europe. He discovered smoking dope in 1950s Colorado and then followed his dreams to San Francisco, where everyone accepted everyone. He'd worked for Enrico Banducci, owner of the *hungry i*, watching his boss showcase every sort of talent because the stage was a Promised Land too, the great equalizer open to anyone who could cut it: Jew or Gentile, black or white. Most of the artists who came through that nightclub were badly managed, including the three guys working the Purple Onion across the street who would become the Kingston Trio. In 1956 they were just wasting away in the trappings of a Weavers wannabe group when Werber, who had moved up to PR, saw his chance.

At the Masonic, Donna's face went from relief to astonishment, and I was a hero as I steered her to our seats: second row, dead center. It turned out we were the only two earthlings in a row of Playboy bunnies (which in those days was prestige); they looked both classy and forward in their jutting sweaters and clinging silks. One row ahead sat all the San Francisco power brokers. We sat marveling about this good fortune until the lights dimmed for the opening act . . . which is the second thing about the evening that would prove indelible.

Onstage, a young girl gingerly made her entrance. At a glance she was oddly attractive, though not pretty, which made her seem odder and more attractive all the time. She had on some kind of a baby doll dress, with something different about the way it broke across her leg, maybe a slit, and a hairdo piled and flipped forward. There was none of the standard performer's hailing the audience; she walked silently and tentatively toward a stool by a microphone like a little girl all dressed up and all alone.

After what seemed like an eternity, she found the spotlight—or it found her—and nothing else was going on: You were just waiting to see what would happen next. She adjusted the mic, moved the stool, pulled the stool closer, fussed with the mic some more, then took the mic and joked, rolling those strange, mismatched eyes:

"It's called *poise*—people tell me I need more of it."

I had heard of Barbra Streisand by then but never seen her.

She leaned into a song, and right away the singing had a precision that seemed miraculous for the danger of the moment she'd created—every bit of her demeanor was *planned*, and yet it felt utterly uncalculated, like she was singing spontaneously just to me.

Even before the first song ended, the spell-casting intensity in her face and in those eyes had me hypnotized, and I thought, it must be so cool. To be that naked and yet in control. You didn't even have to like Streisand's style to see it. I felt like everything I'd ever done musically was chasing the same magic—even if I couldn't have named it when I was thirteen, strumming with Mike in Pomona. And I saw that the way she achieved it was by knowing how to use dynamics. She could be bold and loud or incredibly quiet and sensitive, all within a single phrase. It was like listening to a violinist who could continue to pull on the bow and push on the bow without you ever hearing the change.

Later on, when We Five performed with Herman's Hermits and the Turtles, local reviewers would sometimes remark that our power was refined, pitch-perfect, in danger of being lost in a screaming crowd of thousands. Barbra Streisand may have been corny to some, but she was a goddess of the sacred expectant hush—pulling listeners deeper and deeper toward the promise of a virgin moment. Very much like the expectancy that opens "You Were On My Mind."

There's a concept in music called "playing in the pocket": an infectious ability to feel and respond to the rhythm and flow of a moment. When you find it, it's as unrelenting as a train on rails—the difference being, it can vanish. I think it's a chemical energy just as real as love at first touch, and it happens in all venues of life. One instant a breakthrough doesn't exist, and the next you can't see it *not* existing—whether it's stereo sound or a microwave oven or a call to arms like "The Times They Are a Changin'." And when it happens in the musical realm, vast numbers of people can sometimes hit on a way to lift one another's hopes and visions and share the burden of their times. But it still took a lot of sweat and a lot of structure and a lot of resources and management for that to happen.

At the very least, all of these things reinforced my eagerness to put my faith in Frank Werber. Anything he set his hand to, it seemed to me, was going to be first class. And indeed I would hold that trust long after others in the group began to doubt him.

As for Mike, I guessed he'd spent the evening in the dressing room with John and the Trio. When the crowd filed out, I decided not to hunt him down. I was happy to leave all the musical raw matter for Mike to sort out. Donna and I stopped for burgers, and then we drove to Ocean Beach, where we parked and necked while waves were breaking in the moonlight, and it felt like the right place for me to be.

★ ★ ★

Werber was present a full year later, in October '64, when we recorded a couple of songs at Capitol Records in Hollywood—an opportunity that had been described to me as an "audition." Grammy-nominated music historian Alec Palao[1] just recently informed me that it wasn't an audition for Capitol at all. The Kingston Trio's company, Trident Productions, had paid for the time. Without my knowledge, we were being recorded for a possible release.

We were going to do "I Got Plenty O' Nuttin'" and Mike Stewart's "If You See Me Go," as well as three John Stewart compositions ("Young Man

Go Your Way," "If I Were Alone," and "I Can Never Go Home Again")
that had drums, electric guitars, and a girl. In other words, songs more right
for our generation than the Kingston Trio's.

It was on a break that Werber surprised us, strolling in through the enormous soundproof door in his Oxford shirt, jeans, and Italian boots. Lit from
behind, his longish hair and full beard made an otherworldly silhouette.

"Mike," he said, coming toward us in a purposeful entrance with a sheath
of papers in his hand. "Is there anyone besides you who might be writing?"
There was a very satisfied twinkle in his eye.

"Well, there's Bob, certainly. And Jerry and I have written together."

Frank handed us each a single sheet that turned out to be a sketchily
worded writer's contract with a single dollar bill attached (standard practice in
the music world). For five dollars he had five songwriters under lock and key.

The "Performance and Recording Contract," which followed several
months later, was more complex and required court approval because we were
still minors. I called my father—it was what minors were supposed to do, even
if I didn't feel much like a minor anymore. To his credit, he did not muscle in
or take control. His take was that there was nothing to be gained by finding
flaws in a contract we all knew would be one-sided anyway. Since everyone
else was going to sign it, why make Jerry the odd man out?

★ ★ ★

AND JUST LIKE THAT, I was on my own—the world of my childhood receding into a '50s memory—something that had been trying to
happen for a while. During my senior year in high school, my father started
living up north, studying for a new career. My sister told him about this university program that trained business professionals to become assistant pastors
for Catholic parishes, and it meant he had to live in San Francisco for nine
months. So he gave me the "You're the man of the house now" speech.

That was a year of ridiculous emancipation. My grades dropped from A's
to C's, and I played music with Mike and Susie as much as I liked.

The school even allowed us days off for gigs. We played a surfing event
at the old Long Beach Civic Auditorium with a local R&B duo called the
Righteous Brothers, who'd just released their first record, the hot dance hit
"Little Latin Lupe Lu." Director Bruce Brown was there, too, with an early
cut of his surf documentary *Endless Summer*, which he was narrating live, more
than two years before its theatrical release and his recognition as an innovator
of the genre.

Sometimes we performed till two in the morning, the kind of thing that
would never have been tolerated if Dad were still home. But as long as my

mother knew the people I was working with, she said nothing. In any case, if she did, it didn't stick.

I learned I had the ability to set her off. One day after school, finding the front door locked, I shouted inside for her to come open it. She told me she was waxing the floor in the foyer and that I needed to go around to the back. As I turned away from the door, I muttered some put-down, for no one's ears, but she heard me. She ran across the waxed floor and burst onto the front porch before I even got down the steps, and proceeded to just flail at me, hitting and screaming. *You ungrateful, useless little . . . !*

The phrase went unfinished because my mom never swore. *Bastard* was not in her vocabulary.

I'd only seen her hit one other person before—my dad, over something he'd said—and I intuitively knew there was something about me, as a man, that had to have reminded her of him.

I made a point of not challenging her after that. But pushing a very gentle woman to violence was a skill I apparently shared with my father—some kind of notion that you got to be a man by being indifferent. Sadly, I found a sort of power in it.

After that season, in fact, my dad and I started sparring whenever we talked, and we pretty much kept it up forever. The autonomy had gone straight to my head. He'd empowered me to do my own thing, which led to me thinking I was his equal. And over the years, that gift came back many times to bite him. Whether he was a bigger man than me or I'd just broken him, I'll never know, but eventually he just stopped talking and took it—depriving me of his talent for spotting things that could have spared me forty miles of bad road.

★ ★ ★

Werber's next move was to bring us to San Francisco in the winter of '64–65 for the purpose of unveiling his vision of the band in a town where we were still exotic. The same strategy had worked for Peter, Paul and Mary, and Werber could pull any number of strings in San Francisco. He knew how to get Herb Caen to mention us in the *Daily Chronicle*, and he talked Enrico Banducci into a week of shows at the *hungry i*.

We stayed in the attic of a house near the University of San Francisco, some of us sleeping on couches, others on the floor. We'd go to Chinatown for thirty-five-cent chow mein, then stumble outside—all our eyes widening to the mad-blooming, pre-psychedelic San Francisco scene. Columbus Tower, the Trio's building, overlooked the Purple Onion and Clown Alley. City Lights Books, across Kearny, had become the West Coast's cradle of beat poetry and agitprop, while a block up Broadway, at the Condor Club, nine-teen-year-old Carol Doda frugged topless in a monokini designed by Rudy Gernreich. Across Jackson to the south, beside the entrance to the *hungry i*, we stood looking for our name, which at that time was the Mike Stewart Quintet, on the "marquee"—a hand-painted wall. But reading through to the end of the lineup was a nightmare self-fulfilled. We weren't even listed.

PROFESSOR IRWIN COREY
GAIL GARNETT
JERRY AND MYRNA MUSIC
WE FIVE

We stood there marooned, like the teenagers we were, contemplating this emergency. Then Frank Werber came strolling over from his office across the street.

"Who's 'We Five'?" Michael asked him.

"*You* are," Werber said.

What he liked about the name, Werber told us later, was that it symbol-ized a kind of breakthrough musical convergence: five distinct styles combin-ing into one new sound. Beneath that, he was nursing an even more ambitious dream, that San Francisco, which was becoming a magnet for every kind of social and musical experimentation, would be the birthplace of a musical syn-thesis—incubated by him—that needed nothing from L.A. Albert Grossman had built a mega-folk machine in New York by synergizing Dylan, Peter, Paul and Mary, Ian and Sylvia, Richie Havens, and Gordon Lightfoot; Werber was aiming for a West Coast equivalent. Hoping to siphon power from the Capi-tols and Columbias, he was building a state-of-the-art basement studio, mod-eled after Capitol's Studio B, where he could maintain a hands-on presence in every detail. If he heard a song with hit potential, Trident could publish it. Writing a few new words for folk songs that had never been published, or whose copyrights had expired, generated a constant stream of revenue anytime they were performed, sold on record, played on radio or television, used in a movie, or published in printed form. Meanwhile writers like Mason Williams were under contract composing brand-new material. If the song was wrong for one of Werber's bands, another of them could perform it.

Of course, none of us liked being renamed. But we knew there was a logic to it, and any objections quietly died. That was the kind of impresario Werber was.

We got back to business and hauled our things inside the *hungry i*.

★ ★ ★

It was both more imposing and more storied than the rooms we'd gotten used to in L.A.

Just a black vastness with a brick wall behind you. If any one person in the band got tentative, all the power on that stage could be sucked into the void. Pasadena's Ice House (which notoriously lived up to its name when the audience didn't love you) was big too—but this was bigger, and darker. Everything about the room demanded that the performers project life and light from the stage.

Then there was the fact that the *hungry i* had launched Lenny Bruce, Jonathan Winters, the Smothers Brothers, and the Kingston Trio—which meant now we were following Mike into the shadow of his brother. If I had more sense, I would have been as nervous as he was.

The buildup was intense on night one, but I was able to relax a little watching Gale Garnett sing "We'll Sing in the Sunshine," the breezy folk ballad she'd written about Hoyt Axton. Somewhere in the five years since we'd left elementary school it became okay to sing on the radio about sex without strings. Jerry and Myrna Music, a folk comedy couple, did a set that was something like Stiller and Meara plus banjo, Jerry using the stoned-spacey voice he'd later refine into the voice of Garfield the Cat. Then, in a tantrum of doublespeak from the back rows, Irwin Corey began his squawky-professor routine, haranguing some invisible troublemaker until the spotlight found him—whereupon he flashed an exaggerated showman's grin and took the stage. (I was actually fooled by the stunt.)

The specifics of our own set got lost in a haze of adrenaline. I know the jitters didn't wane until our second or third song, when I finally had some confidence in the sound of the room and our ability to fill it. I guess we opened with something uptempo like "Sing Out!" (the one with the hot gospel clap that record producers didn't like). We must have ended with something similar from our folk repertoire (we weren't yet the We Five of "You Were On My Mind"). In between, we tried to be funny and personable, a challenge that fell to Mike as our ringleader. There were maybe a couple of shaky moments, but after a few nights we were definitely delivering the goods. A week that began singing to empty seats ended with great reviews, full houses, expectant murmurings in the room.

Backstage was another story. It was North Beach Bohemian chaos. We had to change clothes in Banducci's office, because the club only had three dressing rooms for four acts, and alongside the adding machines and file cabinets was an open safe whose combination was taped to the front for anyone too stoned to remember numbers. Naturally, it got robbed within the week—that, or else someone failed to put the night's cash inside of it. In either case, We Five became the suspect, which was ludicrous. I don't think anything Irwin Corey did on stage could match the insanity of leaving a safe wide open and expecting $1,000 in cash to just stay there. Not to mention the stupidity of accusing us in a situation when virtually any employee or any vagabond in the budding West Coast hippie nation could have taken the money and used We Five as their scapegoat.

Or, for all I know, it was Banducci's way of guilting his old friend and combatant, Frank Werber, into paying us out of his own pocket (our fee for the week was exactly the missing amount). Werber was upset with us, and he paid. It was one of only two occasions when Werber would accuse us of something we didn't do.

★ ★ ★

A few weeks later, we found ourselves at Melodyland in Anaheim opening for Phyllis Diller, the hag-haired comedienne-crone ("Can you believe these kids? They're out there singing in a band, being responsible, and I can't get mine to put a cap on the toothpaste! AH! AH! AH!"), a show that, along with the *hungry i*, Frank later wanted purged from our resume. We still looked too much like a transitional folk group rather than the next-wave image he was crafting.

As we took the stage, one Phyllis Diller fan asked her companion, "What's a 'We Five'?" And the bewildered friend exclaimed, "Hey! I've seen that group at the Meeting Place! That's the *Ridgerunners*!"

One night, Beverly ran her pantyhose, and Phyllis Diller loaned her a pair, but not without a scolding about professionalism. "You don't show up with just one pair of pantyhose!" I don't know how that lecture affected Beverly, but I was thinking Phyllis Diller made some sense.

As for the future, you could have made some pretty good predictions by studying the low-watt playground of local television. L.A.'s KCOP-13—whose daytime schedule bounced from sweaty kids' show clowns to reruns of "Victory at Sea"—was home to the first televised appearance we ever did. It was called "Bash," a pre–Animal House debauch on which DJ Emperor Bob Hudson sat enthroned with a crown of laurel leaves, caressed by slave girls and feasting on grapes as he introduced whichever acts were starting to make noise on the Sunset Strip. The Byrds performed "Tambourine Man" when we were there (Jim McGuinn, peering over not-yet-famous granny glasses, had not yet changed his name to Roger). Jackie DeShannon sang "When You Walk in the Room," and Danny Hutton, later of Three Dog Night, previewed "Roses and Rainbows" dressed in early Love-In fashion with an open pirate shirt, beads, leather sandals and the kind of long hair you mistook for a girl's from behind. All of us were going to have hit records within six months.

Frank was still finishing up that basement studio. We'd seen it under construction the week of our *hungry i* debut, stepping over loose tools and two-by-fours one night after closing. It was designed to be the new home for the Kingston Trio when their Capitol Records contract ran out, but We Five would be the first group to record there.

A perfect storm was gathering, and in the meantime, I had fallen in love.

★ ★ ★

It happened the night I got out of the University of San Francisco—following Mike and Bob's move back to Southern California. I'd bought a car (a totally uncollectable 1956 Chevy four-door with pea-green paint and a six-cylinder engine that ticked if you went over 55 mph) and drove down to spend the summer sleeping on the sofa at my grandmother's one-bedroom house in Pomona. On the way, I thought I'd stop in on my old vocal teacher and family friend, Charlie Tonkin, not thinking it would take more than a few minutes and a cup of coffee. I gave not a second's consideration to my grandmother, who was probably waiting up.

I rolled in to the driveway and there stood Charlie, elegant bearing and styled white hair; he was a would-be opera singer before leaving New York. The Great Carlo Tonkinini, he'd called himself. His wife was standing next to him, and they both happened to be heading out the door to catch up to their son.

"When did you get back?" he greeted me when I got out of the car. "We're going to see Jeff singing in a group at the high school. They've got a girl singer who's really good." He was already matchmaking. "She's thin, but *really cute.*"

We arrived at the gymnasium at Glendora High just as the girl took the stage. And I saw her: Debbie Graf.

She had blonde hair in a ponytail, crisp attire—a sort of Streisand sailor dress topped by a knotted kerchief—with legs so thin that people would say they were *too* thin, perfect for modeling, and she was on the edge of tall enough for that, about 5'8" in flats: A blonde, angular, pretty girl with an Arkansas twang. Lauren Bacall with a ponytail. As the Legendaires began to play, she started to move, beautifully (as much as anyone *could* move with both feet nailed to the floor around a single mic, Peter, Paul and Mary style). Whatever she was doing with her voice somehow made Jeff and his partner, Mike Alley, who were never great singers, sound . . . memorable.

Afterward, back at the Tonkins' house, I was dressed slouchy-nerdy (probably an old plaid shirt with jeans and tennis shoes). Debbie was not. Her colors, her lines, that knot on the kerchief—it was all pure perfection. Moreover, she knew its effect. This was when girls were taught hair and makeup in school, and as a creative type, Debbie took the knowledge to art-form levels. You could tell that her look was her canvas. Yet she never looked made up—it was totally natural. I also noticed, while we sat on the couch talking about the performance, how much of the energy and animation she'd brought to the stage was present right there in the room. She was really . . . friendly. And totally without pretense. There was no sense of sparring or maneuvering in her manner like so many of the pretty girls I'd met who sized you up before even agreeing to talk with you. I didn't know her, but already I was comfortable around her.

Suddenly a phone rang, and someone announced, "They delivered your car, Debbie!"

Clearly that was big news. Debbie's cousin, who owned a car lot, had bought her a '61 Falcon at the wholesale auction, and Debbie wanted to go see it right now. The thing was her friends weren't into it. These high school boys were still riding the high of rubbing elbows with the upperclassmen at an all-night party. Whereas Debbie was in college and had been performing all her life—she cared about the car.

I volunteered.

★ ★ ★

We drove my pea-green bomb the six blocks to her parents', where her spotless white Falcon was sitting right there in the driveway, and Debbie started jumping up and down—it was a very smart moment for a guy to be present. She even gave me a peck on the cheek.

A second spontaneous kiss came while I was leaving the Tonkins' house—this one was soft and giving.

I didn't try to take advantage of whatever invitation the kiss implied. But as I walked to my car my head was definitely spinning with possibilities that hadn't been there one day before.

In my whole life till then, I had never known anyone that open and free with affection. I knew that kiss at the door was more than just a holy kiss. But it had no premeditated agenda either.

I had no frame of reference for this. With Sue Davies, long before, it was all about adventure and experiment: blowing minds, taking chances, playing me against Mike on a ride home—*I'll take any roller coaster you want to get on.* With Donna, things were much more tentative: she was a childhood friend and a religious girl, one I might marry . . . untouchable. Debbie was neither, or both.

★ ★ ★

So I became part of Debbie's small community that met at Marge Alley's house up above the country club in Glendora. Marge was the classic stage mother, a small-time actress turned press agent and manager. They had a huge family room where the Legendaires would practice, play, and talk. Mike did vocal arranging, and under the guise of giving guitar lessons I stayed every moment I could, because Debbie was there.

When she wasn't singing, Debbie was a secretary for a construction company. I'd hang around there too, till they told her I couldn't visit anymore.

To get away from the rest of her band, one day we took a drive. I only
vaguely knew where I was going. I'd been taken to Lytle Creek once in high
school. In a bad photo, I'd sat with Susie on a fallen log at a magic spot across
the creek. It was beautiful, idyllic, and only a half-hour away, so we headed
off on a quest for alone time.

Hours went by just driving and talking. We drove east into Cajon Pass,
missed the turnoff, and wound up going all the way to Wrightwood, up Angeles Crest. When we reached Highway 39, Debbie said, "I think you could
get back to Glendora that way. I think this goes down to Azusa." But we
needed a restroom by then.

We found a public Chem Can in the forest with two doors for privacy—
but both holes went to the same tank—and I hunkered in, embarrassed just by
the noise of my stream. I'd grown up with three sisters in an uptight Catholic
home. Going to the bathroom was *private*. Whereas Debbie and her brother,
growing up in Arkansas, used to take baths together to save well water. All
she said, after making her bouncy exit, was that it sure beat the outhouse on
grandpa's farm.

I was floored by her. One time, at a mini-market grabbing munchies
with the band, her pronunciation of "Vienna" sausages rhymed with *hyena*—
and she didn't give a hoot when the guys laughed.

But she knew what she knew, and she commanded respect. After seeing Mike and me chuckling in the back of the audience during one of the
Legendaires' performances—I don't even remember what we were laughing
about—she confronted me. "Either you're mocking someone's work, or
you've got so little respect that you weren't even watching. In either case, it's
unacceptable. And you hurt me."

All at once, the ice felt thin. But she'd made very clear not to take her
for granted.

★ ★ ★

As for Mike, I know he found her attractive, but I don't know that he
was ever romantically interested in Debbie. Maybe he couldn't wrap his brain
around her rural naiveté. Or maybe he was being practical: Debbie kept me
from causing romantic conflicts in the group. Ever the opportunist, Mike also
saw she was a ready instrument for him to sound out the female vocal parts
that were in his head.

He let the old hurts cool on a back burner, and we lived in the moment
making music.

★ ★ ★

With Beverly fifty miles away in Santa Ana, Debbie's versatility as a singer allowed her to pitch in generously with whatever the Ridgerunners happened to be practicing. Meanwhile I just savored being in the same space with her. Talking. Living. Laughing. Touching. One night, steaming the car windows in front of her folks' house, we heard a knock and there stood a cop, rolling his eyes as we thrashed to get shirts tucked in and buttoned. I presented a fake ID that said I was twenty-two, and the cop decided we were old enough to do what we liked. But it freaked us out to realize that if he'd taken the license from its plastic for a closer look, her parents might have been called. Two days later, Debbie gave the document a hand-drawn California seal.

There was nothing else I wanted to do but sing and be with Debbie. And I didn't have to compartmentalize love and music the way I might have with Donna, who liked music well enough but wasn't a musician.

Unfortunately, Donna wasn't going to let me just disappear. Right after she'd found out I wasn't going to stay in the Bay Area, she made arrangements to come down and visit a friend in North Orange County. She wanted to know what was going on.

While the band rehearsed in Mike Stewart's bedroom (the kind of motel-room rehearsal space that eventually backdrops all musicians' lives), Donna overlooked the scene like the art on a TraveLodge wall. I'd known Donna since sixth grade and had sat in her bedroom with friends playing records, each of the guys wishing he was alone with her. We all identified with the Richie Valens hit "Donna" as if he'd written it for us. Rock-band widow was quite a comedown for her.

Eventually the group took a break, and I was left facing her.

"Well, this is really interesting," she said. "Seeing what you do." There was a long pause while I tried to figure out what to say back, and she confessed: "I think I like Jerry the sometime folksinger more than I like Jerry the band member."

I understood what she meant. She didn't see any place for herself in that room.

When I drove her back to the friend's house, she tried to make conversation the way we had after the Streisand concert. Barry Goldwater, the Arizona ultraconservative, was the topic—she couldn't believe anyone would want him to be president. I knew I was supposed to agree, but ever since JFK's assassination, I'd made up my mind I could get by without caring too much about politics. I could even sing a political song without ever thinking of living the message, the same way the Kingston Trio could sing a gospel song on stage and then spend the night with groupies. I didn't care about Barry Goldwater, and I didn't care about Lyndon Johnson either.

For the rest of that summer, Donna continued to write letters. When I didn't answer, she made one last trip to L.A. to find out what was what. It happened that my grandmother was out of town that day, and I'd been looking forward to being with Debbie in the empty house.

So I lied to Donna on the phone. "My grandmother's going to San Diego and she needs me to drive her. There's really no point in you coming over." I figured that was that.

But she came anyway.

The house was a perfect little one-bedroom hideaway next to George's White Way neighborhood market. I stashed my car in the garage to make it look like no one was there. Debbie and I pulled down the blinds (I knew Donna would be hitting town at a certain time) and then we basically sat there waiting.

Donna arrived, knocked on the front door, and when nobody answered, she went around to the back. We sat in the back bedroom, barely breathing. She tried to look in the side windows. She could have easily seen into the kitchen, so Debbie and I didn't wander out there.

It took a while, but Donna finally drove away.

As soon as she did, I buried the thought of how to deal with her. Part of me knew I should have just manned up and told her the truth. I could have introduced her to Debbie right there. I had no desire to keep Donna on a limb; I just felt guilty about having invested so much time only to turn on a dime. I told myself I didn't want to hurt her unnecessarily. Debbie was the only one I wanted to be with that day, or the next for that matter.

I let a year go by without ever finding the nerve to tell Donna the truth. And even then, it was only after she forced the question.

★ ★ ★

There was going to be a learning curve to love. I soon learned that Debbie got migraine headaches. Ruthless and often. Before this, I'd had no idea what the term even meant.

I was at Marge Alley's one day expecting just to play with the dogs and make some music as usual. The dogs were there when I walked in, but no Debbie. Bedrooms at the Alley house were strictly, famously off limits—so my curiosity raged when I was shown to a pitch-black room where I literally tripped over Debbie on the floor.

"What are you doing down there?" I said.

She forced out an elegant straight answer: "Got a headache."

"Can I do anything?" I offered. "Can I get you an aspirin?"

"Aspirin doesn't help."

"Well, have you tried—"

"*Please. Don't make me talk.*"

"Okay." I said. And waited a moment. "But why?"

"I've got a migraine. It hurts to talk."

"What about if I turn a light on?"

I thought I could hear her eyes roll in the dark.

"If lights are on, it hurts and I throw up. Don't talk, please."

Sometimes the headache lasted a week. The trigger might be her period, or a sudden change in air pressure (like a trip to the mountains or an incoming storm). The only remedy she knew was to try to sleep. If she could get her eight hours, the migraine would be gone. But any pill she tried to swallow, she'd throw back up.

My instinct was to get annoyed by the inconvenience. The more bravely she soldiered through a migraine—performing, auditioning, recording—the more skeptical I'd become. How bad could a migraine be if she was handling all that stuff?

Another test of love was that she was a complicated eater. There was a downside to a high metabolism. When Debbie got hungry, we'd have about a fifteen-minute window before she'd be literally too sick to eat. I was exactly the opposite: I could lose myself in a project and stop eating for days. "What's such a crisis about being hungry?" I wanted to know. We'd be doing long treks in the car. The ride from Glendora, where Debbie lived, to the Sunset Strip, where one of us might be playing or auditioning, could take an hour and a half in traffic, and when you parked and got out, there was no fast food. We'd have to go someplace like Ben Frank's on Sunset—where slow service was a sadistic art—and no one counted the minutes like we did, watching the parade of pre-hippie, pre-Manson runaways try to connect with bands or score dope or get stoned on someone else's dime.

Drugs weren't even a remote curiosity for Debbie—Ben Frank's was like doing hard time.

Her Baptist parents opposed her even *dating* a non-Protestant like me. But there she got incensed. She told them, "I'll date a black guy if I want to." So I got invited to the house to meet the family.

I'm not sure they knew what to make of me. Her dad, Woody, was a country-singing farm boy from Mulberry, Arkansas. Her mom made hi-tech monitors for NASA by day and played piano with her husband at square dances by night. Her brother, Gary—an Elvis fan and proud protector of his sister—assumed I was gay because I wore Beatle boots. He was also a mechanic. He showed me his Rambler wagon with reclining seats, which made it a cross between a joke car, a pickup truck, and a rolling motel.

My first real chance to be anything more to these people than the possible homosexual who was incomprehensibly dating Debbie came when they wanted to buy Woody a guitar for his birthday. I took her mom to Wallich's Music City, where in one of those serendipitous moments, we found a Gibson J-50 for only about $250. It wasn't anything top of the line like a Martin, but it had a blond face like what Bob Dylan was playing, so I convinced them it was the most guitar for the money.

I'd hit the jackpot. That Gibson was virtually the same instrument played by Woody's hero, Jimmie Rodgers[2]: not the Jimmie Rodgers who sang "Honeycomb," but the original Yodeling Brakeman—the father of country music. (Until that day, Woody, a well-known picker around Ozark, Arkansas, in his youth, had been content playing a $35 guitar—because that was who he was and where he came from. He was a man who found joy in what he had.)

It just seemed that whatever my differences with Debbie, music could bridge them. Just like me, she'd tried relationships with non-musicians. Her fiancé, who was on his way out when I was on the way in, snapped at her a couple of times just for singing with the radio. As if she could ever not.

Not wanting to send him a Dear John letter, she didn't break up with him until he returned from the service. When she did, we had what both of us seemed to long for: a relationship with no compartments. There were no negatives to us being together. At least not from my point of view.

But there were seeds of conflict. Debbie didn't smoke *anything*. When I smoked a cigarette at a drive-in movie, she reached across the seat and asked if she could try one, then affected a *femme fatale* pose when I lit her up. I smiled with obvious approval: "You look cool!"—but that wasn't what Debbie wanted to hear.

"I was trying to show you how ridiculous you looked!" she said, and threw the cigarette to the parking lot in disgust.

· 7 ·

When I Woke Up This Morning

$\mathcal{A}$s soon as Hank McGill, the engineer who helped build Frank Werber's odd-shaped basement studio, got done with all his finishing touches, Werber sent word for us to come north. He gave us the keys to a little gingerbread-style cottage he'd just vacated in the town of Ross, about thirty minutes north of the city, and we rolled up to a beautiful neighborhood overgrown with trees and shrubs. I couldn't believe he was going to let us just stay there.

We'd been told to bring sleeping bags, and once inside, I saw why. There was no furniture anywhere aside from some lounges by the pool.

Not that any of us minded. We were free of school, away from the world of our relatives, and living in the house of the Kingston Trio's manager, for which privilege we only had to show up at the studio and sing. The only serious challenge was going to be making it through the week on the Phyllis Diller money. Since Frank wasn't giving us a per diem and we plainly wouldn't be cooking meals in the house, I divided the money by days of the week and doled it out to each member of the group.

Most of them liked to sleep in, the sweet privilege of half-adults, but I just couldn't, and Pete Fullerton was a morning guy like me. We'd discovered homemade hash brown potatoes at a breakfast counter in Ross, where I'd watch a guy shred the same potatoes that I'd watched him boil the night before, and then float them in butter on the big grill, and the miracle never got old.

After eating, we grabbed the others and left for the mind-blowing drive to the studio: south through Marin and over the Golden Gate Bridge, through the foresty Presidio, past the Marina district, around Ghiradelli and Fisherman's Wharf, tracing the path that the car would soon find by itself, and then down Columbus to North Beach, with its taxis and strip clubs and carnival barkers.

We walked across Kearny below Broadway—that's where Pete says John Sebastian flung a record from a Corvair convertible, with those classic Euro lines and roof pillars thin as wishbones. "Are you recording at Trident too?" was the only thing Pete could think to ask.

"No, man. Just spreading the word."

The ground-floor lobby of Columbus Tower[1] was a small receiving area with an elevator facing; when it opened, it could barely hold two people and a couple of amps. Seven floors up was Werber's penthouse roost; the Kingston Trio's accounting firm was on the third. When we got to the basement we were like this tiny circus car with clowns stepping out.

Pete set up his bass in his own alcove off to one side. Beyond the alcove was the soundproofed Control Room, dark and futuristic, with only the instrument panels lit and the occupants barely visible to anyone on our side. The studio itself was natural wood, with textured earth-tone fabrics to deaden the room. It was not a real big room, but it could absorb a ton of sound.

That's where we stepped forward to record "You Were On My Mind," just minutes after Jerry Granelli invented the drum track we'd more or less been hearing in our dreams.

★ ★ ★

And now it begins. Granelli pumps out that subtle, urgent drum intro (*AND* ONE), which, alongside the rock guitar's muted staccato, seems to march us toward our fate, and then halts there: a hush, which is the first unforgettable aspect of the song. *Listen*, it seems to say. As if something completely new is going to dawn. It's like those inexorable snare rolls in "The Little Drummer Boy," or in Jefferson Airplane's "White Rabbit," a song that would deploy almost the exact same steady ascent from mysterious quiet to finale. I know I wasn't visualizing drum rolls as an apocalyptic image of soldiers marching off to Vietnam, but I wonder if the Airplane and others were thinking that. It's how the sorrow and promise of the mid-1960s sounded in your gut.

Just drums, muted guitars, string bass, and the suggestion of another body breathing—three measures of daybreak that steals into your room, then stops for the whisper of a young girl at a microphone. And it can't be coincidental that her first six words are these:

WHEN I WOKE UP THIS MORNING

Well. It's the oldest blues lyric, that line. But it's clear from the outset that these blues are not merely gallows blues—in fact, they brim with hope. In the young girl's voice there's an ache, to be sure, but the ache has a confidante, a companion missing and present at once.

YOU WERE ON MY MIND

And as if to shake you in your bed once more with the simple outland-ishness of a *me* and a *you* on the loose in the universe, that confession, in fact, repeats:

AND—YOU WERE ON MY MIND

As if to ask: Did you hear?

It's because of Mike Stewart's vision, funneled through Beverly Bivens's voice, that this indomitable energy has taken hold, and the irresistible thing about it, the thing people will puzzle over for decades, is that the energy in some weird way is struggling to overcome the lyrics themselves. For if the next three lines are taken at their word (I'VE GOT TROUBLES/I'VE GOT WORRIES/I'VE GOT WOUNDS TO BIND), the song remains a lament, just as Sylvia Fricker wrote it. (Actually, she wrote GOT SOME ACHES/GOT SOME PAINS, but we were nineteen years old—what was that?) In-stead, Beverly's joyful sob evokes a whole different sort of dawn, an expecta-tion of healing, an Age of Love in the fallout of a 1950s dream.

SO I WENT TO THE CORNER

Slash! (Bob's first, single bright electro-chord enters the church of folk and remains there to jangle and chime.)

JUST TO EASE MY PAIN

SAID, JUST TO EASE MY PAIN

I'VE GOT TROUBLES/I'VE GOT WORRIES

I CAME HOME AGAIN

Sylvia's original lyric ran "I got drunk and/I got sick and/I came home again," but Frank wasn't going there, not when still smarting over the time Capitol/EMI simply turned the sound off on the word "damn" in the Kings-ton Trio singing "I don't give a damn about a greenback dollar," leaving an infuriating hole in the middle of a song. We were teenagers, and so he thought it best to bypass radio opposition and change the words himself.

Right after that comes another small but crucial embellishment: a one-syllable shift added by Beverly, a note of ambiguity that Sylvia never wrote, a word that slides the focus of the verse from pain to wonder,

BUT I WOKE UP THIS MORNING

YOU WERE ON MY MIND

with more complex harmonies weaving and ascending to new tensions, platforms for catapulting higher still.

Whether it's because the vocal is being carried upward by love's mystery, or because the key shifts, or because the pain of a breakup is being shaken off by an invincible youth that hasn't yet seen the shadow of disappointment, it's ceased to matter. The repetitions mount, sorrows have become freaky treasures (I'VE GOT TROUBLES! I'VE GOT WORRIES! I'VE GOT WOUNDS TO BIND!), and Beverly's vocal opens to a shout:

AND I'VE GOT A FEELING/DOWN IN MY SHOES!
Which is as far down as feeling goes.
THAT I'VE GOT TO RAMBLE! I'VE GOT TO MOVE ON!
I'VE GOT TO WALK AWAY MY BLUES!
Yes, with five shrieking notes pulled from Bob's electric twelve-string—
and a hard stop. But it's only a false climax. The table is reset; the hush re-
convenes. (WHEN I WOKE UP THIS MORNING—YOU WERE ON
MY MIND.) But where that lyric played as mere expectancy at the song's first
gathering, it's now sureness, something cherished, something sublime.

And like the final push over the top of a roller coaster, the symphony
hovers one last time, paying out in a heart-stopping thirty-second finale.
Nothing is finished, say the lyrics (I'VE GOT WOUNDS TO BIND)—
world without end. And yet everything's been said. Copping a George Har-
rison guitar lick (it's "Ticket to Ride," but inverted), Bob has been vamping
through the whole final verse, two chords fighting for resolution, until, with
kick drum pounding, that last root chord expends its chime.

Whatever else people say about "You Were On My Mind," no one
accuses it of just ending. It has one of the most roof-blown finales in the history of popular music. We never wanted it otherwise. Where plenty of rock
records ended with a "board fade," because they were just about getting into
a groove and getting out, we'd had an almost intellectual opposition to that
concept: it implied you couldn't figure out the hidden ending. We'd even
used the same four-chord resolution before—Michael called it a Plagle Cadence—although never with this level of drama.

The final measures took just about everything I had, because I was singing
the moving line in the harmony and it was right at the break point of my range.
If I wasn't in good voice, I had to yell to get the thing out. After too many takes,
trust me, fatigue sets in: you're either singing it flat or just not well. This recording took every one of us to our outer limits. Fans the world over have described
to me how new, in 1965, the song's aural catharsis felt. And to many listeners
the energy of the finale is still unmatched after almost fifty years.

In the aftermath we stood there, drums shaking, hearts pounding.

★ ★ ★

But it took a couple of happy accidents to seal it. What you hear on the
record is take thirteen, with one of the earlier endings (before our voices got
exhausted) spliced on. That fix would be a digital no-brainer today—back
then it took a veteran hand. Hank McGill had to find a spot on both takes
where the group was doing exactly the same thing at the same time. And then
he had to cut the half-inch tape with a razor blade.

So we went searching through the takes until all of us agreed on a promising junction where Hank could do his thing. Then Mike and Bev and most of the others went off to get a burger at Zim's. Pete and I couldn't tear ourselves from the booth. We stayed and watched Hank mark both tapes, cut them, and splice them. It went quick, a simple operation. Then he pushed PLAY. Only something was off, right there at the climax. The beats didn't line up. It turned out the syllable he'd chosen from Mike got sung a half-breath later on one take than on the other, just spontaneously. And since the splices were cut at an angle, like the backslash on your keyboard (/), you couldn't just peel off the adhesive, reattach the original sections, and then cut a vertical inch further along the tape. Peeling the adhesive could also destroy part of the original tape.

Hank looked up and gave us a pitifully sober look. You could tell every possible alternative had been thought of and discarded. "Well," he said, and gathered a breath. "If tape moves at fifteen inches a second, how much do you think that syllable was late by?"

It was evidently a rhetorical question—because he was already leaning down on the blade.

As Pete and I watched in horror, Hank McGill made his cut.

He slid the chopped bit of tape away, history, then spliced the two parts back together. Pete and I were still trying to catch our breath when he re-threaded the reels and played the song back.

Perfection.[2]

* * *

We caught up with the group for hamburgers—a spectacle of stunned relief and comedown from that near-disaster in the control room—and then pulled ourselves together to overdub the vocals.

Overdubbing involved transferring the original recording, which was a live performance on three tracks, to a separate machine and singing along live to fatten up the backing vocals. Turning our three voices into six. We hesitated about whether to double Beverly's lead too or just crank it louder. The answer was to leave her solo lines alone, fattening her only where the harmonies expanded the overall sound.

Now we were hearing what couldn't exist without the laboratory of a studio. Bob had never heard doubling, and it blew him away. You had the aural pressure of six people—two Beverlys, two Mikes, two Jerrys—but syllables pronounced by only three. There's a richness in it that's like the doors of perception are being blown open, or some third ear that you were born with has just crackled back to life.

So even more than the excitement of singing the song into our mics, even more than hearing our own voices first played back, it's another thing to hear it come back larger than life. That's definitely when your skin crawls, because you're hearing the big effect for the first time ever, and when it's good, it's *really* good. You know it's never going to sound like the first time again, but you're hearing it NOW. Plus it bursts on you, the same way it will on the world, what's so brand new and original about the song.

"There's nothing like that being played on the radio!" Bob declared.

We knew it. Frank knew it. No other words were needed. We all knew what each other's smile meant.

There's nothing like that goosebumps feeling. It's happened only a few times in my whole performing life, and the intervals between them just get longer. The first time was at Capitol Records with Mike and Susie when we were still in high school. The song, in the spirit of new awakenings, had been "The First Time Ever I Saw Your Face," way before it was a hit.

We'd traveled some distance, Mike and I, since then.

★ ★ ★

It was the small hours by the time we left on a damp, cool but not cold April night with the North Beach hubbub winding down. Werber went upstairs to his penthouse to bed—ironically he slept in his office while the band slept in his house—and we savored our walk to the car. I remember flashing on the amazement of the moment: to be out in San Francisco in the middle of the night, having cut the Next Hit Record. I must have been thinking, *Somebody pinch me.* I wasn't drinking age, and it wouldn't have crossed my mind to enter a bar. But I didn't need alcohol that night. The city still looked new to me: inviting but mystifying, like Pinocchio's Pleasure Island. Strip joints and jazz clubs and underground worlds I'd hardly even heard about yet.

I was overwhelmed by the idea that my life was changing. We had just made a record, and none of these people we passed on the street knew where we'd been, and none of them had been doing the same thing themselves. There was that glow of accomplishment and pride. We were like kids who'd just discovered sex. Bouncing, talking, laughing. In the next two years there'd be times we'd walk out of that studio deeply depressed. This was not like that.

A 76 station had sold itself out as a parking lot at night, and that was where our car was. Mike drove. It was almost an hour to Ross even in the middle of the night, but we needed every minute of it in order to come down from the high. We passed stragglers milling around the Condor Club after hours, and the Golden Gate Bridge was lit orange in the early morning mist, and I remember the blackness of the water. We went up the Waldo grade and came down into Marin County and the country roads that would take us into Ross, dark, airy, and rural. Rich folk lived there, and they liked it rustic, without sidewalks.

We got ourselves inside and arranged our sleeping bags in the various rooms, going through our rituals in silent proximity. Beverly was as unselfconscious as one of the guys. Pete dragged a chaise lounge from the pool area into the house and plopped himself down in it. Bob was off somewhere smoking a joint. Mike actually had his girlfriend, Cookie, with him, but you'd hardly have known it. All week she'd been the invisible stranger wherever we were. I was thinking: wow. He doesn't treat her like he wants her to be here. They were together, and yet they weren't—not in the way I thought of togetherness. She was living what had been Donna's premonition about a future with me—with the band, but not in the band. Extraneous. Expendable. Window dressing.

I straightened out my sleeping bag and made myself lie there trying to unwind. There was no phone in the place—not that I would have called my parents had there been one. My family was never connected by phones the way most are today. It was Debbie I would have liked talking to. She could have related to what we were experiencing. She was becoming my family.

But she was as unreachable now as my parents were, and whatever had happened to change my life in the studio that night, I was savoring it all by myself, alongside the only other people who knew what it felt like. I had never really identified with those kids in my generation who ran off from home in search of themselves and new answers to life—but it occurred to me, as I drifted to sleep, that here I was doing just that.

PART TWO

After the Trio, anyone could go and get a guitar and a banjo, practice a little bit and go sing together. The Trio ploughed the field so that there could be the Dylans, the Judy Collinses, the Stephen Stillses, etc.

—Frank Werber to Alec Palao, 1997

With "You Were On My Mind," we had given A&M their first hit outside of their own caca creations.

—Werber to Palao, 1997

Trident was at once in the vanguard of rock's next phase, and a victim of it.

—Alec Palao, liner notes to Sing Me a Rainbow

Rock and Roll a Bust for Kingston Trio Man

—Rolling Stone headline, December 1967

· 8 ·

Awe and Shock

$\mathcal{W}$e drove back to L.A. full of ourselves, high on who we were and what we'd done. We weren't high in the drugged sense, because that wasn't happening regularly yet with anyone but Bob, and he didn't make it all that public.

Meanwhile Frank Werber went to work, enacting phase two of his plan to build a West Coast folk-rock empire.

He had put together a management trio. Don Graham, a record promoter plucked from a local Warner Bros. distributor, personified what was then the gospel in making a band climb Billboard's sales charts: small and hyperactive, in loud suits—a young Don Rickles with hair—he had the bounce of a load of ping pong balls hitting a marble floor. He talked too much and too fast and praised you way too highly, as had always been expected of a promotion man until then.

To get the band rehearsed, dressed, and ready to perform, Frank had Joe Gannon, the Kingston Trio's road manager. Tall, trim, and curly haired, Gannon was an accountant and he looked the part, with brogue shoes, pegged pants, and button-down collars. He'd met the Trio at Menlo Business College and even played bass in the band's earlier iteration, until Werber got rid of the girl singer and the bassist. So, Gannon told me, he'd opened a bar called the Library, up the hill toward 19th in a residential area. While he was running this bar, the Trio told him they needed a road manager, to which he'd said, "What do I gotta do?"

They taught him exactly what Gannon soon began teaching me (because he thought I'd be responsible in his absences): how to get a band in and out of bed, onto the airplane, and to the venue with all their instruments, as well

65

as the hard part, how to deal with the contracts. How to check the count on the house to find out if they paid what you were entitled to be paid.

Also, when a show started, it needed to look like a show. Through Joe Gannon, the Kingston Trio had perfected the art of making a concert look like the same folk experience every night, as long as the place had at least one microphone, a table to put the guitars on, and two Super Trooper spotlights with colored gel options. Consistency—that was what he wanted to teach me. Not so much the rest of the group, who gave little credence to this antithesis of the hip musician. I was the one at age twenty who was going to keep a level head in the midst of celebrity chaos.

He set me up with my first Air Travel Card. It wouldn't help you get a train ticket, as I learned in Idaho during an air strike, but you could rent a car with it. He didn't want anyone else in the group even thinking about that stuff.

The Trio had almost mercilessly abused Joe Gannon, because his job was to get in the way of them having fun. The same thing threatened to happen to me. Everyone in the band had an assignment, which Joe or I oversaw. Pete was responsible for the clothes; Bob and John Chambers were responsible for the instruments. Mike was responsible for musical direction and for being our primary mouthpiece to the media. Beverly was responsible for being Beverly, and for getting to the plane on time. I learned to yell for her twenty minutes earlier than I'd yell for everyone else. She would be missing for a midnight departure from San Francisco International Airport, the stewardess profuse with apologies because she knew us but couldn't hold the plane any longer, and then finally Beverly would come running up the ramp.

Frank Werber's job was to cement the record distribution deal, and with considerable foresight he went to A&M on the Sunset Strip. Conceived by PR man Jerry Moss and deft trumpet minimalist Herb Alpert, a Jewish kid from local Fairfax High with Latin-lover looks, the label was already developing a specialty for finding the next musical niche and then widening it to more than a novelty. They had just followed Alpert's Tijuana Brass with the Baja Marimba Band, and had Sérgio Mendes & Brazil '66 waiting in the wings. Whatever was novel and leading-edge, without being rock, A&M was the label that did it. They had good ears, they were lean and lithe, and they didn't have to deal with the corporate bullshit that plagued Columbia, Capitol, and RCA.

Werber secured terms for "You Were On My Mind" that were precedent-setting themselves. The single would be billed as "a Trident production," and instead of a percentage of net profit or gross sales, numbers that record companies easily manipulated, A&M would be required to pay him a fixed number of pennies per record. By simply counting records sold, you earned a million times your pennies for a million-selling record.

Various stories circulate about how Werber did it. Don Graham's is that A&M agreed only if Graham would leave Werber and work for them, which he ultimately did. But others told me Graham left angry over the direction of We Five. Werber wanted the band to move straight to venues like the Bob Hope Show—in the "celebrated artist" mold—whereas Graham believed that model was passing away. The Kingston Trio had gotten trapped in it, as had Bobby Darren and Frankie Avalon.

★ ★ ★

Next, Graham began doing what he'd learned in the folk era: lining up regional radio stations as kindling to build a national fire. He hand-delivered acetates, which play only a few times before wearing out, to KYA, KEWB, and KSFO in the Bay Area, soliciting input from DJs at each stop. The payola era was over, but that didn't mean you couldn't offer people a sense of ownership in the record. In a famous precursor, Murray the K was so invested in the Marcels' "Blue Moon," he played it twenty-six times in one show.

Within days, an unexpected verdict came back. The song, performance, and arrangement were all great, but the hushed opening—Bev's lone vocal over snare drum and muted bass—took too long to gather force and draw the other instruments to itself. If the electric twelve-string could chime in, literally, telegraph the *whoah-whoahs* that reply to *troubles, worries*, and *wounds* in the later verses, then, the DJs were saying, the record would surely be a hit.

The band would not even be consulted about such a thing in 1965. Expediency was in charge.

So Frank Werber called the only Bay Area musician he knew who owned an electric twelve-string. It was a Rickenbacker, like the Beatles and Byrds were starting to use, a very contemporary choice aside from the small fact that it didn't really sound like the guitar Bob Jones had played on record. No matter. A fellow named Rex Larsen added six chords, and the last one was just plain . . . *wrong*.[1]

Mike was the first in the band to get word of it. (I think Frank actually played the opening for him over a phone line.) In a world of MP3s and internet sharing, it's hard for anyone to imagine the long fuse of anxiety that was lit by Mike warning us there was a problem with an added guitar.

"How can they do that?" Bob demanded in Mike's bedroom in Claremont, where we were practicing.

A week later, when the test pressing arrived, Bob forced me to listen. The first new strums seemed foreign at first, but well placed, not really bad by any means. Bob watched me stand there adapting to each chord as it came. "It's okay," I told him neutrally.

"Yeah, yeah," he cut in, his voice getting sharper, "but keep listening." He was pointing toward the turntable like a priest of the Inquisition.

At the heinous final chord overlaying the words *to bind*, I cringed.

It wasn't even in key. At that juncture, the band is suspending an F# minor 7th—while Rex Larsen blares out a proud B7, which contains a half-tone difference, its D# note literally scraping against our chord's natural E. It had all the charm and appeal of a garbage can lid hitting the alley.

We played the record a couple more times, although we might as well have been re-watching the end of a sad movie. Each time, Bob fell into a rage again, storming around, arms waving. "They can't do that!"

Some musicians think we tainted that chord on purpose, maybe to capture the singer's emotion as she headed to the corner to ease her pain. Or that it gave an early taste of the metallic distortion that rock would add to folk on its way toward psychedelia. If so, it was happening by a force I didn't grasp.

But at the radio stations, Don Graham's idea worked to perfection. He buttered up the DJs, telling them their suggestion had made all the difference in the world, which maybe it had. Now vested in discovering the new sound and perfecting it, they waited anxiously for its release, as did we.

★ ★ ★

We were spending that limbo time reconnecting with friends and family and our own agendas in Southern California. Mike was writing a song (ironically called "What Do I Do Now?"— a certain amount of darkness was always right behind him) with Bill Chadwick and Randy Sterling, a ubiquitous L.A. session player whom Frank later tapped to learn arranging and producing for Trident. Bob went back to Palmer Canyon to practice and play. Beverly sunned herself with poolside friends in Orange Country. And I was attaching myself to Debbie, which meant I was doing a lot of tagging along with the Legendaires.

They were playing Disneyland's Mickey Mouse Theater, where the peppier forms of folk music still thrived. Clean as it was, "Mickey Mouse" wasn't a synonym for phony yet. To baby boomers who grew up with it, TV's Mickey Mouse Club had been half glee club, half fraternity—just kids your age who looked good and had fun and went horseback riding. It was the summer camp you wished you could go to. And the park hired legitimate players, from Dixieland to Bluegrass. By the time I was fifteen, the Yachtsmen Quartet had been installed as resident folk group (the guitar that Mike Stewart played on "You Were On My Mind" was bought from a guy in the Quartet who'd gotten a girl pregnant and needed fast money). Mike and I had really arrived, I thought, when the Ridgerunners played on the "Yachtsmen Stage": a submarine's conning tower, with a mast above and lines blowing around. In just a couple more years, on the new Tomorrowland stage, you'd see the First Edition and the Staples Singers and Crystal Gale . . . and Linda Ronstadt singing "Long, Long Time," wearing shorts and knotted blouse and bare feet, like Daisy Mae.

Between Debbie's Legendaires sets, milling and strumming backstage as the hanger-on boyfriend, I found myself talking about "You Were On My Mind," and one of the girls in the show asked how it went. Debbie and I looked at each other and decided to give them a preview of the future. It was just our two voices with one guitar, but two voices could get the basic harmony going, and to a person the place was blown away.

At the same time I felt a pang, as if watching the changing of a season—no longer thinking it would be cool to play the Mickey Mouse Theater, but unaware that it was about to pass into irrelevance. Already, if employees wore anything scruffy that might sully the Disney illusion, they were out. By the time of our third album release at the Disneyland Hotel, hippies were screened at the gate. Our arranger, Richard Tilles, had a Sunset Strip look and an attitude to match, so the confrontation got pretty heated. Finally, we were made to leave the park.

★ ★ ★

Tagging along with Debbie that spring also meant watching the Legendaires work their way to the final round of the L.A. County Parks and Recreation Battle of the Bands at the Hollywood Bowl, a more prestigious event than it sounds today. First prize was a contract with Mercury Records, which Karen and Richard Carpenter won the following year. But it was a source of chronic pain to me and Mike. Year after year we'd been eliminated in an early round by a teenage accordion trio, two guys and a girl whose specialty was to paint their hands in fluorescent colors and then turn invisible under black light. For a finale, the girl moved front and center as both boys wrapped their flying fingers onto her accordion, hammering out "Hava Nagila" and "The Beer Barrel Polka."

I have no idea what happened to them after 1965—I hope they retired. You had the sense that Mike and I would have hung on to win if we'd learned to play "Call the Wind Maria" with, say, Bud and Travis sound effects. Instead, no one could focus on our skill, because of this carnival act from the '50s. I told myself they'd still be competing in talent contests when we were making music that our own generation wanted to hear. And that was just enough to stop having nightmares about fluorescent accordion trios.

Then the Legendaires beat them in the semifinal round. And I figured the judges were finally sick of fluorescent accordions.

But that wasn't really it. The difference was Debbie. The Legendaires' magic began as the lights *came on*. As I watched from a bench halfway up the Hollywood Bowl, an angular blonde girl began to dance—in place—between two guys on guitars: it was everything barely proper about the traditional folk-trio setup, everything holding steady for the previous ten years that was about to be turned loose. The power and animation and chick-ness of Debbie's Arkansas-bluesy voice seemed to lift all the other elements up with it: her dress suddenly full-color, the flash of a sun-bleached ponytail, the sureness of her smile.

★ ★ ★

By the time the awards got handed out, it was too late to go celebrate, not even dinner on the town with family, which must have disappointed Debbie but it was okay with me. I had been stretching my time with Debbie and feeling guilty about it. We Five had to rehearse in San Francisco in the morning, and the whole rest of the band had gone up a day ahead. We had a record; we had a manager—we had an obligation to be someplace that I wasn't.

I made the romantic error of taking Highway 1 through Big Sur, not realizing it would add hours to the trip. It was near dawn when Debbie and I got in range of San Francisco, and I don't remember which station played the song first, but after a ten-hour drive that should have been six, and with the signal as weak as if we were on the boat returning from Japan (long-distance radio goes away when the sun comes up), somehow the magnitude of the event didn't wake me.

After sunrise we walked down a ramp to the Sausalito houseboat where Frank had installed the band: a pre-fab mobile home built on a flat barge, the kind of weekly rental that lots of musicians who worked in the city were now crashing in. At high tide the units floated in a beautiful lagoon with Tiburon to the north and San Francisco Bay to the south; at low tide they floated in a hole dredged out of the mud flats. Inside had a dorm room air. Clothes strewn, dirty ashtrays everywhere.

I was wondering where we could lie down and sleep, but when we stepped through the door, everyone asked, "Did you hear it yet?"

Mike was scanning the radio with a cigarette dangling from his lip, and at the first stop there it was, mid-song. Then it ended, and a DJ told listeners they'd been listening to We Five and its smash hit, "You Were On My Mind," on Color Radio KEWB.

It seemed incongruous that this was really happening—that it wasn't a dream, say. Or just some prank Mike had fabricated.

Bob caught me grinning and got my attention with a scowl: "You haven't heard the intro." The added chords were still a festering wound.

Perfectly exhilarated, and just as perfectly exhausted, I finally asked where we could get a little rest.

"Bev's in this room," Bob said. "Why don't you guys just take the room at the end of the hall till rehearsal? We'll work out who goes where later."

So we walked into the room and shut the door behind us, which felt to me like closing the back cover on a romantic novel. I fell asleep thinking I had the love of my life with me in a houseboat on San Francisco Bay. Maybe I'd live there forever.

A few hours later everyone was still vacillating between old world and new, between "You want some lunch?" and "*Are we dreaming?*" You could only say it so many times before the high started to fade. None of the stations were going thirty minutes without playing us.

Debbie did not trumpet her victory the night before at the Hollywood Bowl, and her face never betrayed anything but joy in our delight. But it had to have been strange, to secure a record contract on the stage of the Hollywood Bowl and watch it become essentially a warm-up act to this.

She paid a different price a couple of days later when her parents picked her up. Cramped quarters with raw trappings on display would have been enough of a shock for them, but the unequal ratio of beds to people conjured images that were just plain devastating. Woody was doing his best just holding his tongue. "Those are some nice guitars," he said on his way out. "We've got a long drive ahead of us."

I learned later that silence reigned as the Grafs drove across Golden Gate Bridge, through the city, and down the peninsula. It was well over an hour before they stopped at a roadside café south of San Jose, where they told Debbie they were sickened by the sight of their daughter in that place.

★ ★ ★

In a few weeks, "You Were On My Mind" had hit number 1 in San Francisco; simultaneously Don Graham accompanied the Kingston Trio to Washington, DC, where he started in on the East Coast stations. As a result, the record would work its way from both coasts to the heartland and be on the charts almost everywhere in the country for the next four months through the summer of 1965. The drawback was that it wasn't peaking everywhere at once, and so took longer to pass a million in sales, which may have kept We Five from winning the Grammy for which we were nominated.

Nevertheless, the song finished number 4 on Billboard's "Hot 100 of 1965," a year that included the Rolling Stones' "Satisfaction" (number 3) and the Beatles' "Help" (number 7) as well as a glut of other electrified folk crossovers that would arrive in that pivotal year: the Byrds' "Tambourine Man" at number 25, Barry McGuire's "Eve of Destruction" at 29, Dylan's "Like a Rolling Stone" at 41. The single that John Sebastian had flung to us in San Francisco a few months earlier ("Do You Believe in Magic") would finish at 89.

All of a sudden, you couldn't *not* hear the song. Arriving at Trident for a meeting with Frank, we heard ourselves on the sound system at Zim's. A flip through the tabletop jukebox menu confirmed we had made it to the streets.

On the sixth floor, Werber's secretary, Charlotte Larsen, blurted a congratulations that needed no explaining, then sent us up the elevator to Frank's penthouse, and en route I had the sensation of a recurring flying dream from childhood; I felt light-headed enough to reach the top without aid of an elevator. In a couple of years, the flying dreams turned to nightmares in which that elevator tore through the roof of the building.

Mike had no trouble accepting our sudden coolness. At long last, the talk was about the group on its merits, with no mention of Mike's junior status to his brother. Perhaps there was something special in the Stewart gene pool, and if so, Michael had it. People wanted to get close to him, hear his process for dreaming a song, know how it felt to pull the future from a hat.

How much Frank Werber understood of the revolution he'd tapped into was hard to predict. Even as he marketed this new sound, he swore by the show-biz polish of the Kingston Trio; not to do so would imply that his experience was for nothing. And so, as the band prepared for its first tour, we bore down to eliminate rough edges.

We got a vocal coach. Judy Davis was hired to give us the same help she gave the Kingston Trio: learning to sing as a group. We drove to a light industrial neighborhood in Oakland to stand in a dimly lit dance studio in jeans and t-shirts doing stretching and breathing exercises. We had to slide our hands as far up our backs as we could reach and then bend forward, a position that prevented air from getting into your lungs anywhere above the rib cage. Beverly, Michael, and I didn't have as much trouble as Bob and Pete, but the point was, you wouldn't be able to breathe in that position without accessing the prized lower diaphragm.

Hyperventilated and dizzy, we moved to phonics. If a group wanted to hold a syllable, Judy Davis said, it was best if everyone held the same sound, and the sound had to be singable, a vowel. *Blue moon* is buh—lee—oo ehm—oo—ehn—ah.

Any modicum of propriety vanished as we heard ourselves *bloooing* and *moooing*; and the entire group disintegrated into giddy, helpless teenaged laughter. Good times.

★ ★ ★

When we weren't doing vocal exercises, we worked on staging and delivery. Beside Frank's pool, on a hill above the Mill Valley Golf Course, we ran through positioning and interplay—even the spontaneity was planned. "If Mike tells a funny story, react as though you're part of the audience hearing it for the first time. Look interested."

Lisa Law, in loose pre-hippie sweater, assembling what would become her ground-level pictography of the counterculture, *Flashing on the Sixties*, was Frank's twenty-something assistant, and she roamed poolside at his house with the Nikon camera he'd given her, capturing us as we worked on stage blocking: goofy hats and sombreros for no reason at all, Mike skinny and shirtless, Beverly in bikini top and jeans, all of us singing into broomsticks.

Then back to the houseboat, which felt like a palace to me. Linens were changed regularly, and we were on the water in Marin County, even if it was a mudflat at low tide. When a storm would come, it was thrilling; when the sun was out, it was serene and beautiful. Down the gangway one morning, I saw Bob talking in the distance with a huge black man in a sharkskin suit, an impossible sight to miss. He had the bearing of an older man, though still in his twenties. Not typical dress for a local, but a lot of visiting entertainers stayed at the houseboats. Bob followed me inside and left the other fellow looking wearily beyond Richardson Bay to the city.

"Who was that?" I asked.

"Otis Redding," Bob told me, half-disbelieving.

I knew that name, but he wasn't Otis Redding, international star, yet. For as many months as Mike and I had been studying the Modern Folk Quartet, Bob had been learning Otis's R&B vocals, note for note.

"He says he's waiting out the day before a gig."

The final recording of "(Sittin' on the) Dock of the Bay" was still unfinished when Redding died in December 1967, with the whistling at the end reputedly a placeholder. But for the rest of our lives, we never had a problem attaching a visual to the song's loneliness. Otis didn't seem to want to be on the dock that day. But I was exactly where I wanted to be, and the tide felt high.

★ ★ ★

The transition to folk-rock was this sudden: we had a hit record with drums, but we had no drummer. Jerry Granelli was doing studio work with Sly Stone and playing jazz with greats like Vince Guaraldi. Abandoning that to play with a bunch of kids didn't make sense.

Frank persisted, but Granelli stood his ground, finally suggesting a young black drum student in the city so gifted he'd sat in with John Coltrane in his mid-teens.

We met him hours before our first show, on the Fourth of July weekend, 1965, at the Safari Room in San Jose. (Over the next year and a half, We Five would perform some three hundred shows in nearly as many U.S. cities, and both the band and the culture would be almost unrecognizable by the end of it.)

John Chambers lived at the corner of Filmore and Golden Gate most of his life, south of the University of San Francisco and a few blocks over from what would later become famous as the Haight, in the heart of an ethnic neighborhood that was virtually all black. He didn't have a car, or a license for that matter, so Bob and Joe Gannon had taken a detour through the city to pick him up at his grandma's apartment in a limousine, creating a stir.

Near the front door, a mix of winos, streetcorner philosophers, and working girls watched Bob carry a full set of drums out to the limo. Joe Gannon wore a three-piece suit, according to Bob, and never got out of the car. "When the time came to pull away, John made a sort of cool final pass before the locals, bantering with the corner crowd and smiling that mildly smug grin that indicated he was pleased with the scene."

With a pre-Hendrix urban wardrobe (t-shirt, overshirt, Indian-style moccasins laced to calf level) and a surrealist's eye for double-meanings (a hotel's motto "On a trip?" once got a very extended laugh), John marched to his own tune and didn't care who he shocked; if anything, he got a kick out of it. That he had a white and pregnant girlfriend—Penny, whom he'd met at Washington High School and befriended at civil rights marches—still drew a few stares in the city, but not like it would anyplace else. He wasn't an activist per se, preferring to dodge battles with a slyer style of subversion. The reason he loved jazz best, Penny told me, was that it didn't ask about color at all. You just had to be good.

I knew nothing about color in 1965 beyond stereotypes and epithets from sailors on the ship to Japan. The word *black* wasn't even in use yet. I knew that Bob, who grew up a haole in Honolulu, had taken crap from his non-white classmates. I caught up with him eating some pizza before we started tuning up.

"Do you think it's going to matter?" I asked.

Bob thought for a long, cryptic time. "I can't think why it should. He's a good drummer and he seems to be a good guy. What else could matter?"

Years later, he told me where he'd gone during that pause.

"I was interested in playing in a folk group partly because folk music seemed to be the leading edge of social change, and I wanted to go where it was headed. Growing up, one of my favorite bands had been Booker T and the MGs, and it always bothered me that the album cover didn't show their pictures. No one ever admitted it, but I somehow knew that one of the reasons was because it was an integrated band. When the Ridgerunners moved beyond folk, and then the next musician we added was a black guy, I was thinking, cool. I'm in a band that's on the leading edge of everything. I remember standing behind the curtain before we played our first set, and as the button was pushed to raise the curtain, thinking, 'Here we go!'"

Pete Fullerton and I were probably the slowest to adapt to the onstage power. But there was a compatibility, and setting up for our first show, with drums flanked on each side by amplifiers like the Byrds or the Beatles, we looked as much like rock and roll as folk.

★ ★ ★

The Safari's owner, Paul Catalana, looked like a Vegas wheeler-dealer, and the club felt like a front for other things. Everywhere were chicks with big boobs and small outfits and furs where they didn't belong.

A workingman's rock group called the Nooney Rickett IV, chasing the Bobby Fuller dance sound, was playing a gig in the adjoining bar, and when Frank Werber insisted that we have an opening act, Catalana made them drag their amps from the bar into the showroom to do it, a small border crossing. Rock bands didn't play the same kinds of rooms that folkies did (or places like the Troubadour and the Cellar Door, where pre-hippie beatniks mingled and blended), and folk bands didn't play this kind of showroom.

Remembered as one of the first promoters to book the Beatles in America (at the Cow Palace in 1964), Catalana also brought the Rolling Stones, two months before our gig, to the San Francisco Municipal Auditorium. The Stones didn't sell out—this was pre-"Satisfaction"—but they drew exactly the new audience of seekers that would soon be typical of places like the Matrix in San Francisco's Marina district, where an unknown band called the Jefferson Airplane would debut in August.

We didn't sell out either, at least on our first night, and I felt embarrassed to the point of apologetic. But Catalana seemed unworried.

"Don't worry about the crowd," he said. "That's my job. I booked the Beatles, and I made a lot of money."

Each night we'd wind down with a whisper-quiet version of "My Favorite Things" sung a capella, then move to "Somewhere Beyond the Sea," with folk guitar and banjo opening up to big driving vocals and a finish that always arrived with a YES! With the audience revved, John tapped his sticks, and from the opening cadence the crowd knew we were playing "You Were On My Mind," which brought standing ovations.

Catalana knew that the music world was undergoing a changing of the guard that was going to turn into new niche audiences. He had his bases covered by owning a low-end bowling alley with a rock band and an adjacent showroom one step better (not the Coconut Grove, but not just a coffee house either), while at the other extreme he could book the Cow Palace. He believed he had identified a new audience that would show up and see us, and they did: fans who would click with both "You Were On My Mind" and with the eighteen months of folk-rock that were going to follow. By the end of that week, it was standing room only.

★ ★ ★

In fact, there were an awful lot of people now on a collision course for where the Eagles would end up in 1970–1975. Trini Lopez was doing folk music on an electric guitar; Johnny Rivers was doing a somewhat similar thing, but with a higher dose of R&B.

Doug Weston's Troubadour in L.A. saw the change coming and invited us on stage for the standard rate of $600 a week—but Werber (unlike James Taylor, Elton John, Carole King . . .) refused. Had we done the Troubadour with a folk hit, I still believe the reviews in L.A. might have been resounding. Instead, in September, Werber would book us into It's Boss (formerly Ciro's and now the Comedy Store). Future Monkee Davy Jones, on his first day in L.A., attended the show on the Sunset Strip and declared that he'd found where he wanted to land. Before the show, Sonny and Cher's manager parted the crowd in a limo.

"You'll never see me waste your money like that," Werber told me.

After the Safari, Mike and I headed up U.S. 101 in the Falcon wagon to Eureka to case the next venue, called the Bambuco Club[2]—basically a storefront with glass blacked out, World War II style, not the *hungry i* by any stretch, not even the Safari Room. The town of Eureka is a nineteenth-century gold-rush seaport a hundred miles south of the Oregon border, an uneasy mix of restored Victorians and lumber-mill roughnecks. We got there about 1:30 a.m., Trident having made us a motel reservation for "early morning arrival," but the No VACANCY sign was lit and the motel was locked up tight.

Like kids whose parents had gone to bed, we leaned on the doorbell, waking the manager, who informed us what early morning meant: *11:00 a.m.* And they weren't about to throw a sleeping guest out of a room to make way for us. They directed us to a downtown hotel, so we got back in the Falcon— tired, hungry, not happy—and drove away from where any sane person would spend the night. Finally we arrived at the shadow side of a Victorian mining town before an old building with a sign that flashed ROOMS. It was the kind of hard-edged world Sylvia's lyrics hinted about.

The hotel clerk looked like a character from a Bogart movie: face lined from years of cigarettes, alcohol, and all-nighters at his post. "I've got one room left with a double bed. Take it or leave it." He made no apologies for the appearance of the place or the obvious indignity of the sleeping arrangement.

We handed him the $8 and climbed up dark stairs to a long hallway with numbered doors and one communal toilet. The reek made me not want to go further, but we were tired and supposedly grown up so we pressed on. Like an insult in the middle of the room, the double bed stood on a dirty threadbare carpet covering the raw wood floor. It was self-evident to me that people had died in this bed.

There was nothing to do but pull the blanket back, and we were surprised when the sheets underneath were clean.

"I know, but you can *see* through them," Mike said. And the tint of the mattress only reinforced my scenario about it being a death bed.

Senses dialed to high, with the sign blinking outside, we crawled in, fully clothed. The pasteboard walls were no filter for the sounds of someone's ruined lungs hacking in a futile attempt to clear themselves back to health. I considered how many coughs I'd have to listen to in the eternity before sunrise. Then the slurry monologue of a drunk in the next room broke in, and with every passing moment the phantom-itch sensation grew that there was something alive in the bed that was not named Jerry or Mike.

"Let's get out of here," Mike said, bolting upright.

We jumped up, bounded down the stairs, suitcases banging against the walls, and we never looked more like two kids from St. Joseph's in Pomona, speed-walking to the Falcon wagon. Mike drove us away, and we parked in the lot of the modern motel to wait for sunrise in a sitting position.

★ ★ ★

The landscape leaving Eureka was like a lost continent. Within minutes all signs of civilization were replaced by a primeval forest that stopped at the edge of an endless coastline littered with gigantic fallen trees that had been washed out to sea by storms and then left on the beach by the tides. The size and symmetry of the scattered stumps and logs suggested a giant had been doing freeform sculpture—there were hundreds of them as we drove along watching the setting sun flicker between the dead branches before it was absorbed into the blackness of the sea.

Then we were sunbathing in the desolate triple-digit heat of Sacramento. When John Stewart came up from Mill Valley to catch the night's show, he found us all in the water.

"Busy practicing your craft!" he cracked.

"It's hot, John!" I said.

"Yeah, yeah. Sacramento in summer isn't paradise for me either. But Jerry—just don't forget. It'll always beat working."

"Heard that," said John Chambers at poolside. Then: "Anyone have suntan lotion? I don't want to get burned."

A stunned hesitation, followed by howls from the group.

"You're joking, right?" I asked uncertainly. "You've got a permanent tan."

Chambers deadpanned: "That's a mis*conception*, Jerry."

He had to explain to me that not being able to see the damage had gotten him sunburned many times. He was one of the first to leave the pool.

The Berry Patch was a jazz club—read: bar—and technically we couldn't work, because we were underage.

"So bring in some food—make it a restaurant," Frank demanded.

But a line had been forming there since mid-afternoon, teenagers swarming everywhere, and the owner got nervous. He canceled the show.

I wound up seriously drinking anyway—my first time getting beyond drunk, after all those chances. We went to see the Travelers Three, a folk group that ruled Sacramento, and got invited to the after party. The guitars came out, but I drifted to the open bar.

"Stop the bed spinning!" I kept yelling from the hotel bed. God knew how late it was.

"Stop whining and go to sleep!" Pete had had it.

Bob Jones just said, "Jerry, stick to dope."

★ ★ ★

So we were debating drugs versus alcohol now, but Don Graham was still devoted to getting us proper haircuts. He would pour us drinks and show us records ranging from the Four Tops to Gil Evans and Kenny Burrell, and it wasn't their music that he thought was so instructive. He wanted us to look and act professional at all times.

He took us all to a barber shop that did razor jobs only. We were told to sit in the chair and keep our suggestions to ourselves.

Considering what the Beatles were doing, along with everyone else who was emulating them, getting any kind of haircut seemed like a dubious idea, and having no opinion about how you wanted to look was simply crazy. We all sat in the chair—once. Bob was the first to rebel, and the first to morph from preppy folksinger to acid-hip. Don Graham and Joe Gannon couldn't process long hair as rebellion even if they tried to. Frank Werber let us slide, perhaps because of his own longish hair and boots, but he wasn't happy about it. One concession he did make to our complaints was freeing us of the pullover shirts. We hated those outfits, hated the velours and turtleneck dickies. They were hopelessly dated within months. So Frank sent Joe Gannon out to get us quality matching suits, and we were genuinely excited to go—until Gannon couldn't wrap his head around the expense of the clothiers.

"A jacket's a jacket," he scoffed—and he took us to *Sears*.

For six, seven months, we wore what he bought us, rack suits. There was no shared vision of who we were.

But we were being met with ridiculous enthusiasm wherever we arrived. Walking into a coffee shop for lunch, we'd be followed by whispers and furtive looks. At a PR appearance or a record hop, excitement coursed through the room, culminating in shrieks and cheers as we stepped onto a dais.

On a visit to my folks' house, I found a friend of my sister's hiding in a closet. She'd seen us on the cover of *KYA Beat*, and when she heard I was coming over, she either panicked or stowed herself away.

We could go into a club thinking we knew no one, but people would know us. Hanging out at the Trip, I wound up dancing with the six-foot-plus folk-blues powerhouse Judy Henske ("If Linda Ronstadt's a torch singer, Henske's a flame thrower," crime writer Andrew Vachss wrote) while her then-husband, Jerry Yester, played with the Modern Folk Quartet, who'd just gone amplified. Henske was barefoot and even in my Beatle boots I didn't come up to her shoulders. It was not a bad view, but a little embarrassing. When I finally sat down, a group of girls were studying Mike and me from across the room. One of them approached us.

"Hey, our friend went to St. Joseph's with you guys," she said, pointing to an embarrassed-looking girl across the room. "Do you want to have a drink with us?"

Mike looked in the old friend's direction and then back at me. "I don't recognize her—do you?"

She had dark, mysterious eyes that I did indeed remember, though I'd never met her. I said, "Yeah."

"Too weird for me," Mike said, without waiting a beat. "Knock yourself out. I'm out of here."

That left me without transportation, which only encouraged the girls. They pushed their friend to give me a ride back to the motel—inevitably, the Sunset Sands.

The simplicity of the whole thing was staggering. She got out of the car and followed me to my door. But as we talked, it was clear that her friends were the ones with the vision. She was conflicted about the whole thing and did not really want to be there, let alone have sex with someone she didn't know. At the same time, she did not want to leave and have to lie to her friends about the night—or worse, admit failure to launch. We circled around the shared history of St. Joseph's. She was living in Hollywood now, working at a department store, waiting for her break. I stood there at the door to the Sunset Sands motel room, wondering whether to go inside, and why. When the small talk mercifully ended and she left, I felt a stab of tormented regret that I was not thirty miles east with Debbie.

I never found myself in that situation again.

★ ★ ★

After a concert some months later, wondering if it was too late to phone Debbie, I overheard some girls arguing about who they wanted to score with, and my name was conspicuously omitted. I approached them and, trying to affect an air of nonchalant wisdom, said, "You girls appear to be on a mission—I'll let them know you're waiting." I wondered if they thought I was gay. I couldn't help adding: "I'm curious though—what am I, chopped liver?"

"Oh, no." Their leader switched to a very conciliatory tone. "But you're not available."

Shocked at her directness, I asked, "How did you know that?"

She smiled, and in a very friendly, nonthreatening voice she said, "We go to a *lot* of concerts."

★ ★ ★

We played the San Francisco Civic with Herman's Hermits and the Turtles on August 14, the first time I got the feeling that we might be riding a larger wave than I knew how to ride.

A new road manager, Bob Joseph, drove us to the gig in his Lincoln Continental, enacting a conversation entirely with himself about its superiority over a Cadillac or a lowly Chrysler Imperial. I resigned myself to what amounted to a cab ride. I was twenty years old, inarticulately wishing we were driving with a manager who was into who we were and what we could be—I felt pretty sure someone had simply told Bob Joseph to babysit us.

The auditorium was an enormous and weirdly ornate barn, with embellishments that might have been appropriate to another era but somehow didn't translate to a suburban kid in 1965. The far end held a temporary stage, like you'd see in a high school gym set up for a dance. The Turtles were doing a sound check as we walked the full length of the cavernous hall past rows of folding chairs to the bomb-shelter tones of drums and electric instruments played through too-large amplifiers reverberating in a room. Whatever they were playing was totally indiscernible, and brought back a host of bad experiences with the Ridgerunners in arenas and gyms. I couldn't even imagine, let alone worry deeply, how our little folk-group-turned-rock-band would fare. Like everything else right now, it just seemed totally out of my control.

Our sound check was not good. You could probably hear our voices through the house system echoing about the room, but I doubt you could understand the lyrics unless you already knew them. Our more upbeat, electrified stuff might sound somewhat like the Turtles, if less boomy because we had smaller amps, but my acoustic guitar could not be heard at all. On songs like "Beyond the Sea Tonight" and "Softly as I Leave You," where my instrument had a critical part, it was like unplugging one of the speakers on a stereo. This was not us.

But there was no time to dwell on that. As afternoon wore into night, we watched the venue take on life. Bob Jones was standing outside having a cigarette and thinking about the situation, watching hundreds of teenage girls circling like gulls around a fishing boat. By the stage door, a lone security guard was all that stood between them and a glimpse inside. As Bob tells it, a figure walked through the hallway behind the door and a scream rose up from the crowd. Someone else screamed (whether declaring or asking was unknown): "It's Peter Noone!"

At once the crowd swelled in numbers while coalescing outside the door where the guard was standing. Fascination turned to concern as Bob saw the look of fear on the guard's face. It would have taken several minutes for every person now running in his direction to fit through that door, but it was equally apparent they were all committed to being first. Whoever got crushed, it wouldn't be them.

I'm not sure which side of the door the guard was on, or even if he got it closed, as the mass of humanity bounced off one another like tomatoes in a truck, apparently without serious injury to anyone present.

It was time for us to ascend the stairs and take the stage, and we were warned to move quickly and hold tight to our instruments—under no circumstances should we drop our guard and stop. If we did, a runner would try to crash the rope and the human security line would break down. I made the mad dash and felt arms without bodies or faces slapping and pulling at my velour shirt.

Suddenly we'd reached the stage, with the house lights still fairly bright, so unless a spotlight happened to blind me, I could see the whole scene at once. The building was full, with most of the people in back standing or pressing forward, arms waving and girls jumping and screaming with fathers next to them trying to make sense of it all. The madness would subside for the space of a song, then just as quickly revive, like a TV show with lighted signs reading SCREAM. Given only thirty minutes to play, we cut some of the quieter material, but not all: We Five was still essentially a vocal group. As the Beatles had already learned, concert audiences in 1965 were more interested in being somewhere than in hearing precision and harmony.

Peter Noone, seventeen, looked to be hopelessly drunk. Onstage he staggered through the cutesy motions of "Mrs. Brown," but the voice was a wavering, chirrupy bellow. As we made our way out, I caught a rearward look into his dressing room, booze bottles on the counter, frat-party sounds. In the car, I couldn't let it go.

"Guy was awful!" I complained.

"Well," said Beverly Bivens.

"Worse than awful—he's drunk! Jesus!"

She said it was that his managers weren't taking care of him.

"What's he thinking?"

"What's his *management* thinking?" Beverly said, and she turned to face me. "He's seventeen, Jerry."

· 9 ·

Trouble Every Day

$\mathcal{T}$he next day's *San Francisco Chronicle* review matched my reaction. The Turtles were a great stateside counterpart to the British invasion; Peter Noone had issues but was charming; and We Five's hit song held up live, but the reviewer would have preferred to hear us someplace intimate.

Instead, our experiences kept heading toward *surreal*. Even TV's dance shows were turning on to electrified folk, as plugged-in former folksingers started playing to screaming youth.

We did American Bandstand—Donovan Leitch teasing his jumble of curls into perfect Dylanesque randomness and order before going onstage to sing "Colours." We were driven to Malibu for "Where the Action Is." En route, Bobby Goldsboro kept throwing his voice to simulate a cricket loose in the limousine.

On "Shivaree," Raquel Welch lost the extensions from her wig during a dance, then picked them up and swung them overhead like an undergarment. We did a semi-live lip synch on "Shindig" (a virtually impossible task for John Chambers, because no one much understands how Jerry Granelli plays drums, let alone matches him), and that same night I had the gift of my first migraine. I lay on a bed afterward wishing I could die, beaming apologies to Debbie, wherever she was, for all the times I'd secretly judged her headaches. Meanwhile A&M took the rest of the band out on the town—all but Bob, who wished they were out seeing unknown bands doing original music.

We had a pressing common goal with A&M, to get us into the boat with artists that had more than one hit. We'd put out "Cast Your Fate to the Wind" and "Somewhere Beyond the Sea," which weren't rock at all. When it was clear the second folk-rock hit wasn't on that first album, the burden fell to a new single: "Let's Get Together (and Love One Another)," which Werber had published and which the Trio had recorded in 1963. We recorded three versions, finally releasing one in November '65, two years ahead of the Youngbloods' magical version. There was airplay sufficient for our sales to reach number 31 on Billboard. But what sells in December is either Christmas music or else stuff being purchased as Christmas presents. When the onslaught dies down in January, there's no way to revive a two-month-old song.

Our status as an overnight sensation didn't mean much to bands who were already there. We opened for the Beach Boys at the Santa Clara County Fairgrounds, the first time my teenage sisters could attend, and like the SF Civic, there was plenty of screaming—but without walls and a ceiling to hold it in, it tended to disperse. I think the disembodiment went both ways, because our material must have felt really weak across the track to the distant stands. After the show, my sisters told me what I already figured but still feared: we were fun to see, but sounded lost.

The Beach Boys were older than us, of course, but the gap was more enormous than that: we were a group of kids with one hit. There was no camaraderie as we were hustled onto, then off of the stage. What I pictured as a great experience ended with me disappointed, both at the music we made and the failure to connect. There's a way to succeed in arena-sized shows, but we hadn't learned it. You don't flicker your eyes to get a reaction; you wave your arms.

And I wasn't sure who we were in an electrified world. The Kingston Trio's approach to miking three guys with acoustic instruments wasn't going to work in the places we played now. I began looking for alternatives to my acoustic Martin—reinvention was needed, and fast.

On a pawn shop wall I saw a guitar with a black tobacco sunburst face like John Lennon played in *A Hard Day's Night*. On inspection it was a used Gibson J-160E—exactly what the Beatles, Chad and Jeremy, and Peter and Gordon had been photographed playing on stage. It had the body of a Gibson Jumbo acoustic like Woody's, but with a built-in pickup along with volume and tone controls. I played a couple of chords, noticed it didn't sound very good. The shopkeeper agreed.

I gave him more than a week's wages and bought it on the spot.

Anxious to get approval from the only electric musician I knew, I showed it to Bob. He played some jazz licks up and down the neck and said, "Ooooh, this feels nice. This may be the best playing guitar we have in the band right now. Let's plug it in."

So we did, and there were issues: it sounded like an electric guitar playing through a magnetic pickup. But other successful people were using the model, and I wanted to look like them. Not willing to accept that image wasn't everything, I vowed to find the secret to making it sound as rich and bright as an acoustic.

During sound check at the Masonic Auditorium, the place where I'd seen Barbra Streisand years before (Frank took heed of the bad arena reviews and booked us as an opening act for Bill Cosby), Joe Gannon stopped us and said, "Something's wrong with Jerry's guitar."

I was defensive. "I'm playing what I always play."

"I'm not talking about you. I'm saying something's wrong with the sound of the guitar."

Bob and I explained that this was a newfangled thing, an electric/acoustic designed for use on the stage. We told him who was playing them.

"That may be what the Beatles play on stage, but it doesn't sound like Jerry's acoustic—and I don't like it! It's too tubby, too electric, too . . . wrong."

Did that mean we were never to evolve? Joe's point was moot, because I didn't even have my old guitar at the auditorium. We Five was going to turn in the direction of an all-electric band with that show.

Probably looking for a chance to prevail on something, Joe turned next to Bob's new Rickenbacker twelve-string, purchased because Bob's old twelve-string wasn't as versatile on stage. Ricks had begun turning up in bands everywhere, a pale-red model so recognizable that Bob was constantly asked how he'd ever achieved the sound on our record using that Rick—the tiresome answer being, "By not using a Rick." In a bid for individuality, he'd at last decided to fool with the audience. He bought twin rolls of two-inch graphic tape—one black, one yellow—and covered the entire body with a custom arrangement of alternating stripes.

"Is that a new guitar, too?" Joe confronted him.

"Nope," Bob replied.

"Well, it looks different. What happened?"

"I wanted it to look different than all the other Rickenbackers out there."

Joe shook his head and announced that the look was unacceptable. It didn't fit We Five's image.

"That, my friend, is ludicrous," Bob said calmly. But being an accommodating guy, at least at that stage, he knelt down and peeled off every strip of tape.

Nevertheless, he chalked the incident into the "this is stupid" column. I believe a fissure of distrust was born in that moment.

My problem, that night and thereafter, was my guitar's tubby sound. Too many low tones were getting in the way of what I was playing. The circuitry of Pete's bass amp, which he and I both played through, was actually designed to minimize treble frequencies, making my guitar sound like crap on stage. If we were in a studio we could amplify other frequencies; it's known as active equalization, and today almost all acoustic guitars are equipped with it. But the idea hadn't occurred to guitar manufacturers in 1965. The industry was scrambling, inventing as it went.

Then I started plugging myself into a thing called a treble booster, a chrome box about the size of a Mounds bar. It didn't sound folky enough for Joe, but at least it didn't muddy up the bass and Bob's lead, a decent compromise.

The point was, I was changing. Phil Ochs could cling to his folk purity— I was throwing in with all those guys I'd been resisting since high school.

★ ★ ★

No sooner did you make sense of one form of change in 1965, no sooner did you spot a branch to hold onto in the rapids, than that gave way too.

Eleven days after the Beach Boys concert, we were dropping John Chambers off at his apartment in San Francisco, near Golden Gate and Fillmore, when we saw groupings of people on the streets just kind of hanging in the late afternoon—like they were waiting for something to happen. There was a weird energy, not exactly menacing but giddy, uncommitted to any normal activity at all. John was never an excitable guy, but he was suddenly apprehensive. "Something's wrong," he said. "Something's going on."

One of us suggested we switch the radio to a news station, and that was where we found out that rioting had broken out in Los Angeles in the black community known as Watts.

Even as we listened, the clusters of people outside the car seemed to combine in larger groups, looking for some center of mass.

"Do you want to stay with us, John? Are you thinking there'll be trouble here too?"

"I don't know," he said. "I think I'll be okay. But some of these guys, when they start to hang out like this, stuff happens. I think you need to get out of here."

A lost feeling took over me, like that of being in a foreign country and the driver is worried, so you are too. John had been our artful dodger—the one who knew how to stay out of trouble, land on his feet, find daylight. Soon, he and his girlfriend, Penny, would move a few blocks away to the buffer neighborhood between ghetto and wealth, on Haight Street, about to become the epicenter of the hippie revolution.

He got out, moved quickly through the front door and up the stairs. And we drove, pensive as we left, hearing the thoughts spin in our heads, back to our hotel, leaving John in his own neighborhood. Which was not a comfortable distinction.

Only later would we learn how L.A.'s police chief, William Parker (who coined the term "thin blue line"), had ordered officers to intimidate as many black teens as possible, to establish dominance while they were still young. A statewide repeal of fair housing laws added extra friction the winter before. Racial anger in L.A. was one more phenomenon previously off my radar that was suddenly mushrooming, as if from having pushed the thought into the dark. Now, on August 11, a police encounter with a twenty-one-year-old drunk driver had gotten out of hand when backup police started arresting hecklers on the street.

Frank Zappa, then living in Echo Park, saw the riots on TV and composed "Trouble Comin' Every Day"—a song that would secure him an MGM contract in March '66, because producer Tom Wilson thought it sounded like white blues. All these cultural lines were breaking down.

But I understood very little about the roots of the violence. In 1965, according to opinion polls, as many people blamed "communist groups" for the Watts Riots as racial discrimination. I confused NASA with the NAACP, and Mike made fun of me.

What I did learn was that the printing press that made our album covers was in the fire zone. This delayed our album release till mid-September (and, not insignificantly, put us three months behind the Byrds' debut).

Only when the chaos settled down did we head back to L.A. for a launch party at the Gene Autry Hotel, later to become the Continental Hyatt, the infamous rock dormitory on the Strip. "You've already done your part," Frank said. "Just be there, be friendly, have fun." We were told the trade papers would be there to catch everyone who'd come to see and be seen. Mostly there seemed to be Hollywood office workers who'd gotten passes from a boss or a friend. On a stage set up in the banquet room, we played a few songs, shook hands, and signed autographs. We posed for a picture with Chad Stuart and his wife, but beyond that the most striking visual was Barry McGuire.

Once the squeaky-clean Christy Minstrel who sang "Green, Green," he was now in his black-leather, doomsday-rock, "Eve of Destruction" glory. But for all the prophetic thunder of that song, it seemed like coffee-shop philosophy as Barry schmoozed the room, sampling hors d'oeuvres and getting stoned.

I felt like a kid out of place—I had no idea how to be a celebrity.

Nor did I want to admit that We Five and McGuire were at similar crossroads. We both had overnight folk-rock hits—songs that met a national mood, reached millions, and rode forces way bigger than the people who recorded them. McGuire was placing hopes on a follow-up, on which four of his friends sang harmonies, but producer Adler offered to find him something better suited to a soloist, so the backing singers took this number. Its title was "California Dreamin'," and the singers became the Mamas and the Papas.

There would be no more solo success for Barry McGuire. He was living in a trailer in Mama Cass's driveway when the call came for him to appear on Broadway in *Hair*.

(We Five, in similar fashion, had just turned down an offer to record "Along Came Mary," which became the Association's first hit.)

The air still felt volatile in San Francisco when we went to John Chambers's apartment for a rehearsal—stepping over winos and hoping they weren't dead, which was part of John's doorstep routine. I asked John how he handled it, and he said, "I go to my room, get high, and tune in to Sly." Sylvester Stone was, among other things, a hypnotic Bay Area DJ in 1965. "And I let my mind drift out the window, and down Golden Gate, and I go to sleep."

But later in the afternoon, starving and thirsty—probably the munchies— I decided to hit the coffee shop across the street for some Cokes and sandwiches. Dressed in jeans, Beatle boots, and a bright pullover, I couldn't have attracted more attention if I'd been waving a French flag. I got stares and a few hoots as I walked up Fillmore and entered the place, which looked like more of a pool room than a coffee shop. When I asked about getting a sandwich to go, the friendlier patrons laughed out loud. A hostile group was more direct. "What choo thinkin', boy? This ain't no burger joint."

I said I was just across the street with a friend and hoping to get a sandwich and a Coke to take back. But their dead-cold glares disabled my mission. I bought a bag of potato chips and held my breath all the way back to John's.

★ ★ ★

Which was nothing like what John experienced. At the start of October, we were going to spend two weeks traveling around New Mexico, Texas, Louisiana, and Oklahoma with the Righteous Brothers—not the Old South, but it would still be our first taste of being an integrated band in the Heartland. But first there was the Hollywood Palace.

We'd be sharing a stage with comedians Bill Dana and Paul Lynde as well as Rudolf Nureyev, and there was a lot of concern about getting us in and out quickly. But when we arrived for blocking with our guitars, amps, and drums, everything came to a standstill. They'd been expecting five hootenanny-type singers with hand-held instruments—not amplifiers and certainly not drums. There may have been other apprehensions as well.

The director was good and he was fast. Rather than putting John on stage behind us in the traditional setup, they set him up offstage, somewhat in front of the band. They took the opening shot across a silhouette of the drummers' hands playing the intro. Then the camera zoom-lensed past the drums on to the singers and stayed on us for the remainder of the song. It pulled back out again for the twelve-string-and-drum finish with the drummer still in shadow. I never thought deeply about it until seeing the video some thirty years later.

John was just a silhouette.

★ ★ ★

What was veiled in Hollywood was flagrant in southwest Texas. The State Teachers College (now Texas State University) in San Marcos produced Lyndon Johnson, who went there in 1930 and was now on his way to championing the Great Society. But after playing there, we had to wonder how that happened. We were sitting in a green room while some of the student reporters decided to grill the Righteous Brothers about why they were singing "that nigger music." Nothing was said directly to We Five or to John, who was right beside us. But the questions were a grenade lobbed at Bobby Hatfield and Bill Medley with no concern for them. Only how far the shrapnel carried.

In Lafayette, Louisiana, summer was a party. Pete and I joined Bill Medley and a couple of his band members for a fish fry on the bayou. The boats were low—canoe-like skiffs that kept us above the brown water, but not much. We were cautioned to keep our hands out of the water because of alligators, and after Bill chugged down enough beers, he fell in the water. Desperate efforts were made to get the lanky singer back into the skiff without turning it over and dumping the rest of us in the murky water. There was talk of real alligators and the need for speed, and everyone got pretty anxious. The other skiff that was with us came over and grabbed the far side of our boat so that when Bill was pulled in we wouldn't roll over and join him.

Nor were we harassed overtly in Dallas, at Southern Methodist University, and we started settling into the bonding rituals of musicians on the road. When a band would set up and tune up and show off, everyone else would watch like players from a dugout, listening and sizing themselves up. Sometimes a jam would take shape, which happened when Bob first met John. More often, someone with a point to prove would throw out a musical challenge, seeing who'd take the bait. It was an undeclared game of "Can you top this?" John was a drummer's drummer, and he wasn't going to back down, but while surviving every volley of rock exhibitionism in one of these musical games of Horse, he was quietly seething. He laid down his sticks and glided outside into the Dallas summer heat of 1965, and cursed. "I hate that shit! Why couldn't we find something to play together?"

★ ★ ★

We swallowed another dose of reality on November 5 when we entered the Louisville Fairgrounds Coliseum for our first rock concert since the San Francisco Muni.

For almost a month, We Five would be joining a traveling bill that piled together the Byrds, Bo Diddley, Dale Wright and the Men of Action, Soul Inc., the Results (a mod sister act in go-go boots), and Paul Revere and the Raiders. Dubbed "The Dick Clark Caravan of Stars," it was a lineup that, for the most part, somehow clicked. The opening acts would wake the crowd with journeyman exuberance; then Bo Diddley would slide onstage, chopping his syncopated rhythms in closely guarded tunings beside the Dutchess and her soul singers, whose sexual audacity was unprecedented for a Dick Clark production: their outfits were slit to the navel. When show manager Jack Nance insisted they wear something underneath, Bo had them flaunt fluorescent bikini tops, which was probably more conspicuous from a distance than if they'd been nude.

Next came the Byrds, shedding more of their hootenanny roots each day for a darker, more credible edge (David Crosby had been a folksinger the year before, and Roger—then Jim—McGuinn was an accompanist for Judy Collins and the Chad Mitchell trio that John Denver later joined). Crosby now had taken to swooping his arms in a green leather cape. The image elicited shrieks of delight from the girls, while the rest of the band loitered in Dylan-like mystery as they played their driving set of protest songs and love songs, all with those rich floral harmonies that sounded like the armies of liberation.

It left us to close the show's second half after Paul Revere and the Raiders—a problem, because we were following a band that used any device possible to incite an audience to frenzy. Paul Revere, Mark Lindsay, Fang, and company threw cream pies, did the Boogaloo atop amplifiers, and generally trashed the stage, anything they could think of, all to the relentless drive of pure unadulterated rock. We were utterly unprepared to follow the electricity this whole experiment was taking on, no way to feed the constantly growing hunger. Only "You Were On My Mind" rose to the task, and it came late in our set. After the first night, we opened the second half of the show.

None of this bore any relation to the life we'd lived just weeks before— Disneyland, hootenannies in living rooms, a bowling alley bar that wasn't even full.

But it would be a blueprint for the next twenty-three days. We flew from Louisville to Chicago across time zones, arriving earlier than when we left. We shot a segment to air on Lloyd Thaxton's L.A.-based TV show, Mike taking questions from the media as the rest of us sped away to McCormick Place. He arrived to meet us just in time, and we closed that night's concert running late for the bus that would be our home. Scrambling down a back stairwell, we almost fell over the fallen figure of a girl who'd been hurt in the crush of fans running for autographs. She was in tears.

When she recognized us, she started to half-smile through the pain, maybe at the weirdness of holding up her book for us to sign.

"Not now!" our escort ordered. "We've got to get you to the bus. Let's go."

Mike was kind of evaluating. "How long can it take?"

My reflex was mostly about getting to the bus, although if I got a word out, it was pointless, because Beverly was already stooping to take the girl's hand.

But it was Mike's response that I will always remember. He took in the moment, the way a genius takes in a word problem—something Mike always did, whether he was trying to gauge the feeling of a room or the meaning of his times. "We'll pass the book around, but it feels cruddy to leave you like this." Then you could see the light come on. "We could sing to you."

The song he picked was "My Favorite Things," which made perfect sense: it was a lullaby, it was a capella, and the situation in front of us, after all, was the bedtime scene from *The Sound of Music*. Still my reluctance didn't wane until we started singing. Then all thought of the waiting bus faded to irrelevance. At the closing line, "then I don't feel so bad," the girl's sad face warmed to amazement, like a time-lapse flower; the echo of the stairwell brought back the coffee house days, and we were like kids for that moment.

· *10* ·

Appalachian Thanksgiving

*T*he Dick Clark Caravan of Stars was the most up-to-the-minute thing in the world of pop, and it was the most woefully unmodern contraption, the age of Greyhound bus travel clattering toward the age of electrified rockfest, with thirty or more rock, soul, and R&B players in transport, some devising the future, some clinging to their moment as it was starting to pass. Plus whatever we were.

We boarded in Chicago past midnight on November 6, with Mike's lullaby to the injured girl still in our ears, and the first thing apparent was that the bus was overloaded. It practically tipped when you climbed up the steps. There were exactly six seats for the six of us, but the aisles were filled solid with equipment. Beverly stopped dead in her tracks and whispered to me—I was our de facto road manager. "Jerry, this is not safe. At all."

I asked Jack Nance if it was filled like that when the rest of the players drove up from Louisville, and he said yes. "There's only the one bus. We can't fix anything until we get to Nashville."

None of these soul legends and famous rockers had voiced the spoiled-seeming complaint that now fell to a twenty-year-old.

"Jack, we can't get on the bus like that," I said as bravely as I could.

They called Dick Clark, who happened to still be at the arena, and he walked across the lot and to the bus. To his striking credit, it took him only a glance down the center aisle. "They're right," he said. "Rent We Five some cars and go with them. And when you get to Nashville, rent a truck for the equipment."

He looked like who he was: youthful, reassuring, inseparable from his instincts. I could have been watching a movie version of the man, this clean-faced icon who'd made peace between the public and each new fragile musical revolution, one perfectly historic decision at a time.

Now I felt good about what I'd done, but being behind the wheel of a car instead of on the bus made for a different kind of long night's journey to Nashville. I sat tall, driving the second of two Ford wagons south in the pre-dawn hours while Jack Nance drove the first. We were pressed for time to reach the hotel for check-in and get some sleep before setting up the next show, and it was Sunday, with no one on the road, so the speed limits were pretty much taken as a suggestion. In Texas with the Righteous Brothers, I'd picked up the bad habit of straddling both lanes on a divided highway to straighten the line and keep your speed up, but I had never driven ninety-five this long. It was like blowing off the doors to a secret room where all the forbidden stuff was, to have that rush of freedom and motion with the center line ever holding. I was still wide awake and shooting ahead in Jack's jet stream when an Indiana state motorcycle trooper pulled up behind me. Lights were flashing and the siren was wailing and everybody who wasn't driving woke with a start. I went from outlaw to guilty child.

Beverly was frantically concerned. "What are they going to do? Are we busted?"

"I don't know," I said. "We'll see."

Jack Nance's wagon in front of us was also slowing down, and I could see the guys shuffling around trying to get ready for an unwanted search.

By the side of the road, the officer had me get out. He looked at my California license and let me know this was not California, and there were speed limits in Indiana that didn't care where you were from. "Where are you staying in Indiana?"

I told him about having to get to Nashville. "I don't even know where we're going, so I had no choice but to keep up with those guys."

He wasn't having it. "I'm dealing with you, and you were exceeding the posted speed limit by more than thirty miles an hour. I've got to give you a ticket."

"I understand. How do I go about paying the fine?"

His next words hit me like ice water. "There's no fine set for the excessive speed. You'll have to appear in court. A judge will decide if there's a fine or if you go to jail."

"But I can't come back to Indiana, because we're on a tour. And I can't go to jail because we have a show tonight in Nashville." I became a very desperate young star.

He left me with my words hanging, and walked over to talk to Jack. I watched a brief conversation and a bit of head nodding, and then the trooper went back to his patrol car and got on the radio.

After what felt like an eternity, he told us to follow him, and our caravan of three crept over the median to the other side of the interstate, headed back in the direction we'd come from, then exited the main highway onto a two-lane country road. That eventually became a dirt road that took us to a farmhouse surrounded by trees. It looked like the set for the original Lassie TV show. If it wasn't for the situation, it would have been charming.

It was about 7:00 a.m. with no sign of life, but there were dogs barking like they would kill you if they could only get loose.

"Look," Jack coached me when the cop went inside the house by a back door. "This trooper is a pretty good guy. When we get inside, be polite and act remorseful. If you don't cause any problems, they'll just scare us and fine us."

The courtroom was built onto the back of the house belonging to the local justice of the peace: a fatherly guy wearing wire-rimmed spectacles, pajamas, and a bathrobe and slippers. He pounded his gavel and said, "This trooper was doing his best to enforce the laws of Indiana, but he is not without compassion. He contacted this court with great concern reminding me that it is still very early on a Sunday morning. Why don't you tell me your story?"

I spoke like the Jerry I still somewhat was. I apologized for being there and told him how much I appreciated him getting up at dawn. I was sure to mention the overloaded bus and how I'd spoken up in Chicago to insist we be given rental cars to do the responsible, safe thing. I was wrong to be driving so fast, but there was no one on the road, it was a high-power rent-a-car, and the speed sometimes crept up. I ended by saying I lived in San Francisco and was on tour, so I couldn't be sure when I could get back to Indiana.

He briefly scared me about what blatant disregard it was to the citizens who'd elected him judge that I drove ninety-five miles an hour when the limit was sixty-five—then concluded, "You seem to be a good young man." And I wanted him to know that I really was still a good and responsible young man, even though I felt guilty to be getting special treatment for it, and for being on the Caravan of Stars.

He added, "I don't see any merit in making you come back to Indiana, either—in fact, I hope you stay away until you learn to read a traffic sign."

He fined me $100 for court costs and left the room while Jack Nance pulled out a roll of bills to pay the trooper. As I drove away, I saw in my rearview the trooper peel off some of the bills for the pajama-clad judge in the house's front doorway. We drove without further event and arrived in Nashville as most of the world was eating a late Sunday-morning breakfast, and I let myself admit that my true fear was that those station wagons would have gone on without me and left my career to end.

★ ★ ★

The suede-coated Byrds broke down and rented themselves a blue Winnebago, where they could get high and strum guitars in peace, and a full-sized truck had been procured to carry the equipment overflow that so worried us in Chicago. So from Nashville on out, there was room for us to get back on the bus with all the others—still a packed situation, but with two empty seats and a luggage rack above where a couple of people could lay out after the shows. (Pete Fullerton and Marc Lindsay and I would usually jockey in a friendly way for two spots in the rack when we had an all-night drive.) We crisscrossed every backwoods road from the Ozarks to the Appalachians that way, sleeping a full night maybe every other day.

Walls broke down; friendships formed. Other than the Raiders' infuriating quest to raise the level of stunts on stage every night, there was mildness and brotherhood here. Bo Diddley was Pete's new confidante, and Bob Jones and John Chambers passed the waking hours talking blues with Bo's band in the wide backseat of the bus.

But it wasn't about music alone. Bo had a different view of life.

He was moving toward round from stocky when I met him. I remember him generally in dark or black clothes, though on stage he wore fabrics that caught the light. His face was hidden, always, behind those dark, horn-rimmed glasses and shadowed by a wide-brimmed dude hat like the one James Caan's Mississippi character wore in "El Dorado"—but with an embroidered pattern on the front that gave it a crown-like finish.

He was totally natural and easy to be with—until you tried to engage him about his sound. I knew how to play his famous five-beat rhythm, but watching him tune, I asked if it was his use of reverb and tremolo that gave the guitars that floating effect. That was not a topic he'd discuss.

"Don't you ask me about what I'm doing. It's for me to know and you to wonder about. And don't you come around here when we're getting ready to play."

I learned later that after touring with white artists, he was distressed to find elements of his performance turning up in the songs of people who had opened for him—like a rising young band called the Rolling Stones.

Bo had a protective mentality that extended beyond his troupe. He wouldn't let his girl singers go out with *anyone*—although in hotels he let them visit Bev—and when he found Bob Jones lighting up in the woods, he warned him, "You don't want to get caught smoking that stuff south of the Mason-Dixon line. Some local sheriff'll lock you up and lose the key." Still, I never pushed for any more trade secrets. Once, when some of us were listening to Howlin' Wolf on Bob's portable player, in a gymnasium adjacent to the showers, Bo came in astonished at the sound echoing down the hall. The sound was so big, he thought Wolf was there. Seeing that wasn't the case, he lavished some high praise on the quality of Bob's speakers, but then reverted to his suspicion that we were stealing the bluesman's material.

I did hear that he softened a few years later as he realized that unlike the record companies of the '50s and early '60s, who had no problems exploiting black artists, more and more young rock acts were both recording his songs and giving him credit, which he described as "giving me a living."

We were pulling our luggage off the bus in Atlanta when Bo called to John Chambers from beside a cab. "Get your stuff and come on. We're going to a hotel in town where you'll feel more comfortable."

John said no thanks, but Bo persisted. "You won't be welcome here," he repeated.

It was written all over him that he was a veteran of things we'd barely heard of. And I certainly wouldn't have dismissed him as stuck in the past—but it also seemed to me he might be clouded to the facts. We were a safe pocket, a full white contingent that even the deep south wouldn't dare to disrespect. And John I don't think had any interest in living a world apart from us.

"It's okay—he'll be with *us*," we waved, assuming responsibility. Bo left, not looking utterly convinced.

Doormen and bellboys stared as we entered the hotel and got in line for our room keys: Pete and I; Bob and John; Beverly alone; Michael. At Bob and John's turn, there were looks, but still no questions. The next morning was another story. As the six of us waited to be seated in the wood-paneled hotel restaurant, every head in the room turned and there was not even an effort to veil the shock.

"Five for breakfast?" said the maître d', looking us over. *Five.*

"Six," several of us replied, just by reflex, and he looked as if we'd confirmed what he feared but didn't really believe.

"I'm afraid we can't accommodate six."

We looked around. "But there are tables everywhere," Pete said.

"What *is* this?" Bob said stepping in, his voice beginning to rise.

Maybe not knowing which choice would cause the louder scene, they seated us, but when the waiter arrived he made a point of taking everyone's order in turn, skipping John.

I'm not absolutely sure who started it, but that's when we looked at each other and got the idea to start ordering extra food items, *very loudly and deliberately*.

It wasn't that we were any kind of freedom riders, and it wasn't that we were stars—I think it was more that we were kids from California, and suddenly on our own, that we were part of a generation that was discovering we were a force, and could wear down the traditions of our elders, whether by numbers or naiveté. We had no idea what could happen to us, which meant we were sure that nothing could. It was like goofing on my teachers, pushing to see how far you could go.

After making sure the whole restaurant had heard us order our food, we divided it all to share with John, and ate our meal verbalizing every private thought we had ("Those are dumb-looking wood panels—*have you ever seen such dumb-looking wood panels?*") as loudly as we could, until finally we left, without tipping.

Bo Diddley heard about it from John that night when we were setting up at the Atlanta City Auditorium, but he didn't really process it the way we did.

"You were lucky," he said gently. "There's no point getting hurt trying to stay where you're not welcome. If you'd come with us, you'd've got a great reception and better food. And they give special treatment to musicians. Next time."

It never happened again, but the point hit home. We might have been tolerated because we were musicians on a Dick Clark tour, but we'd crossed a line that was still very well defined in Atlanta.

★ ★ ★

Mike was becoming ever more the peripheral genius. In hotels he roomed alone, like Beverly, which I assumed was so he could bring in girls and not do it dorm-room style. His girlfriend Cookie had been out of the picture since the gingerbread house in San Francisco—I had no idea why. He was keeping me in a cone of silence about his personal life now. If a girl entered a room with both Mike and me in it, Mike left. But to this day I get phone calls from girls he met on the road.

Others on the tour were feeling their freedom, too. Guys who were inclined to make advances on the younger girls made advances, although Bev drew a very firm line. I passed some time with Mark Lindsay and Pete Fullerton in a hotel room as the girls from the Results popped a list of sex questions to see how experienced we were. When they got to bestiality, I had to ask them what it was.

Mark Lindsay knew.

The rooming-alone routine changed when Mike phoned me in the middle of the night saying he was sick and asking if I could help. I was still the one he called.

When I got to the room, there was no place he had not thrown up. I called the front desk clerk, who brought in a doctor, and Michael was hospitalized for the better part of a week. We never got the full story on what caused his liver to rebel—whether an infection or a toxic substance. But it was serious, and he couldn't perform.

Frank suggested we cancel one show and then pick it up the next night, continuing without Michael until he was well enough to rejoin us. Suddenly, for a stretch, we were playing without him.

This had been a heady six months for Mike. For so long he had brooded in the shadow of his brother and suffered his snubs. The sense of inferiority was so acute that in 1964, when John began to play a version of "Rally Round the Flag" at a Troubadour Hoot Night, Michael seethed beside Fred Thompson in the balcony. "That's my arrangement! And all he has to do is walk on stage and they go crazy!" With that, Michael alarmed Fred by putting his head on his shoulder, collapsing into sobs.

"He doesn't have your brains," Fred told him. "You'll do fine. Just give it time."

But now the Kingston Trio hadn't had a real hit record since "Greenback Dollar" ("The Reverend Mister Black" was their last single even to chart), a fact that was increasingly being talked about at the Trident studio. We were the new wave. Many of the singer-songwriters who'd followed John Stewart and even emulated him were now eclipsing him. Like Gordon Lightfoot, they wrote big hits for other acts; or, like Dylan, they wrote for themselves. Meanwhile the Trio, having left Capitol Records, saw its recording quality tank. And those who knew John Stewart said he started to feel trapped.

Decades later, at Mike's funeral, John Stewart would say something that struck me as very telling: that he never understood, and therefore had huge respect for, Mike's genius for vocal arrangements—that ability to hear the whole choral thing in his head at one time and sort out all the parts. Mike had been a threat to John Stewart on that count. Like John, he'd sold songs to the Kingston Trio, and they were good songs. But now, in the fall of 1965, Mike had dragged a group of his own to success—something John had never done.

He would never be a jock or a film star, and he couldn't find the other side of a room without his glasses . . . but he did switch to hip wire-rimmed frames on this tour, leaving the Buddy Holly look behind. Interviewed by *Tiger Beat*, he played his aloof comic timing to the hilt, holding back any vital connection until he found the opening to jump through with a double-entendre or a joke. And he was letting his hair furl to the bottom of his ear and his sideburns to the jaw, a look that, along with the wire rims, was an affirmation of the Byrds.

Their music had to have influenced him too. The effusion of harmony and power in "Mr. Tambourine Man" (released nationally in April, just as "You Were On My Mind" was being recorded in San Francisco) finally had gotten the press to invent the term *folk-rock*. Soon the label was retroactively extended to the Beau Brummels' buzzy San Francisco harmonies, as well as to Barry McGuire and Sonny and Cher. By midsummer, it was common vernacular. Repeatedly, DJs asked Mike if we were trying to emulate what the Byrds had set in motion. Mike made sure to say we weren't copying anyone, but if it helped anyone to remember us, that was fine.

Ever since we'd appeared with the Byrds on "Bash," of course, you could see that what they were doing was the new cutting edge. When the Beatles still were wearing Beatles suits, the Byrds weren't. For the first time with any confidence, bands were discovering a map to success beyond Brian Epstein's template. And the Byrds got to this electro-folk fusion of American roots and British Invasion before the Beatles did. They got there before Dylan, who didn't know his songs were rock until other people turned "Mr. Tambourine Man" into rock. "Wow, you can dance to that!" he reportedly said.

What they did was simply take Dylan's rhythm and straighten it out to a flat four beats per measure—like Roy Orbison's "Pretty Woman," only less quick. And they added a drummer and a melodic lead bass that slid like oil (instead of bumping like an old string bass). Whereas Mike's instinct as an arranger was to give "You Were On My Mind" a syncopated, danceable jump, the Byrds' hit was as simple and as straight and as banging a rhythm as you could get.

Even I succumbed. I didn't usually react well to the absence of my favorite thing, acoustic strings, from a pure folk composition. But the sound was perfection, and "Tambourine Man," much like our own hit, filled peoples' ears in so many ways timely to 1965. There just wasn't anything else being played with that pure energy, continuity, and suffusion—not to mention the Pied Piper conflation of meaning and sound in the words "jingle-jangle morning." It was a nearly perfect aural fanfare for a changing time.

The other thing that impressed me—something our own performances got close to while Mike recovered in the hospital—was that they were able to achieve all that full studio sound on stage every night using just two guitars and Gene Clark's tambourine. (The first Byrds recordings, like the Beach Boys', let studio musicians worry about the instruments while the band focused on singing their epic harmonies—only Roger McGuinn actually played guitar on "Mr. Tambourine Man.") Since Michael and I strummed and picked just as aggressively as in our acoustic days, we sometimes got in each other's way, and there'd be too much going on. Using one less guitar, the Byrds' rhythms sounded super-clear, and each guy on stage could actually hear what the other was doing. I stared at McGuinn's technique on the twelve-string, trying to break it down—a combination of flat pick plus two fingers that I'd seen Glen Campbell use once in studio—and I swore I'd learn how to do that.

Walking outside after our first show without Mike, I kept after Bob until he stopped in his tracks and stared at me.

"I hope you're not suggesting we don't need Michael."

Of course, We Five was not We Five without Michael. Bob's point was not lost on me.

But I made a personal commitment to learn more about playing a better, cleaner electric rhythm. By the end of the tour, I was also learning the tambourine.

★ ★ ★

One night, I begged a ride in the blue Winnebago, an act of genuine boldness. I assumed grass would be involved. Whatever else went down would at least be a change from the bus.

I sat myself at their kitchen table nook, shooting the breeze for a few minutes, realizing this was no more comfortable than the bus, when McGuinn and Crosby and Clark and Hillman drifted to the open bed area for what they called a meeting.

Now I really felt stupid. For someone to talk with, I moved up and rode shotgun beside Roger, the Byrds' roadie/driver, and we hadn't traveled far when I heard the curtain yanked shut across the aisle, cutting the back of the Winnebago from the front. The hiss and sulfur of lighters and matches gave way to the sweet tarry oil scent wafting through the bus as heavily as fog on a lake.

"Do you ever join the band's meetings?" I asked Roger the roadie with an ironic tone. He laughed and said he didn't need to, in order to get the fallout effect.

After a couple of minutes, the curtain snapped open and David Crosby ambled back to the dining nook to marvel at his latest arrival into the altered state. The others found places to lie down and things got peaceably, sacredly quiet. Within twenty minutes there was total silence that lasted until we arrived at the next hotel.

In parking lots, or out back of a theater, when John and Bob and Mike joined the ongoing dissection of subjects like Shankar and Coltrane and everything to do with music, the Byrds' stash was shared freely. But not here, when I was by myself. I was not hip.

Somewhere in Tennessee our tour bus rolled to a rest in front of a lighted neon bar sign made up of intense colors that flashed and spiraled, the way cartoons show you that a character's been hypnotized or knocked dizzy. It was a seriously psychedelic image for 1965. Someone on the bus yelled the obvious thought: "I wonder if the Byrds noticed this!"

Someone else joked, "Noticed! They probably parked here for fifteen minutes!"

★ ★ ★

The country outside was a very different reality. We knew about the poverty in Appalachia, which is nothing like meeting it up close.

"At one point," Pete Fullerton remembers, "the bus stopped in West Virginia so bus driver Harold could rest his head with a power nap; we all piled out into the fresh November air. We'd been holed up with the nasty reek of an overflowing toilet, and B.O. from performers who hadn't showered after sweating bullets on stage. Harold gave us an hour to check out the beauty of the backdrop, and it was stunning—then the rest of it hit me. The human need. The homes without windows or doors. Dirt-caked kids in ragged clothes shuffling around and staring at me with benign interest."

It was hard to deny, on the one hand, that this was the grassroots world that folk songs harkened to. This was what folk-rock borrowed its dignity, substance, and true "hipness" from—from life and death, common striving and brotherhood. At the same time, we were hard at work forgetting it. The Byrds and We Five were in so many ways just passing through—in our case, three days ahead of playing with the Rolling Stones in Pittsburgh. Suddenly here was this alternate reality, both mirror and time warp.

Pete had a notion of getting a pair of his pants sewed up, after ripping them in a stage bow the night before. He asked some of the kids outside if there was anyone around who could do the job.

"Oh, yeah," one of the boys said. "The lady that sews lives just up the hill."

The local shopkeeper gave Pete directions, and after hiking half an hour on unmarked dirt roads to find the house, he was ready to give up. Then suddenly it appeared, a log cabin with no windows or doors about a hundred yards ahead. She sat on her front porch in a homemade rocking chair, smoking an actual corncob pipe and doing some kind of needle work.

She greeted Pete's request with a completely toothless smile. "Yeah, I spotted you comin' up the hill. I'll do it fer fifty cent."

Pete remembers watching her sew. "She had the skill of a professional violinist. Her beautiful gnarled hands spoke volumes of the hard life she'd had. Her satisfaction in simply doing a good job for me was apparent as she returned the pants. She didn't have to say anything. I was struck by the beauty of her kindness, her existence, and thought I'd like to have some of that kind of peace."

He got back to the bus, and everyone saw that something had happened to him. It was as if he had been put back in touch with who he was, or who he wanted to be. Maybe he had been waiting for this to happen to him, ever since he was the little boy who, when told that a dry nose meant a dog was ill, toured his neighborhood licking dogs' noses.

"The bus still smelled like ten miles of bad road," Pete says, "and that shocked me back into real time, but I still hung onto that memory of the woman's pride of teaching her family the art of self-sufficiency. Maybe it was something she said as she talked about life living in those back hills of West

Virginia, or perhaps it was her peaceful love as she returned my pants. She gave me a glimpse of a future that, in time, I knew I would explore more deeply."

For me, it was more like this: we were far from home, and the weather was turning dismal. It got worse as we drove, and then it was Thanksgiving Day with the mountains preparing for winter. The fall colors had gone lifeless and gray, blurring into a sky just as dim that occasionally spat raindrops on the roads and windows as we clambered along. Jack Nance announced that he'd arranged for us to stop for dinner, so I started watching hopefully for any sign of a hotel, even a wannabe Holiday Inn with coffee shop as the bus crawled along the darkening streets of Empire, West Virginia. When we stopped in front of a pool room, Jack got out.

Probably asking for directions, I was thinking. Beverly gave voice to my apprehension: "This can't be it . . . can it?"

In a minute Jack climbed back into the bus, shaking off the drizzle, and announced, "It's not the Ritz, but there are people eating turkey. All you can eat for $1.14."

But the room we entered was not a restaurant. It was not even a café. It reminded me more of that billiard place near John Chambers's apartment.

In Southern California, Thanksgiving Day had meant playing football in shirtsleeves until being called into a festive dining room overflowing with friends and relatives, air filled with the aromas of spices and turkey dressing. This room was probably swept regularly, but it certainly had not seen fresh paint in quite a while. Hundreds of Naugas must have sacrificed their hides, as the joke went, for the padded booths. You could almost feel your arms sticking to the Formica tabletops before you sat down.

Our busload of thirty-two grumbling show people entered the dining room in twos and threes, and the murmured conversations of the locals stopped as they took us in: four rock-and-roll bands, a black R&B revue, and our support crew must have been a little overwhelming. Much of the clientele appeared to have been there for hours, or days, drooping over their plates. Some looked to be homeless—or close to it. But the flagging hush was soon replaced with our own critical swagger.

"Well, this isn't like any Thanksgiving I've ever been to!" said someone from the tour, sitting down. "Unless you count the time we passed out food at the mission."

I cringed as I heard it, and stole a glance at the locals, many hovering closer to their food. The mood among the performers was not one of thanks for anything, except for not having to be outside.

Until the food began to do its work. Then the raw nerves were calmed, and the group was about as jovial as it usually was. Peter, on the other hand, looked beatific. I had no idea what he was grinning about.

When I'd had enough to eat, I stepped out into a dark, dirty street with a biting wind blowing. Pete took a walk to check out the Empire building, a newspaper operation that had burned down, leaving only the rock facade. The dismal goo of the rainy evening finally got to him, too, and he said that while he knew he wasn't any more lonely than anyone else, he couldn't stop imagining California, walking at home with his fiancée, a thought I could relate to.

Thanksgiving 1965 became a complicated joke to everyone on the tour. Years later, I wrote a song called "Lonely Afternoon" for the 1977 *Take Each Day* album; it was a hot summer day in Pomona when I wrote it, but I saw there was still a piece of me back in Empire, West Virginia, trying to work out the riddle of how loneliness could make you less alone if you saw it like Peter in the restaurant.

> Old Mrs. Robbins watches
> As the mailman fills the boxes
> All but one
> She'll smile again tomorrow
> But today I'm not the only one alone
> On this lonely afternoon

• *11* •

The Lonely Crowd

$\mathcal{A}$s major as the Rolling Stones already were (just when people thought "This Will Be The Last Time" had taken a repetitive lead guitar line to the level of rock Nirvana, here came "Satisfaction" in June to reset the bar for all eternity), their staying power into the next century was no more foreseeable in the fall of '65 than anyone else's. They'd released three U.S. albums in two years when our tour met up with them in Pittsburgh, and the suddenly acceptable musical potpourri that could throw together everyone from Keith Richards and Mick Jagger to bass pickers like Pete Fullerton and Midwestern Go-Go girls like the Results was either gloriously eclectic, or ultimately unsustainable, or both. Only USO tours and the Ed Sullivan Show had ever done anything like it.

The Stones were still too harsh for me at twenty. Gentle folk harmony, synergy, agreement . . . my Everly Brothers childhood still defined how I looked at every musical risk. I liked the Beatles. I liked Simon and Garfunkel. I liked the Pozo Seco Singers: laidback country, like Rooftop Singers on Quaaludes. And I liked the Righteous Brothers, the depth, the wall of sound. On "You've Lost That Lovin' Feeling," even though you couldn't swear you heard an acoustic guitar, you had the sense the whole thing was built on its vestige, a flowing acoustic rhythm, the pick noise missing under all the generations. Phil Spector would layer more and more stuff, soaked in echo, and when his records got close to finished, they'd have to put percussive sounds like tambourine back in, for clarity and motion, because you couldn't find it for the overdubbed drums, strings, and voices. All these things, I liked.

But hearing "Satisfaction" on the radio, when the Stones gave what sounded like a Stax saxophone hook to a fuzz guitar, Bob and Mike and I first had to debate what the instrument was. (Bob said, "Whoah. It sounds like a Fender played through a blown amp.")

Later their repertoire would fold in harpsichords and recorders, funk, roadhouse, folk, disco, and everything between—their eclecticism would survive where ours didn't. And maybe other people's experiments were destined only to add fuel to theirs. But on some level that went to the heart of their charisma; Jagger and Richards seemed to take their destiny for granted in a way I never could. They were making things happen. Like with the Byrds, there was more than just music to them—there was a mentality, and they were singular in their pursuit of it. They were the apex of cool, and I was hoping they'd be good guys, too.

We did our sound check and then found them near the dressing rooms behind a small band of hangers-on, Mick Jagger holding a basket of French Fries and chewing a hamburger, Brian Jones, somber as an English garden, standing alongside him in a green velvet military jacket—more Sgt. Pepper than Winston Churchill. On Jones's shoulder a pet monkey, of all things, perched beside an epaulet. Someone announced our arrival, and Beverly extended her typically gracious hand to both Mick and Brian, saying, "Very nice to meet you, I'm a great fan." She was acknowledged, but with no recognition of why they should care.

Pete Fullerton stepped forward then. When Jones saw the handshake looming, he dipped his shoulder, extending the monkey's tiny hand instead of his own. A surprised Pete dutifully shook it.

I was holding back, like a beggar meeting royalty, when suddenly, in a scene from "The Scarlet Pimpernel," one of the Stones' handlers informed Mick that his dinner was ready and flung upon a door to a room with a banquet table set for ten. Pivoting to go in, Mick handed Pete the burger in the French fry tray, and said, "Are you hungry?"—but not waiting for an answer.

The French fries were cold, but no more than the remarkable greeting we had just experienced.

Later, when Jones was found dead in his swimming pool, the obituaries talked about his despair watching the band that he'd founded become Mick and Keith's ride to superstardom and not his. You wondered if the monkey was his substitute for a friend in the band. Marianne Faithfull has spoken of another incident involving monkeys: an acid-tinged visit to the Rock of Gibraltar,[1] to which Brian brought a tape-player with some music he'd just composed for a movie featuring his girlfriend, Anita Pallenberg. According to Faithfull's account, the famous Gibraltar monkey colony gave a "collective shriek" at the sound of the first few bars, then "ran pell-mell away, tearing off into the distance. . . . Brian screamed at the monkeys, trying to get them to come back, and then when they wouldn't, he began to revile them in terrible language.

It was awful. And then he began to weep, a kind of madness, shouting, 'The monkeys don't like my music! Fuck the monkeys! Fuck the monkeys!'"

I was dealing with my own alienation that night. The Civic Arena was the largest venue We Five would ever play, beneath the world's first retractable-roof dome (reportedly inaugurated by Carol Burnett in 1962 with the words "Ladies and gentlemen, I present to you . . . the sky!"), a cold, gray hydraulic flower whose metallic petals unfolded to the sky like a gargantuan vegetable steamer. The stage was two flights higher than the dressing rooms; none of our amps or instruments were miked; and there were no monitors for us to hear ourselves play—a problem that was academic, because the screaming started early in the marathon lineup and never stopped.

That was a rush, but at the same time weirdly impersonal. When the acts from the Dick Clark Caravan had finished, some of us strolled into the arena to join the audience, as if we were arriving at a hockey game fashionably late. The anonymity was eerie: nobody had any idea I'd just been singing to them on stage. God, I wished Debbie were there, to joke with me about this circus the way she would.

You could almost make out the tender, peppy/sad vocals of the Cyrkle ("And I think it's gonna be all right/Yeah, the worst is over now/The morning sun is shining like a Red Rubber Ball"). But when the Stones took the stage, an inhuman shriek rose from the nine thousand fans, and you couldn't hear anything again after that.

★ ★ ★

Adding injury to insult, $200 in cash had been taken from the room, because I hadn't used the safe (I never left money in a room again after that)—and by the time we rolled into New York, which was nearly the Caravan's end, a strange emptiness had settled in.

I wasn't tormented like Brian Jones, but who *was* I? I walked around Manhattan like a phantom, wearing my California coat in the December cold. Our date was in White Plains, but we stayed in Manhattan, because it was Manhattan. I wanted to buy a stereo copy of our album for my old music teacher, Gil Robbins, who was living and playing folk music in the Village now, and when I found a little record store, the expert at the counter said what I wanted didn't exist. "That's a rock record," he let me know. "Rock records aren't produced in stereo."

"I happen to know this one is," I said, "because I have one."

He shook his head definitively, and kept right on pressing me to buy the monaural.

"Look," I said. "I'll buy this because I need it for a friend, but I'm in the group and I can assure you it's available in stereo." And he *still* wouldn't concede the point, until I showed him my picture on the cover. Even then, I'm not sure he saw much chance that he was wrong.

Heading on through the village to meet Gil, I passed a jewelry store with a silver signet ring in the window bearing "JB" in great big letters. That seemed like fate, so I bought it, and a pendant for Debbie as well.

Then I went to see Gil. When the Cumberland Three signed with Roulette Records at the dawn of the decade and came to New York, he and his actress wife loved it, and they were never going back to Pomona. Even when John Stewart left the band for the Kingston Trio, and Mike Settle went his own way (later to found the First Edition with Kenny Rogers), Gil remained in the folk world, recording with Belafonte and the Serendipity Singers and Tom Paxton. Then three years with the Highwaymen. He was living the folk life that the young Bob Dylan had popularized. But folk was on a collision course with 1965, and folk-rock, and—us, really.

I found him heading out the door of this church where he was leading a choir. He looked a little older now, with a big fuzzy winter coat, and his first words were "Come on—I've got to take you somewhere." He had discovered Greenwich Village, and he had to make sure I had a proper slice of New York pizza.

We then needed to swing by the theater where his wife was directing children's theater, then back to his apartment for dinner. We went up four, five flights, a walkup, and when we got inside there was not a square inch of unused space, because Gil's family had continued to grow and they'd moved everything from the house in Pomona—books and magazines and all his old musical artifacts and just *stuff*, like it was the Nutty Professor's library, but utterly comfortable and utterly lived in. Tim Robbins, who was then seven years old, came in, ambled around, and left. Gil played me some new stuff he was writing and singing, and it was good, but it was very early '60s folk music. I didn't connect at all with where he was heading musically, because it sounded like every other folk song—and we had already moved on.

What the Robbins family did have that was exotic to me was conversation. We had dinner and the kids were all there, bantering about art and politics and other heady things. I actually felt a bit uncomfortable because I didn't know how to do it. Not so much that I think it showed, but I couldn't stop marveling how everyone in this family just seemed able to go their own way yet come together, talk, and grapple with the realities of life. I sat in this snug, homey, comfortable New York walkup with this family that had found their place.

All I knew was that I wanted to find mine.

★ ★ ★

The thought rarely arose to phone anyone back in California. For one thing, my per diem barely covered food. When my day began, it was too early on the West Coast to call, while by the end of my day, they were all asleep.

Nor did my parents and I have the habit of communicating deeply. They supported without question my being plugged into music and touring. My older sister had left home for the convent, which eliminated another prime mover for family chats. And my next sister, Kathy, was five years younger than me so we didn't share much.

Mike Stewart's story had led him to a similar spot. His family may have had charged, super-intellectual dinner talk . . . but when a child got beat down for throwing in with them, he took his opinions elsewhere. He compartmentalized, daring to trust a few people in one arena and a few more people in others.

Maybe like a lot of kids in my generation, we never knew the rapport that we were missing. I'd never practiced the art of it. And so if I was lonely in New York, it wasn't for my family. It was for Debbie.

No doubt my father felt I'd turned my back on him. Missouri stonecutters, he came from. And even though my mother missed me, I never learned that from her directly—it was my sisters who told me she followed reports of our tour. She came from a broken home in New England, and you could always tell by watching her shift the food around on her plate that she wanted it to last as long as possible, a carryover from when they had so little. She was the heart of the family, but she alone couldn't make us a loving family. Born to a mother who hated men because her husband deserted her, she herself grew up to marry a control freak. A nice guy, a compassionate guy, but a control freak. And people tell me I'm just like him.

For my parents' pre-therapeutic generation, absolutism was hope itself. Kids were told their place. *This is the truth, and that is not. Lawrence Welk, not Elvis Presley. No options or shadings.* Mike's family were masters at shutting one another down with a snappy comeback. Hand over hand on the baseball bat so that your hand wound up on top. My family just let go of the bat.

Then somewhere along the line, kids like us got enraptured by the words *everything is relative.* And I embraced that thought whenever I said, in my mind, *Forget them—I'm going to find a way to marry Debbie. A Baptist. You think I'm going to hell, but I disagree. Watch me.*

★ ★ ★

In that state, I went with Pete, Bob, Mike, and Marc Lindsay to see *Dr. Zhivago,* Pasternak's timeless story of lovers separated by circumstances, which for me was playing with fire.

As we got in line with the early show just letting out, here came David Crosby, cherubic and happy and inviting us to come hear the Byrds' recording session over at Columbia when we got done. Uptightness was never on anyone's radar when Crosby was around—he had that what-me-worry grin, that willingness to say whatever he thought, and if anyone took offense it was their problem, not his. Just like on stage with the green cape, he had a genius for the next cool visual slogan: Thomas Jefferson hair and Sunset Strip jeans and scruffy shirt, stuff you wore if you knew where to go . . . stuff you couldn't get at Sears.

Now I had a pretty exciting night ahead of me—the movie, the chance to watch the Byrds work on their next record, a night off in Manhattan—but something made it incomplete. Watching the movie, seeing Julie Christie's sculpted face and long blonde hair, which were a shocking match to Debbie's, tracking Omar Sharif's longing for her, it was almost too much. I sat in the dark theater and found I was crying, less because of the storyline than because I wanted Debbie to be seeing the movie next to me. With other girlfriends, the longing could be quelled by a phone call. But I had never missed another human being so much that it physically hurt.

When the movie let out, we found our way to Columbia, and there was plenty of energy in the air. Even though the Byrds had only one more hit record than we had, they had the advantage of a label that was anxious to get stuff out of them and that had studios on both coasts to help them do it. Crosby was tuning up, excited because rather than use session players, they were all going to play their instruments this time. He greeted us. But producer Terry Melcher was not so carefree. He took one look at the leaders of We Five and dispatched an assistant to tell us to leave.

This was the kind of worry the recording industry was running up against now. The last thing Melcher wanted was to be ripped off by a good rearranger. He would at the very least have suspected that We Five was interested in east-meets-west instrumentation. And he knew what to fear: the Byrds themselves had latched onto Ravi Shankar via the Beatles, and would soon release a jazz synthesis in "Eight Miles High." They had found the secret to rearranging Dylan's "Bells of Rhymney." It used to be songs that needed protecting; now it was sounds.

Had Dylan slipped quietly into Columbia this night, I very much doubt he'd have been thrown out. As a songwriter, he might have brought something to the party, but he wouldn't have been a threat to take anything away from it.

In any case, we got thrown out, Bob, Mike, and me, and wound up heading separate ways. Bob figured he'd go check out a blues club. I don't remember if Mike went with him. I know it was cold, dark, and late.

But not so late out West.

I raced back to the hotel and phoned Debbie. I told her all about the movie, about Julie Christie, how Zhivago's love for her rivaled his love for his family. And how I related.

"Will you be coming to L.A. soon?" she asked.

That didn't seem likely. We were scheduled to record in San Francisco, and I didn't know when we'd be back down south at all. "Why don't you come up and visit during the two weeks when we're back in San Francisco?" I asked.

It was that easy to get back on track. Bonded as we were, we didn't freak out over not talking—if I was with you, I was with you, and if I wasn't, I wasn't.

The Legendaires were on their own ride. They'd sung at the New York World's Fair, where the mayor gave Debbie a key to the city. Mike Curb, founder of Curb Records and the future lieutenant governor of California, was producing them; he handed Debbie the Dylan tune "She Belongs to Me," although, as the title implies, it was proving an unworkable choice for a 1960s female singer. They'd done the Regis Philbin Show and the Art Linkletter Show and auditioned for the Dean Martin Show. They'd even done a Scopitone—a video-jukebox precursor to MTV, where for a dollar instead of a dime, a bar patron could both watch and listen to a hit song.[2]

But we had no special need to talk about any of that career stuff when we talked—we just made plans to get together in San Francisco. Career for Debbie was a joy, but it was never a need. It wasn't a white picket fence with three kids and a dog.

Which was all she'd ever wanted. That plus a husband who would direct the church choir. Whereas I more or less wanted it all.

★ ★ ★

The problem was that from the moment we got back to Northern California, I began having a harder and harder time making sense of who I was.

Except for Mike, who stayed with his brother in Mill Valley, everyone had begun to settle down romantically: Bev with Fred Marshall, the avant-garde jazz player, under whose influence even the cutting edge of folk-rock must have begun to seem childish; John Chambers with Penny in the Haight; and Peter with his fiancée, Susan, a nursing student who was becoming Debbie's new best friend. When Pete and Susan jumped to a bigger apartment, Bob and I took over theirs, an aging two-bedroom woodframe flat that suited us. It was while living there that a number of things started to change me.

For the first time I saw pot used as casually as coffee. Bob would wake up, light the pipe, drop a record onto the KLH stereo in the dining room, sit for a minute, and then start foraging for food. If we didn't have a rehearsal or a recording date, John Chambers would show up with new records by Ornette Coleman or John Coltrane, and while I couldn't begin to find the tune amid the etherea, John would locate the melody line and sing it back precisely as played, sometimes with Bob gleefully layering a harmony line on guitar. They talked about how Dylan had taught the Beatles and the Byrds how to market elusiveness, and how the Beatles had meant the long in-breaths in "Girl" as an insider's allusion to drawing a toke. The two of them, John and Bob, slung free verse just to see where it would land; a line that sticks with me, though it never got into a song, is "It will be glass/It will be happiness at last."

By the time Bob brought home *Rubber Soul*, recorded in October and November and released December 3, I was smoking whatever was offered. I accepted Bob's extra headphones and a pipe and I settled in and watched the needle drop and bob atop the vinyl. With the first three whole-spun notes of the acoustic twelve-string in "I've Just Seen a Face," which opened the American release, you knew what you were hearing: the Beatles had been taken by folk-rock. Maybe a little more Russian folk than American—but folk-rock. "Norwegian Wood" was an even bigger revelation. I'd been used to hearing sitar anytime McGuinn was around, but only in the context of a raga. Suddenly I was flung into a different realm. My choices were to struggle against the newness or hang on for the ride.

The first side ended, and we both sat silent for what felt like minutes. Finally Bob removed his phones. "Every one of those songs is a hit record!"

We let the words streak like tracer fire, and then fall into a glassy lake, and it was a long few seconds before I managed to respond.

"That's not really rock. They used acoustic instruments."

I even thought, presumptuously, that the Beatles might have heard our album. I didn't know about their roots as a skiffle group. They could parody almost any genre well enough to play it.

As the ridiculous range of what we'd heard began to settle in, Bob said, *"There's another side."*

I began to listen to records in a whole new way. And I was fascinated, amazed by how randomly Bob and John could glide across a conversation, or a day.

At the same time, it made me uncomfortable. I was curious about these new enlightenments, but not ready to go there full-time. I'd been used to keeping regular hours, having structure in my life. I tended to eat dinner sometime near dinner time. When Debbie confirmed that she was coming to visit, my head boomeranged to conventionality: I got right up and bought some bags full of groceries—and an electric blanket with two controls.

No sooner did she arrive than the feel of the place, and the sight of Bob and John constantly stoned, hit Debbie like a bomb. She was actually too stunned to say anything. We got out and did stuff, went down below the Golden Gate Bridge and to Fisherman's Wharf, and spent some time just singing together, Debbie and me and Mike. But she couldn't wait to get out of that apartment. I learned later she was making up her mind never to see me again. She'd seen what drink and drugs had done to some of her relatives in rural Arkansas—where drugs were, she did not hang out.

Intuitively I must have known she'd never come back to see me under these circumstances. So when she left, I found a studio apartment that was closer to Trident, on the other side of the Broadway tunnel just up from Pacific and Franklin. I went to Cost Plus and bought plates, silverware, sheets, and towels. I took full advantage of the store across the street and made real meals: steak, salad, vegetables, bacon, eggs. Right then and there, at age twenty, I took a stand to be myself, to not be like Bob or John Chambers or anybody else. And that was the very day Frank Werber gave each of us, as matching Christmas presents, a coffee-can-sized beaker of high-grade marijuana.

Just like that, it was not necessary for me to be with the band to get stoned.

Now I was rudderless. I was Dustin Hoffman (two years ahead of the movie) floating in his parents' swimming pool in *The Graduate*. Joe Gannon, thinking he was being helpful, reminded me I had no responsibilities but to show up on stage when we had a date, and I took to wandering the city, looking to purchase an identity. I went to the Emporium on Market Street, bought some faux Beatle boots at Flagg Brothers for $10 because Frank Werber had some. I'd wanted to buy a Brooks Brothers shirt because I thought they were cool, but at Brooks Brothers I realized businessmen shopped there, not musicians. That wasn't who I was supposed to be. And I started whittling away at the thought: What *should* my image be? I was just this twenty-year-old kid from St. Joseph's who'd been singing in a folk group. I didn't have a clue.

So I dropped that quest, and, on the doorstep to 1966, began to spend my days in an intoxicated state. The compelling fact was, I thought it helped me musically. At least it helped me relax enough from the cerebral weight of being Jerry.

Back in summer, when we were on the houseboat trying to learn "Love Me Not Tomorrow," Bob had halted us in frustration. "We-have-GOT-to-find-the-GROOVE!" he cried.

I didn't even know what he meant—*which* groove? He pulled out a pipe. "We should get stoned."

When we got back to the song, instead of following my intellect (two strokes down, one up), all I had to do was feel, find the wave and surf it. I was doing the same things I'd always done, but just following the flow of the music. I was in the great Unconscious.

I listened to "Like A Rolling Stone" again, this time with headphones and a pipe, and I was so blown away by the band, I didn't even hear the whiny snarl I used to hate, the Dylan voice that Debbie and I once made fun of.

"Wrong is right," John Chambers liked to recite, the jazz truism, and I was trying to absorb what it could mean. Over time it might change everything, your perception of what's fun and not fun, good and not good.

New Year's Eve was the first time I performed stoned, on a bill with the Kingston Trio at the Circle Star in San Carlos, and it was the first time I got paranoid, feeling naked and alone before four thousand fans and no monitors, hearing just bass and drums and my own voice trying to correct itself to the echo that came from the back of the room to the stage, across which Bob and Mike were battling the same thing. But I blamed the environment, not the grass.

At Werber's hotel room afterward, a big place in Burlingame, we added champagne and hard liquor to the mix; and I staggered to my room too bombed to find the thermostat, quaking in a blanket with the temperature somewhere in the forties. In the morning the thermostat was right there by the door, and I blamed the alcohol, not the grass. I stuck with grass.

Night after night I came home to my studio apartment, played the inexhaustible *Rubber Soul* album, played Dylan, played Simon and Garfunkel, played the Journeymen, pot issuing through the walls, which was a calling card, just like the music and the Patchouli that everyone used to cover the smell. I killed the lights one time and was drifting into Neverland when there was a knock at the door. Somehow I mustered the courage to open it. An attractive young woman, thin and blonde like Debbie only not Debbie, sized me up through the partially opened door. "Sorry to bother you," she said. Her expression changed from curious to concerned. "Look, I was just walking past and smelled the smoke. I don't know how many people in this building would know what it is, but you should probably block the crack under the door just to be safe."

I nodded okay, scanning the hallway, and she came inside to avoid us being heard.

The place wasn't bad with the drapes closed, but when you opened them my view had all the charm of a New York fleabag, so I kept them closed. A brick wall stood just a few feet past the window.

She smiled, "You're new here, aren't you? What do you do?"

"I'm a musician," I said.

"Really. Where do you play?" She looked curious, but not exactly in a fan's way.

I sensed the opportunity to tell her the name of the hit song that was ours. But when the band wasn't around, it made me uncomfortable. People would gush how they loved the group, how it was their favorite song, how they'd made love to the song, how (always) they loved Beverly. Once you played that card, it was your last, and you'd never find out why—or if—they liked you. I think I was unconsciously avoiding that endgame.

"Well, we don't play much in the city," I said. "We just live and record here."

"Wow. I was at a recording session last night at a cool little studio in the basement of a building in North Beach. The Kingston Trio were recording. Do you know them?"

Not wanting to give away too much, I said, "Really. Who were you there with?"

"Oh, just some guys I met at a party," she said casually.

There was an uncertain pause. I wasn't sure what it was about, on the part of this good-looking neighbor. I didn't know if I was dropping the baton, but I was very locked into the certainty and the hope that I was going to be marrying Debbie.

"We'll have to get together sometime and talk about it," she said finally. "But I've got to get some sleep. Don't forget to seal that door."

A couple of days later, Frank confirmed there'd been a couple of girls at a Kingston Trio session—adding: "Some hookers, actually. And those were some expensive girls."

When he found out one was my neighbor, he tacked on his usual advice. "Stay out of trouble and don't get your name in the paper."

We remained casual friends. She woke me on a Sunday morning to offer breakfast, and I followed her into her apartment—really an enormous living room—and everything about it was white: carpets, couches, walls, even the plants. Unlike my unit, she had a picture window with an utterly breathtaking view of the bay. Amazed as I walked over to get a better look, I heard a disgusted half shout from the kitchen.

"The cheap son of a bitch took the eggs!" Without stopping to explain, she collected herself and said, "Well, I promised you breakfast. Let's walk up to the Hippo and see what's on the menu."

Once, after Debbie and I got married, she knocked on my door again. "Who's the beautiful girl I've seen going in and out of your apartment when you're touring?"

"That's my wife, Debbie," I announced proudly.

"Wow! Good job!" She seemed genuinely impressed.

I only saw her a couple of times after that. But I always thought I was living a really adventurous life, being next door to a high-priced call girl. I liked how it sounded when I told people about her place done all in white, and the egg breakfast we never got to have.

★ ★ ★

It was February when Debbie and I got married. It was a couple of weeks later when she found the beaker of dope.

My not living with Bob anymore had given her just enough faith that I was solid; it also didn't hurt that I helped her walk away from the bad-news manager, Marge Alley, who'd double-crossed her. The Dean Martin Show, we learned from the Legendaires' booking agent, had offered to hire Debbie solo, without Marge's son, and Marge never forwarded the request.

When Debbie at last told Marge she'd had enough, Marge, who knew all about manipulating the legal system, filed suit. But I brought the papers to We Five's lawyer, who saw the holes in Marge Alley's case. Marge backed down, and I came out looking very much like a candidate for husband.

For her part, Debbie didn't go on to fling herself at the Dean Martin show, or at anything else—it was on principle that she broke off with Marge Alley. If career opportunities came her way, she was grateful; if they didn't, she sang in the kitchen. Cutthroat was never going to be her style.

We set the date for February 16 (which was three days after Beverly Bivens, at nineteen, married Fred Marshall). We'd been waiting to be twenty-one, the legal age in California: I knew my parents wouldn't approve a non-Catholic marriage, so I didn't want to have to ask permission. She turned twenty-one in early December, and the first opportunity I had to meet her in L.A. after turning twenty-one myself was the week of my father's birthday. Considering his role as a Catholic lay pastor, it was a pretty tough gift for him.

Debbie picked me up at LAX, and I figured we were heading to a courthouse in Pomona. But other plans had been made—we were going to see her Baptist pastor in Glendora, so he could find out what kind of guy she planned to marry.

I'm sure he was underwhelmed. He said, "I understand that you were raised as a Catholic. Do you consider yourself a Catholic now? Are you going to church?"

My cavalier response was something like, "If I was a good Catholic, would I be sitting here talking to you?"

Rather than excuse himself from the whole business, which he could have, he asked about my understanding of God. Did I consider myself a Christian—and what did that mean?

I told him that while I was raised in a Christian home and went to Catholic schools, I had some issues with the church that seemed insurmountable. I said I knew Debbie and her family to be good people with as much faith as anyone I knew, so it seemed wrong for my Catholic priest to have told me I should break up with her. When he asked if I considered marriage to be a lifelong relationship ordained by God, I said yes.

I must have said yes to just enough things. The next night he married us in front of the fireplace at Debbie's parents' house, with Deb's mom and dad, her brother, his future wife, Carol, and Debbie's best friend from high school as witnesses. I wore the sharpest thing I owned, a green sharkskin suit my uncle once brought back from Hong Kong, and we spent our wedding night at a motel near the Ontario airport.

Alone with her, I still felt like a school kid. Like marriage had changed nothing. Would the cops come through the door? Would her folks?

But Debbie acted as if being married and spending the night was the most natural thing imaginable. This was the first night of the rest of our lives together. I was amazed at my good fortune.

★ ★ ★

The day she found the pot, she said nothing. "There was a glass beaker in this closet," I said.

"Yes," she said. "I threw it away."

"That wasn't yours to throw away."

"Well, we're married now. If I'm going to be in this house, it can't stay."

"That was a gift," I said. "From Frank Werber. For Christmas. It was worth a lot of money."

"I'm sorry. I'm not going to be around that. I can't stop you, but it's not going to be here. Or I'm not going to be here."

Tongue-tied, I announced I was going out. I looked in the closet for a jacket, and realized I still didn't have a real jacket. I need a jacket, I said, and went out shopping again.

I came back some time later—with a tacky vinyl jacket that I did wear some, not hip and not leather—and beheld Debbie's ability to put a painful thing aside and move ahead. I could have concluded that she must not have been so bothered, but it wasn't true. She was extremely bothered. But she was working to live out her obligations in faith—never approving, but not brandishing the disapproval. The message was: you don't ever have to ask if drugs are still unacceptable—they are. Let's stay close to what we agree on, because it won't be that.

I never again brought grass into that apartment. But if we were time-hopping from the East Coast to the West, I found it very hard to get to sleep.

Otherwise, I never missed having it at home, except musically. I hadn't quite learned how to get lost in music, that Wonderland effect, except with grass. Always, Bob and Mike had been able to hear things in a recording that I'd have to study or have shown to me. Debbie, a right-brained being, could pick out sounds that had been shrouded from me like 3D puzzle pictures. Which might explain why she had no understanding of my "grass opens my ears" argument.

Eventually I kept some in a little film can in one of my guitar cases, which was usually with the band equipment. Years later, when we were staying at her folks', her dad, probably looking for a pick, opened that can. He never opened the case again without asking. He let me know, without saying so, that I'd done the same thing to him in his house that I'd done to his daughter in mine.

★ ★ ★

When draft notices first loomed, Frank's PR-whiz idea had been for me to marry Beverly (not Debbie, mind you, but Beverly!). But marriage was no longer a valid deferment unless you had children. One friend of mine, a conscientious objector, fled to Canada (where he is now the president of a religious university). But leaving the country wouldn't help us stay on the pop charts, and there was no question but that this mattered most.

The war was another dark contradiction that wouldn't go away. As with the Watts Riots, it was as if parallel decades were exposed: everything was flowering, anything was fair—and yet the ethereal promise of the mid-1960s never quite seemed to reach fruition; the war raged on.

Werber knew a doctor in Sausalito who took draft deferrals very seriously, and after an in-depth interview, we came up with X-rays showing an extra bone in my foot, plus a wear pattern on the soles of my shoes suggesting the bone could be problematic. A way to stay out of the infantry, perhaps. Still probably not enough for a deferral.

Buying time, we got a venue transfer to the Oakland Induction Center and kept trying to build a medical case: asthma for Bob and Mike, a hyperactive stomach I'd been treated for at St. Joseph's, which could open the door to a psychological deferral. But all in all, I looked pretty healthy on paper.

When the day arrived I drove to a dreadful section of Oakland armed with my X-rays and medical records, not realizing what was in store. The first thing that mystified me was no parking lot. It hadn't entered my mind that most guys, like my friend Mike Higdon, boarded buses at their local draft board and passed through the induction center not expecting to go back home.

I felt like a log floating toward a waterfall, poked and probed and tested along with everyone else, when finally I got pulled out of line for review of the records I'd brought. But stomach and foot issues didn't matter to this doctor.

"I still think everyone should serve who possibly can," he said. "So I'm giving you a 1-A classification, pending a retest for high albumin levels. Come back in three weeks, and we'll test you again."

I was one of the few who left with my freedom that day. Mike and Bob were sent home, legitimately, for asthma. Bob told me, "The doctor asked if I ever woke up with phlegm and handed me a paper cup—I almost filled it, and handed it back."

Pete got a temporary delay while the band's personal doctor had him keep a record of bedwetting "accidents." Setting a glass of water on his bed, he'd climb in, and then write, honest to a fault: "An accident last night. Soaked the bed. I had to change the sheets and blankets."

My case wasn't so easy. Joe Gannon had heard that if I stopped eating eggs and meat—living only on pancakes and milkshakes—my albumin would go up, and I'd be home free. Maybe the source of that advice was the doctor who thought everyone should fight. Albumin is just undigested protein, and when you stop eating protein, your albumin drops. Luckily my doctor found something else: a hernia that had earlier been misdiagnosed as a hydrocele.

"Yeah," the induction doctor agreed when I came back to Oakland. "You should have that fixed right away, and let us know, so we can reclassify you."

"You'll be first to know," I said smugly as I dressed to leave. I had lived for about eight years with that hernia.

I used it as an excuse to not lift equipment on the road, but I postponed having it repaired until I was a dad, and draft-exempt.

My father once said he became a Republican only to cancel my mom's vote; if that was as deep as politics ran, I thought, what's the point? I was out of touch with friends from high school, and I didn't hear news of anyone who went to Vietnam to risk their lives until some of them started coming home in pieces, or in bags. Stopping the domino effect of communism carried an echo of logic from the air-raid drills of my school years, and I hadn't begun to suspect that talk of the Soviet threat might not really add up. Had Mike Stewart not brought a guitar when I came back from Japan, I might well have reconsidered the Navy and just joined.

If you're not a liberal when you're twenty, runs the quote, you have no heart; if you're not a conservative when you're forty, you have no brain. I thought it was my responsibility as a twenty-year-old folksinger to be a liberal, even though I didn't know what in the world it meant. We were straddling separate cultures. I didn't know the difference between the laboratory of the stage—where youth unrest was the stuff of a new awakening—and the Iowa airport, where just waiting for a plane connection in our San Francisco street gear could cause alarm. There we became aware of suspicious security people increasing in number and appearing to surround us, while reporters with cameras waited on the tarmac for a politico taking forever to deplane. Only when we went outside did the security appear to shift along with us, and not until we were safely on the plane, watching from our seats, did the politico emerge and the cameras roll.

And all across America there were settings like Debbie's Aunt Aline's. There we sat for Sunday dinner with a dozen relatives when Debbie's Uncle Clyde went off about "the cowards who went to Canada." He had firm roots in the Arkansas farm where he was raised, and he was a good, decent man, but he'd lost friends and family in battle and his opinions in the area of service to God and country were not debatable.

I was only thinking about my friend Pat, who'd been willing to face jail on principle, but had been pushed by his family into crossing the northern border. "Well, a man has to follow his conscience," I began.

I saw Debbie's brother Gary wince as though a vase were about to tumble from a high table. Clyde's voice rose twenty decibels as he squared to face me. "They ought to all be hunted down and arrested for treason! They're a bunch of stinking cowards—that's just what they are. And how come you're not in the service? Don't you know there's a war on?"

Before I could mount a defense, Aline, in a tone at once commanding and gracious, said, "Did everyone get enough turkey? There's plenty more. Jerry, why don't you tell us where you've been traveling and playing shows?"

After dinner, Gary took me aside and said, "He means well. Listen, Jerry. Uncle Clyde was standing at attention on the Missouri as the Japanese surrendered before the eyes of all the sailors who'd seen friends die. He takes the sacrifice of soldiers very seriously."

"Can you imagine if we'd been drafted?" Bob Jones said. "I can still remember Michael at college in his ROTC uniform, like a ten-year-old trying on daddy's suit!"

The world was probably safer with Mike Stewart and me restringing guitars than field-stripping an M-1 rifle, but I know that I was spared an experience that destroyed lives in ways that are still surfacing in the twenty-first century. My son Chris would be born that fall. Of course, I did go to Vietnam—on a record. The youthful optimism pressed into that three-minute song made Mike's arrangement of "You Were On My Mind" a part of the dreamscape of almost everyone who went to Vietnam in person. Forty years later, a not-atypical email from a veteran told the We Five web site that playing the *You Were On My Mind* album was the last, joyful memory he shared with his wife before leaving for the service in 1965.

Jerry with tenor guitar in 1958.

Ridgerunner Jerry in 1962.

"Teen Trio" with Sue Ellen Davies doing a home recording (choreography by M. Stewart).

Ridgerunners Trio, and Triangle, perform at prom in 1962.

Concert with Eileen Duffy and bassman Pete Fullerton, 1964. Note: Mike is playing the acoustic twelve-string Bob amplified and used to record You Were On My Mind.

With John Stewart at a "Quiet Fight" high school assembly.

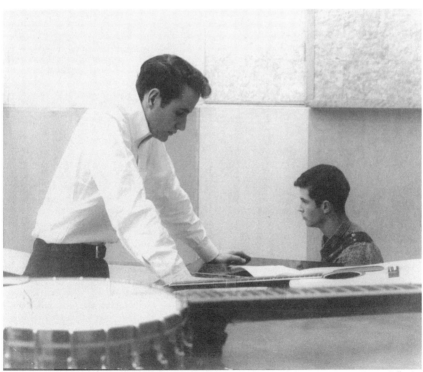

Jerry with John at Capitol Records.

Folk Trio, Satirist, To Open
At the Meeting Place Tonight

UPLAND — The Ridgerunners, a local folk singing trio, will perform this weekend at The Meeting Place, folk music center at the Sierra Athletic Club, 1275 W. Foothill Boulevard.

They will share billing with another local entertainer, satirist George Yanok of Pomona.

Shows will be presented at 8:30, 10:30, and 12:30 tonight, tomorrow, and Saturday.

The Ridgerunners are Mike Stewart of Claremont, Jerry Burgan of San Jose, and Beverly Bivens of Santa Ana, all graduates of Pomona Catholic High School, as is Yanok.

Stewart, leader of the trio, is the brother of John Stewart of the Kingston Trio. He has written five songs sung by the Kingston Trio and the Modern Folk Quartet.

He was musical coordinator for the documentary film, "With Their Eyes on the Stars," which has been nominated for Academy Awards. Mike and John wrote and arranged the score.

Burgan plays the guitar and sings tenor. He has worked with Mike Stewart for 5½ years.

Miss Bivens, the newest member of the group, ranges from low alto to soprano. She has "the tremendous spirit and volume that are the Ridgerunners trademark," according to her press agent.

Yanok has lived in Pomona since 1951, but this is his first professional appearance in the area. He put on comedy acts in Pomona while in high school, and continued to perform at the University of Santa Clara and San Jose State College.

As a soldier, he competed last year in the all-Army entertainment contest with 350 other soldier entertainers and won first prize in individual specialty and was voted best individual performer of the show.

Yanok has performed at the Jazz Masque and the Kerosene Club and at San Francisco's Burp Hollow. After his show at The Meeting Place he will appear with The Four Amigos at The Tin Pan Alley near San Francisco.

RUNNING THE RIDGE — The Ridgerunners, local folk song trio, open at The Meeting Place in Upland tonight. They are Mike Stewart, Beverly Bivens, and Jerry Burgan.

Beverly Bivens joins the group in 1964.

Jerry with Debbie and friend at Legendaires rehearsal.

The Legendaires: Jeff Tonkin, Debbie Graf, and Mike Alley.

Legendaires winning Best Vocal Group and Mercury recording contract at the Hollywood Bowl 1965 Battle of the Bands.

All the players in place with the Mike Stewart Quintet on Fountain Avenue in Hollywood, 1965.

The group, now renamed We Five, at "band camp" doing blocking and rehearsing segues beside Frank Werber's pool.

Houseboat rehearsal on the dock of the bay, 1965.

First performance with a hit record, on stage at the Safari Room, July 1965.

Touring KYA radio studio (under construction) at the Mark Hopkins Hotel with DJ Johnny Holliday in summer 1965.

TV and Touring: We Five lip-synching on a dance show. The guys now in suits, Bev still had on velour.

EXCLUSIVE INTERVIEW
WITH
WE FIVE

CROWELL-COLLIER BROADCASTING

KEWB/91
—BOSS—30—

Volume 1, Number 24   ON THE BIG BAY   October 29, 1965

When You Woke Up This Morning -
What Was On Your Mind??

By JOHNNIE "G" (6 - 10 p.m.)

Well, if it wasn't the WE FIVE it should have been as this young A&M recording group is causing much conversation in the music world.

It started approximately three years ago when Mike Stewart whose brother John is one-third of the famed Kingston Trio formed *The Ridge Runners*, a largely folk oriented group. Their first effort in a folk saturated field fell on deaf ears. John, who had great faith in his brother's ability, repeatedly brought his brother's group to the attention of Frank Werber, manager of the Kingston Trio. Months of hard work, endless hours of rehearsal, and countless revisions and refinements, resulted finally in the nucleus of an excitingly individual music concept. By this time, Werber had formed TRIDENT PRODUCTIONS, INC., a Kingston Trio owned independent production company and succeeded in obtaining the services of Don Graham as National Promotion Chief, and it was agreed to sign the group to a recording contract.

On April 20th, 1965, Werber brought WE FIVE into the Columbus Recoding Studios in the basement of the Columbus Tower in San Francisco. Here, in the same area once occupied by the original Hungry i, in Trident's new ultra modern studio, the initial recording steps began.

(Continued on next page)

MIKE   PETE   BEV   BOB   JERRY

KEWB/91 promo paper, October 1965.

WE FIVE HAVE ARRIVED!

(Continued from Page 1)

After six long hours spent in total dedication to the final product, the record was as ready as human effort could make it. This was WE FIVE in *Thought and Soul*. This was *You Were on My Mind*."

With the new record completed, it now became the job of Trident Productions to arrange for distribution through a national record company. Aftee close scrutiny of all companies in business today, A&M Records became "most likely to succeed." This enthusiastic young company, owned and operated by Jerry Moss and Herb Alpert, who had experienced a phenomenal two and a half year growth with Tijuana Brass, agreed that the sound of WE FIVE generated such

(Continued on next page)

KEWB's BOSS MAN JOHNNIE "G," welcomes WE FIVE on a recent visit around KEWB's Jack London Square Studios.

WE FIVE IN ACTION as seen on TV show 9th Street West. Here they belt out "Love Me Not Tomorrow" from their current A&M album. The LP, entitled "You Were on My Mind" is currently a San Francisco best seller.

TAKEN DURING RECENT Hollywood press party in honor of WE FIVE . . . they are shown here talking with Chad Stewart and his atraticve young wife,
— Photos by California Photo Service.

Burgan Collection.

MUNICIPAL AUD. 7:30 P.M. SUN NOV 7

ADVANCE TICKETS $2.50 - AT THE DOOR $3.00

DICK CLARK'S ★ CARAVAN OF STARS ★

THE BYRDS
"TAMBOURINE MAN"

WE FIVE
"YOU WERE ON MY MIND"

BO DIDDLEY

THE DUCHESS

PAUL REVERE & THE RAIDERS

★ ★ ★ ★ PLUS AN ALL STAR CAST ★ ★ ★ ★

TICKETS ON SALE HERE SHONEY'S DRIVE - IN

November to Remember . . . twenty-eight shows in twenty-five days. This 1965 boxing-style poster was created for the Nashville performance. Photograph taken by Jerry Burgan of original poster designed and printed by Hatch Show Print.

You Were On My Mind *album release party at the Continental Hotel with Frank and two-thirds of the Kingston Trio.*

At a taping for The Bob Hope Show.

The boys in the band: Mike, Pete, John, Jerry, and Bob.

The Asthmatics.

You can look at it two ways . . . this way, or that way.

So tell me again, is it We Five or We Six? Alec

Always on a trip . . . of some kind.

. . . and always ready to play.

Jerry, Mike, Bob, Pete, and Bev doing overdubs in the studio, 1966.

The mysterious Bev before a concert.

With Fred Marshall in the studio.

The Return of We Five *group (Rich, Frank, Debbie, Jerry, and Pete) dissolved into a garage band until Mike returned to produce* Catch the Wind.

One of Pete's neighbors identified the source of the noise.

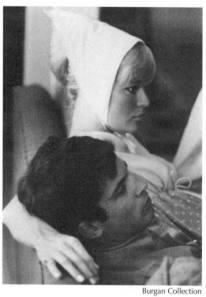

Debbie and Jerry, 1966, at a photo shoot.

1976 at home.

Debbie in a chukar feather choker, 1981.

With the band in 1973.

Feel Factor

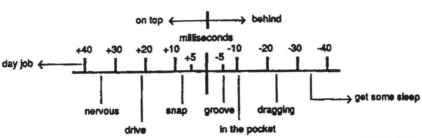

This chart is a classic example of Michael Stewart's creative intellect at work—but never with humor too far from mind. Model for programming synthesizers and drum machines based on observations of how the bass and the kick drum influence other musicians in actual recording sessions. From an article by Michael Stewart in Electronic Musician.

Michael "feeling" laid back on a yeti-skin rug.

Jamie Stewart carries on his father's tradition.

Mike's last We Five show in 1981 on the Tomorrowland Stage with Tholow Chan and Rico Lozano.

Bob joins Jerry, Debbie, Terry Rangno, and Chris Burgan for a reunion show at the University of San Francisco in 2005.

Burgan Collection

Bev and Jerry's last visit with Bob in March 2013.

Stewart Collection

Mike jamming in 1990.

Fullerton Collection

Pete taking a break on the beach in 2011.

John Chambers, d. 1985.

Michael Gassen Stewart, d. 2002.

Robert Paul Jones, d. 2013.

· 12 ·

Ad after Ad after Ad

$\mathcal{E}$ven despite Vietnam, the dawn of folk-rock remained green, as did Trident's hope to stay in its vanguard in the winter of '66. Already We Five had become San Francisco's highest-charting electrified band ever (a distinction we'd hold until Creedence Clearwater arrived in '69). And the same new collision of styles that could make the band's playlist sometimes get a little bit ethereal and formless had the equally powerful potential, through soaring folk vocals and mountaintop idealism, to seemingly harmonize Everything. You could hear it in the Seekers' "Georgy Girl" as readily as "You Were On My Mind," the rising spirit, the world-uniting effervescence. Madison Avenue heard it, too.

"Coca-Cola called. They want us to do a rock spot!" Werber greeted us one afternoon at the door of his office.

To my memory, only Beverly looked openly worried.

Werber was ebullient. "It's just the beginning," he went on. "I'm gonna make you guys bigger than the Kingston Trio."

McCann-Erickson had been commissioning youth-market radio ads for Coke since as early as 1963—sung and played by everyone from the Limeliters to the Supremes, Jay and the Americans, the Moody Blues, Jan and Dean, Roy Orbison, Pet Clark, and Ray Charles. In six more months, of course, such partnerships would be deemed selling out. But the hip metamorphosis hadn't happened yet. In 1966, a hit commercial still offered, if anything, more staying power than did a hit song. The Andy Williams model for entertainment success had not crumbled, and Werber, in position to make San Francisco ground zero of the folk-rock revolution, was determined to funnel the future through that past.

He did what Werber would do: he upped the ante. Offering Coke a bigger deal than what they'd asked for, he secured an all-or-nothing partnership, along the lines of what the Kingston Trio had with 7-Up in the late '50s (madcap TV spots where they mugged and joshed and gave each other noogies beside a soft drink machine, or wobbled on swaying girders above San Francisco like Charlie Chaplin).

The agency brought us to New York and played us their Ray Charles ads, which did nothing to shame the enterprise. On the "Things go better with Coca-Cola" line, "Coca-Cola" came out just like "Georgia," sung sideways—of course, Ray Charles could sing the phone book and make it sound credible. They set up a Coke machine in the studio, to induce *transference*, because when you sell anything in life, you choke on the words unless you find a way to believe in them.

So we cut a pretty-sounding piece for the Rose Bowl game on January 1, and we figured we'd create a couple more spots that would satisfy the Coke people and sustain us—still drawing an unspoken line against committing the one unconscionable sellout: that is, to take Coke's initial brainstorm ("Coke Was on My Mind") and sing it *verbatim*.

Beverly's husband, Fred, undoubtedly questioned the integrity of the undertaking, and the purity of Werber's motives, and the soundness of Werber's business vision—although in some ways that only clarified the challenge, which was to deploy our creativity to ensure that whatever we did to satisfy Madison Avenue would not offend or hurt us artistically.

Frank assured us we could do that. And we believed Frank.

★ ★ ★

Ironically, we were starting to take more creative risks that winter than ever before. Mike Stewart was still Mike Stewart, and his approach to the Coke challenge was to throw away the rulebook. "We're not going to do the expected," he told us.

We got to practice across Columbus at the Little Fox Theater, which the Kingston Trio's company owned. Bev would drive in from Berkeley, Mike and Bob from Mill Valley, and John, Pete, and I from the city, and we began our mornings doing what working musicians did: inventing on a stage of our own, unsupervised.

If you listen to these Coca-Cola takes today, you can actually hear a hint of the "San Francisco sound" in some of its finest flower—not what it became known as, in the Grateful Dead and Big Brother, but what it first was and still is to me. There was bossa nova and there was Broadway and there was folk and there was British rock, and there was garage-band rock. There was, as Bob Jones has pointed out to me, the new way Bev's voice came at a note, a way she'd recently brought to our cover of Judy Henske's "High Flying Bird," from below the note lifting upward, at once soulful and distressed, that pointed forward not only to psychedelia and Grace Slick's emergence from the Airplane but also fifteen years beyond to punk-rock.

"Bird" would become Bev's signature song (as well as a standard for the Jefferson Airplane and for Ritchie Havens, who would sing it in the film *Easy Rider*). It was the essence of the more ragged psychedelic stuff to follow, better live than in studio. Perhaps it was the studio version's relentless, flogging acoustic groove that constrained Bev; the faster we played, the less time for her to explore that lower melodic edge, and the more the voice just sounded flat. But on stage! We got slower, with a howling electric guitar, and drums doing the work of keeping time—music is all about being ahead of or behind the beat, without ever moving that beat. And the bigger the instrumental pad we brought in, the more surely Bev rode above, like a boat on rising water.

There was Bob Jones's answering lead guitar, playing blues fills that bent or built to the floor of Bev's next note, crazy in small bursts, plus folk-picking arpeggios on the electric twelve-string that created a mind-blowing, almost orchestral intricacy dancing around the vocals.

Naturally, there was an awful lot of "Things go better with Coke" too—but the point was, the adventure of all we were learning musically in that phase spilled over unmistakably to these ads.

We sent the songs to Coke, a half dozen of them. But Coke had a problem.

Their dream was a campaign based on "When I woke up this morning, Coke was on my mind." And they weren't speaking figuratively. They wanted the one thing we absolutely could not do.

Incredibly, Frank Werber was unworried. Perhaps it was the fact that, after his resistless first success with the Trio, he'd only ever seen commerce won over by creativity before; perhaps he knew he'd have Coke on the hook legally for at least a sizable share of the money they'd promised even if we failed. Perhaps it was pot. For whatever reason, Werber liked his position. If we just were adventurous enough, stuck to our guns, Werber was certain, we'd soon come up with a lyric or a musical hook that the Coke people would like just as well as "Coke was on my mind."

Ten or fifteen more failures soon followed—each of which we'd thought was pretty good—and now the war between Frank Werber and McCann-Erickson had become entrenched. One hour of rehearsal led to two; two hours led to a day; two days led to weeks and weeks.

Then Bev came down with tonsillitis. It wasn't an immediately devastating concern, because I could always get Debbie to help us work out vocal

arrangements until we had something ready to record. Frank even suggested
we build a spot around Debbie. But you could almost hear the band not smile.

"I need the whole five octaves of Bev's voice," Mike said sharply.

And the more Debbie was around, the fewer opportunities for creativity
via the hash pipe. Bob and John Chambers, in particular, had come to resent
her presence.

Spring arrived.

★ ★ ★

The "Debbie isn't Beverly" problem came to a head in Albuquerque,
on May 21. Beverly called me to her room in agony one night and I found
her lying face down on the bed wearing only a bikini bottom. She had not
been out in the sun in months, and now, at high elevation, after a day by the
pool with no sunscreen, she was bright red and had to be hospitalized with
a second-degree sunburn. Again, Frank offered to fly Debbie in—but Mike
drew a line. No. Not anymore, not ever. We'd wait for Bev.

★ ★ ★

Between college dates in Ohio and Oklahoma and Montana and New
York, between taping the Lloyd Thaxton show and Hullabaloo, in the desert
wilderness of Coke sessions, We Five still managed to record some adventurous material toward its next album, which was rapidly seeming overdue. We
recorded "You Let a Love Burn Out" and "There Stands the Door," both
of which were released too slowly for the raga-rock leading edge, and "Make
Someone Happy," the album's bossa nova title track, perhaps the best we'd
done in that vein. It wasn't that we *couldn't* record our own stuff—it was
that the daily frustration of Coke commercials boiled over into a rebellion of
which we were both beneficiary and victim: *now* we were going to do what
we wanted. When what we wanted under the circumstances was to make noise
and break stuff.

Bev's voice had recovered, but by now we were openly directing our
frustration toward the soft drink. One morning, Mike arrived and told the
group, "Repeat this word a hundred times: Tercoke-aff." He wasn't smiling.

And we did so: Ter-Coke-af-ter-Coke-af-ter-Coke-af-ter-Coke. . . .
We were going crazy like that.

After close to fifty unique rejected radio spots, Coca-Cola dispatched a
hand-picked producer of its own. Billy Strange was a session guitarist from
L.A.'s famed "wrecking crew" who'd fed the twelve-string craze with an
album devoted to the sound. He had just produced Nancy Sinatra's "Boots,"

and he seemed to think that gave him rank. Starting from outright aversion (whatever Billy Strange said, we were against it), we finally ground out one arrangement we could live with—not as creative as the others, perhaps, but with a Bo Diddley shave-and-a-haircut beat that we liked well enough to take across Columbus Street and into the Trident building to record. Werber showed up now, expectant. He had a speaker in his seventh-floor office that relayed whatever was going on in the studio; if you'd created something he especially liked, or especially didn't, he might mystically appear. Whether it was that, or whether Billy Strange roused him with a phone call, it seemed we'd crossed the finish line. Hank McGill ran tape copies, and at long, long last we sent Billy Strange on a redeye flight to New York, where he strode into McCann-Erickson's office the next morning to play the final version for his bosses.

Before it even finished, the reaction was uniformly funereal.

Billy. This isn't what we sent you to do.

And Frank told me later that Billy panicked, swearing to the room: "Those Trident guys must have switched tapes on me!"

The Coke episode would prove not just an unlucky bet for Werber but also a turning point. Like every other folk-rock act we'd been stretching our repertoire, learning to be extemporaneous. Musicians would ask, "What was that jam you were doing *before* the show started? Can I buy *that* on a record?" Each day the call of invention sped past us. Audiences wanted creation in the moment. They wanted to hear what Bob Jones was discovering on guitar. They wanted to see this drummer named Chambers who had jammed with John Coltrane in his mid-teens.

And our hearts began to sicken into a pall of inevitability every time anybody asked, "Why isn't the radio playing *that*?" Like prizefighters, though, we kept hoping.

Herb Alpert sensed trouble as early as April 14, at the Unicorn in Boston. It was the first time ever we weren't in "uniform." I'd found a store that afternoon called Kennedys (every other establishment in Boston was a Kennedy) with a Carnaby Street display and bought an electric-blue corduroy double-breasted blazer with brass buttons. Back at the hotel, someone in the group egged me on: "You should wear that thing on stage—it's only a club in Boston."

Somehow, we all picked up the rebellion: "Why don't we all wear whatever the hell we want?"

It was by fluke that Alpert walked in for our last set: a Tuesday night, not a lot of people in the club. We were getting loud and electric and definitely rowdy for a folk club. I wouldn't have recognized us either. This was not the gentle mix of June '65.

"We Five is over," Alpert reportedly prophesied to Jerry Moss shortly afterward. We watched him leave mid-set.

★ ★ ★

The Frank Werber we'd revered at the apex of the 1960s—in aviator shades, biker boots, short suede coat, and hipster beard, like a Jewish Peter Fonda—cut an image nearly irresistible to an aspiring teenaged artist. Both hip and accomplished, he'd epitomized the progressive but refined hipsterism of the Playboy era—the idea that you could be a daring thinker and wear a three-piece suit—and he'd used this natural sense, a sort of managerial perfect pitch, to help the Trio's white college audience feel . . . safely edgy. To draw an analogy to standup comedy, which Werber studied intimately at the *hungry i*, he believed (and argued) that the survival instinct of a Bill Cosby or Jonathan Winters meant greater impact, in the long run, than the death wish of a Lenny Bruce—even though, personally and culturally, Werber saw more of himself in the irreverent outcast. Black comedians like Red Foxx and Slappy White played to a tiny, however voracious, audience; it took Cosby to move that line, gently. And Cosby's genius created space for Flip Wilson and Richard Pryor, who flourished with a candor far exceeding the degree that doomed Lenny Bruce. Bob Newhart and Shelley Berman, too, were daring, but to Werber's mind, they knew, unlike Bruce, how to push a line without crossing. The two men had spoken about it.

In the glow of the We Five launch, Frank Werber again thought he would guide, rather than discern, a cultural shift; and until 1966, his own rules had always applied. Yet, as Bob Jones has noted, Werber missed something that began to be apparent that year: the oncoming shift was tectonic. A mass media tsunami could not be led. Rather than saying, "Paddle like hell and get on the wave," Werber believed he could control it—perhaps even believed, through his early success, he had formed it. As a result, for the first time, he now risked drowning.

Bob in particular was becoming alarmed. Before his eyes, the music scene was blossoming into something utterly new and vital, a laboratory of dreams, yet he was helpless to take part in the experiment. This despite belonging to a band that less than a year earlier had been in a leading position to redraw the rules of both folk and rock. It was Mike Stewart who'd dared to leave folky lyrics behind and plug in; it was Bev Bivens, at seventeen, enthralled as much by blues as by Streisand, who'd first embodied a way to channel both vocal styles while copying neither.

But We Five's incubation led us to discover what others, too, were beginning to learn, that it was not just new music being born, but a whole new way of creating, playing, and living it. We Five had merely entered the scene a few seconds earlier than did the folk-rock, psychedelic, and roots-rock artists who followed. And on this score, Bob felt helpless—like he had jumped a train, only to find it was heading away from the center of the action. The fact that it was making good time only made matters worse.

The band wanted to play the Fillmore—Werber forbade it. He didn't want the public associating us with unruly cousins like the Airplane, the Grateful Dead, and Big Brother. The "San Francisco sound"—the term Werber coined when he launched We Five—was to him a kind of trademark, to be protected against scragglier elements in the Fillmore and in Berkeley, as well as in Southern California counterparts like the Doors and Buffalo Springfield, who stood to cut us off from the territory Werber knew.

In this manner Werber divided the world, hoping to conquer: having managed the Journeymen, he turned down a demo from John Phillips, without even listening to it ("You're a pain in the ass, and I'm afraid I might like it"). He passed on the Mamas and Papas. He turned down the Charlatans. He turned down the Jefferson Airplane, who sounded similar to We Five then, but whom Werber considered not as "classy," and less controllable. Witness the Airplane's antiestablishment graffiti campaign that soon painted "Jefferson Airplane Loves You" on walls all over town.

Other artists were going overseas to reimagine themselves. The English tabloids ran pictures of Sonny and Cher standing on the street in their fur vests, having arranged to be 86'd from their upscale hotel; the next day, escorted by photographers, they marched back to the front desk as celebrities. Paul Simon wrote "Homeward Bound" in the north of England, waiting for a train; he offered it unsuccessfully to Chad and Jeremy before deciding to record it himself.

Werber took an opposite tack—assembling a stable of singularly inventive acts he would tout as homegrown. At that point in the San Francisco scene, aside from We Five, only the Beau Brummels, first produced by Sly Stone, had found viability. Werber hurried to fill the void before anyone else could. He signed Blackburn and Snow, a boy-girl duo with British-soul harmonies whose Bond-meets-Byrds treatment of "Stranger in a Strange Land" (David Crosby wrote it) sang a cannabis-flavored brotherhood. He signed the Mystery Trend (formed by a San Francisco Art Institute professor) and Marin County's horn-heavy "Sons of Champlin," whose frontman, Bill Champlin, later joined Chicago. Most promisingly, he added the Justice League (known in the pre-hippie scene as Captain Zoom), who, emblematic of the trouble on Werber's horizon, would spend three years storing rich masters that somehow missed their moment for release.

The first constant among these acts was eclecticism. To Frank, the San Francisco sound meant every influence at once, capable of going in a multitude of directions, but finding something in common between all of them. In each of his acts, Werber placed two hopes: that they'd be creative enough to turn over some new rocks, under which he would find some edible bugs, and that they would simply stay cooperative. He had enough trouble keeping We Five in velour sweaters and under his control.

Nor could Werber seem to merge, to the media's satisfaction, his coinage ("the San Francisco sound") with theirs ("folk-rock"). Folk-rock, literally speaking, was only about two-fifths of what We Five represented—and some of our repertoire (Broadway, pop) was stuff the rival scene was rejecting out of hand. Within months, San Francisco would be known for Quicksilver Messenger Service, the Grateful Dead, and the Jefferson Airplane—none as eclectic as We Five, and none embodying the safe next step that Werber foresaw. Though his bands made possible all the others.

The other constant was pot.

★ ★ ★

It both defined the San Francisco sound and sabotaged it. With the band, it was never simply in the background. Marlboros were half-emptied and laced with grass to be smoked anytime, anyplace. On airplanes we'd parade to the restroom as soon as the seat belt light went off; the vacuum in the sink sucked out all hint of what we'd done.

Outside an auditorium in Denver, a policeman doing security asked for a cigarette; Bob carelessly pulled out the special pack. Lighting up, the cop reflected, "If I didn't see that it's a Marlboro, I'd swear this smelled like pot."

John Chambers said, "Yeah, you get that sometimes—hemp grows like a weed in the tobacco fields," and we hurried to the dressing room, leaving the policeman with the loaded cigarette. He probably really enjoyed the music when the show started.

Heroin never made its way into my body. I took some methedrine one night at a rehearsal, after which we'd planned to go to the forbidden Fillmore; Debbie wasn't part of the crew, but the prospect of going out on a date was novel enough, and she'd gotten us a babysitter. At the promised hour, the band was still rehearsing; first thirty minutes went by, then an hour, and then it was gone. When I got home, Debbie was dressed, dinner was cold, and she was unhappy. She didn't beat me up about it. She didn't have to. When I went to bed a few hours later, my heart was pounding so hard I thought it would wake *her*—if I didn't die first. I never did speed again.

At the house one afternoon I found the band in the kitchen smoking opium: it had a heavy, sticky smell and was an incredible downer. Bob plodded to a piano and began to play "Let the Good Times Roll," hampered partly by lack of skill, but I suspect it was the smoke, because we all dredged up our instruments and joined in at a pace that would have struggled to keep up with a dirge. When we gave up, John Chambers said, "Man, opium is a downer. You can have it."

LSD made an appearance early in my experimental phase, with Pete and I visiting Mike and Bob on the houseboat. As with my first time on grass, at least an hour passed before I realized my perceptions were changing. I began by reading *The Tibetan Book of the Dead*, but soon got bored and headed for the stereo. I had the inspiration to listen to "Like a Rolling Stone" again—if grass heightened Dylan's sound, it had to be incredible on acid. Instead, the once-lush guitar and organ sounded ragged, and when he started to sing, I saw Pinocchio on Pleasure Island, complete with donkey ears and tail, braying from the speaker. Revolted, I turned off the stereo and wandered outside. Dawn was breaking on Richardson Bay, the houseboat squatting in a mud hole at low tide. Beyond a rock-faced retaining wall the parking lot, too, looked like a cartoon, tinted in junkyard purples and pastels. Pete figured we ought to go, and he drove me back over the Golden Gate Bridge during rush hour—a spectacular sight seldom seen by musicians—when I was suddenly overpowered by the existential curse of facing the day: gazing at the people in the cars all dealing with the tedium of bringing themselves to one more workday, I began to wonder if they were crazy for doing it. Then it struck me: I must be the crazy one, because there were so many more of them than me and they looked like they knew what they were doing. I was sure that I didn't. Almost instantly I slid from being amazed by the sunrise on the bay to questioning my own sanity, to realizing that I wasn't the first crazy person to conclude atop the Golden Gate Bridge that life was too much to bear. Plainly the thing was to jump—that's what crazy people did. As I began to strategize my escape from the car, I realized Pete wouldn't be stopping, and I'd probably get hurt. A frustrating dilemma. I thought, "Well, I have to do something." At that instant, I proceeded to throw up, like a fountain, coating the very ample passenger side of Pete's wife's '57 Plymouth.

In slow motion, Pete looked over at me and asked, "Feeling sick?"

Emptying myself had brought a certain armistice, approximating peace, but when Pete stopped in front of my apartment, I was seized by remorse for what I'd done to Sue's car. I insisted he wait while I got a towel and cleaned up. I'd have been furious if I were him.

"Don't worry about it," he smiled. A very Pete moment. "You needed to get that out of your system. I'll clean it up later."

I never did acid again.

Mike, too, was changing. On grass, he was either immune to speed limits, or I was paranoid. The morning after an all-night drive to L.A. in his car, he showed me a footprint on the dashboard, passenger side, where I'd been riding the night before. Bracing myself for the crash that did not come.

★ ★ ★

Meanwhile we put out no album.

One night, the car radio picked up what I knew at once was acoustic finger-picking, and I reached to turn up the sound. It might have been ours. And that became, *This could have been us.* "Listen to that!" I said to no one in particular. "We've got to find songs like that!" It had a folk character but still enough drive to be played on the radio, with drums that placed it squarely in the folk-rock genre: "Homeward Bound" by Simon and Garfunkel.

The luxury of time and the freedom to experiment on stage was vanishing, and even the creative process started to feel like work. On our once well-oiled fast track, Mike began to strain. We tried rehearsing in different locations. We stayed for a week at a resort in Boulder, Colorado, to be "free of distractions." We rented a house on the hill in Mill Valley, where the band could work in freedom.

But we were tired. Tired of flying at midnight to perform twenty hours later in a different time zone. Tired of being asked when We Five was going to have another hit. And the pressure Mike felt was enormous.

Hoping to think outside the box, Mike added an experimental sitar bridge to his banjo, but when we arrived at the studio, it was as if he'd brought in an accordion. "The banjo is a dead and archaic instrument," Frank announced, with a professorial laugh.

A&M offered to record us in L.A., to get us another producer, to send us some writers. But they were new to big-time success relative to Frank, and Frank wasn't about to surrender control.

Mike continued to work with Randy Sterling on "What Do I Do Now," the title seeming more and more a taunt. The song dealt with waking up to loss, a theme that, in "You Were On My Mind," had tapped a vein of liberation—only this time, resolve gives way to fear: someday freedom, but what now? Alec Palao has quoted Pete Fullerton pronouncing some of our post-Mind material "whiny." Along with "There Stands the Door," this tune certainly qualified.

We recorded it several times looking for the magic, and the instrumentation and arrangement were cutting-edge contemporary. But the more force and conviction we added to the music, the more it simply bounced off the bewilderment of the words.

• *13* •

C'mon People Now

*W*hen Debbie's pregnancy started to show, our landlord told us it was time to plan on moving. Neither of us still felt comfortable in the city anyway. We had a stick-shift car that always had to be parked on some hill or other, and the weather always felt more or less cold.

The two-bedroom, two-story place we found on Highway 1 in Tamalpias Valley cost $10 a week less than the studio apartment I'd rented in the city. It was on the leeward side of the coastal mountains, and the fog pouring over to our valley most afternoons engulfed our apartment like a scene from some weirdly gorgeous horror flick.

Here Debbie began, uneasily, to live my dream. She was beautiful, sweet, and there for me whenever I got in from touring. We took day trips to spectacular places like Point Reyes and Samuel P. Taylor State Park to the north, and of course San Francisco to the south. But she was isolated from her family, and living with a guy who'd changed from the one she fell in love with. Only Pete's wife could she really call a friend. She could find company at my folks' house in San Jose, where she came to love my mother, brother, and two younger sisters, but it meant being berated by my father for seducing me from the Catholic Church and condemning me to eternal damnation.

One of the first areas of non-musical common ground we discovered was the Busvan Storage Company in the funky warehouse part of North Beach. We'd spend hours going through a square city block of unclaimed goods for little and large treasures to furnish our apartment, prepare for the baby, and create a shared life that had nothing to do with We Five. It was going to be frilly curtains and colonial furniture for the bedroom no matter what I thought (I thought: *It's got a bed in it*). But for the living room we could agree on a combination of Mediterranean and distressed Mexican furniture with a touch

131

of Cost Plus brass. Neither of us cared they didn't match. A random employee at Sears vouched for me as belonging to We Five, which was good, because I was about to have my credit denied for not having a "job."

I'd been on the road, only intermittently plugged in to the pregnancy. Debbie had an OB on the corner of Van Ness and Pacific, across from the Hippo restaurant, walking distance from our old apartment in the city. Now it required a day trip. On September 16, just a year after the release of We Five's first album, we made the drive over the bridge to St. Mary's Hospital—only to have Debbie spend a day in false labor, refusing sleep even after they doped her with a pill. I sat with her and talked, but she hated, *hated* the wooziness of being intoxicated. This was Debbie they were treating. Around 10:00 a.m. they convinced me to go home and get some rest. Fathers were hangers-on in those days, a tradition that was changing like everything else, but St. Mary's was a traditional hospital, run by nuns.

I'd finally fallen asleep when the call came that the baby was in stress and delivery was being induced. So I raced back, but the drive was too far, and I missed the wondrous event—the breaking of the water, the forceps pulling Chris into the world (he was fine but bore tiny capillaries on his cheek for years). Only when both of them were out of the delivery room was I allowed in, and while Debbie beamed and encouraged me to hold him, there was nothing I knew yet how to do: it was just me and this baby with a full head of dark hair ("He's a Beatle!" I cracked)—would I accidentally break his neck? All too soon the nurses swooped in and sent me out again.

Everything about our new role felt tentative and awkward. Debbie's folks were coming the day after we brought Chris home, and we were terrified he'd die before they got there.

Over time Debbie created a new domestic routine. She found a church up the road and a place to pick blackberries to make cobbler. She brought Chris to my folks' and wore down my theologian dad by citing more scripture than he knew. We learned to barbeque using a Hibachi, or thought we learned: one night when the ventilation fan got turned off, Chris went limp. "I feel strange too," Debbie said. "I'm taking him to bed." I wobbled behind her, closing the bedroom door behind us. The doctor later said that closed door saved our lives.

In this way, the band became a compartment in my life. Counting John Chambers's new daughter Miya on Haight Street, we now had four family units competing for time with the band—I was witnessing the whole flower-power scene as a distant, suburban observer. Folks in Iowa assumed we were part of it, but I was barely even part of the business. I first heard Big Brother and the Holding Company on Tom Donahue's underground FM radio show, and saw them for the first time on a local PBS TV show. Going to the Matrix was not on Debbie's to-do list.

★ ★ ★

That left Mike and Bob shaping what music we took to the studio. In the hillside house that the band rented for rehearsals, the creative coupling of the twelve-string with electric banjo and dulcimer took form. More vocal melodies were carried by Mike, with Bob adding harmonies. Werber, to put it mildly, was displeased.

"What do you *mean* Bev's not singing lead!?" he freaked, interrupting the recording of "There Stands the Door."

Her husband's jazz friends were venturing far outside the mainstream now. As light shows became the rage at the Filmore and the Matrix, Fred Marshall joined Jerry Granelli and Bill Ham to conceive the Light Sound Dimension (LSD), taking music, as that year's "Star Trek" debut might have put it, to places no man had gone before. Fred's seniority and proficiency, Bev would later tell me, could sometimes feel intimidating. It all required her to change gears drastically when working with us. Anything with conventional voices and instruments started to look like the same old thing to her—or perhaps just not intimidating enough.

Even so, the creativity that was within Mike's reach can be appreciated on the unreleased tracks finally available on *There Stands The Door—The Best Of We Five*, released in 2009 by Ace Records Producer Alec Palao (Big Beat CDWIKD 286). Had the title track, a raga rock anthem with pulsing modal harmonies, been issued right away in January '66, it would have preceded rather than followed a glut of "me too" raga arrangements—by everyone from BJ Thomas ("Hooked on a Feeling") to the Cyrkle ("Turn Down Day")—in which electric sitar was a cheap afterthought, closing the window of originality Mike and Bob had worked to open.

We were missing our moment, while in another sense we were evolving beyond recognition. As 1967 began, we were booked for a concert at ultraconservative Baylor University to cap their "Baylor Beauties" pageant, for which we'd be featured as guest judges. The Beauties, dressed in formal wear and eating crumpets in a wood-paneled hall, were supposed to meet and shake hands with the visiting band before all the bigwigs of school and community—another concept brokered by Werber that had worked fine for the Kingston Trio. Our first concern arose at the Dallas airport, where a welcoming party had been sent to take our equipment and speed us to the pageant. There was no time even to check in or change clothes. The band on the cover of our album looked a little like a church's youth group in bright sweaters and close haircuts; the band at the terminal looked like an integrated San Francisco rock band. Two years had passed in the wink of an eye. We had dirty traveling clothes and a black guy with big hair. It was, as if overnight, February 1967. And it would be the mid-1970s before hippie fashion found Texas.

John Chambers in his rough-out jacket and moccasins. Bob in heavy sweaters, Bev in baggy sweater and pants. My hair went afro in humidity, and I wasn't taking advantage of that yet, so it was merely scruffy. Bob's was early Beatle; Mike's had already progressed to stringy, lanky to the collarbone, with bangs.

"Jerry, there's nothing to it," Werber said, a thousand miles West, when I phoned from the terminal. But then, he hadn't seen us.

"I'm really concerned about the tea party—or reception, or whatever it is they want to take us to," I tried to tell him. "We might need showers. But they're taking us straight to the event."

In the months since the Coke episode, Werber had subtly begun checking out as a music manager. It was becoming clear. He could have anticipated this.

Someone hollered, then, for "the five of us" to climb into a car. Here we went again.

"Actually, we have six."

Faced with the reality of John Chambers's presence, the face of the liaison tightened like a preview of the social hall. "Can he arrive in the other car? With the equipment?"

I fed more coins into the terminal pay phone.

"Frank. These people are acting like this is really a fancy thing. We need to go back to the rooms and dress, and they won't let us."

You could practically hear him toke. "The Kingston Trio have done it. You'll be fine."

The problem was, we were not the Kingston Trio. You had to wonder if he'd really thought this through. And now here we were, in Waco, TX, ushered into a paneled study. Most definitely high tea. Faces, taking us in, with expressions of What. Is. This.

You could have cut the tension with a knife.

We made a kind of shrunken approach and were joined by a guy who seemed to be the emcee or publicist for the event. He was trying to give us a crash course on the event format.

"It's like a beauty contest, then?" Bev asked.

"No, not a contest, because there's no official winner—I mean, there won't be a queen crowned. We Five is going to have tea and talk to each

Beauty and then rank them, based on points." It wasn't adding up for me. There'd be no winner, but we were judging?

"Not judging," he clarified. "*Rating.*"

This wasn't clear to any of us, but there seemed no way out anymore except through. We had tried to sound alarms at the airport. We had asked if it wouldn't be better to bypass the tea and go to sound check, and they'd reminded us we were under contract. We had apologized for our attire. Now it was too late. We were simply us.

After some further commotion about whether John was also a band member and thus a judge, and how to account for the album cover showing five members while six seemed to have shown up, the Beauties in their formals made their individual entrances, each announced in turn, and approached us to shake hands. Then they stood by as we held up our shameful cards showing sixes and fives—all but John, who had moved to a different zone entirely.

He held up zeroes.

Maybe he reacted to some aversion on the part of the girls, a few of whom shook hands as if they were afraid the black would rub off.

Beverly remembers him laughing.

I was thinking: What are we going to do? We should not have been in this position. Baylor was a Southern Baptist university, which at the time meant racially separate and who cared whether equal. But we were here, and if John was going to be asked to judge, his judgment was: this is a fiasco.

I don't think any person in the room wanted to be there now. And still our hosts were determined to finish celebrating the emperor's pajamas. Nobody knew another way out.

It was John who came closest to candor, by holding up those zero cards. He didn't call names; he didn't make speeches. By now I knew how to read John: he was not scared, or even pissed—Mike and I were probably closer to that. He was just dumbfounded to be in a time and place where, as uncomfortable as everyone was, no one could acknowledge the discomfort.

Eternally slow transition out of the room. All of a sudden our hosts seemed to be in perfect agreement that we should be allowed to go do our sound check and get on with our concert. We changed into the neat herringboned jackets and pressed shirts we'd perform in, color-matched, and after the concert, since we still hadn't ever made it to the hotel to get clean, Mike Stewart took off a relatively clean shirt to put on a shirt we'd left San Francisco in, and that looked like he'd slept in it.

Fred Dale at Perenchio, the agency who'd booked us, forwarded to Frank a letter from Baylor University dated February 8, 1967:

In the first place . . . since their appearance was so slouchy and unkempt, they passed by a group of our students [at the airport] without being recognized. They looked nothing like the publicity pictures you sent!

WE FIVE had agreed to attend a tea and judge our Baylor Beauties. They came to the tea exactly like they had stepped off the plane—which would have been all right had they been neat.

My greatest disappointment came, however, when they presented their entertainment. There were six of them instead of WE FIVE. They had added a drummer along the way! The music was loud and by the time the first intermission came, almost half of our audience had left. . . .

I would appreciate your assistance in helping us to avoid such embarrassment in the future. If you know that a group would not be suitable for our campus, please do not hesitate to tell me.

Numerous students and administrative personnel have suggested that we not secure entertainment from your Company again if that is the quality that you have to offer.

At the concert itself, we'd done encores; we got screams. But the local paper published a snide interview-profile rather than a review, barely mentioning the show, and gave readers the general impression that the audience had yawned and left early. Just as John Chambers gave zeroes to the Baylor Beauties, so did the Waco press score us.

★ ★ ★

With our second album, *Make Someone Happy*, stuck on hold, several songs had been issued as singles, but never charted. Only "Get Together" penetrated the top 40, peaking at 31. It had been composed by Dino Valenti in the early '60s in New York and recorded by the Kingston Trio well ahead of its time. A half-decade later it seemed a perfect anthem for the changing era—a reaching, almost scriptural vision of flower-child spirituality and universal love, with allusions to the Second Coming ("When the One who left us here returns for us at last . . .").

Our version back in '65 had gotten stuck at number 31, partly because of the timing of its release before Christmas, but in retrospect there may have been issues with the arrangement as well. Unlike "You Were On My Mind," we never found the marriage of lyric, mood, and instrumentation that would capture and define a generational moment. We just kept making it bigger: John pounding out drum rolls on a timpani he'd found under a blanket in Capitol's Studio B, the rest of our voices yelling at the listener about peace and love. While not as bitter as "What Do I Do Now?" it was more scold than invitation. By contrast, the Youngbloods' meander three years later may have better romanced the vibey brotherhood of the words.

Driving to rehearsal one day, Pete said, "Jerry—are you in We Five for security? Do you think any of us has security in the group?"

I had no idea what he was getting at, so I cut to the happy, obvious fact that went without saying: "All we need is another hit, and we'll be right back on top."

Pete nodded slowly. "Yes. I'm sure that if that happens, 'We Five' will be back on top. But what is We Five? Is it you? Is it me? Does the group need you to be We Five?" There was a new, basement register to his voice, concerned but also wise, as if he'd already surrendered to an outcome I'd never even considered. I'm not sure I answered him at all.

In fact, he was struggling. Too much musical diversity in the group had become a problem; Pete often felt like the scapegoat. His style wasn't where the musical wave was going, and he knew it, though in small acts of defensive assertion, he clung to it more. He told everyone who would listen that he missed playing standup bass, and that he didn't get, or like, the kind of R&B parts he was being told the new direction of the band required. Ampeg, our amplifier company, actually sent him a prototype of the Ampeg Baby Bass— the first practical attempt at making a portable string bass. Pete loved the idea, but it didn't really sound very good and there was no justification for carrying it on the road.

I did know the scene was changing. The euphoria and TV attention we once enjoyed now spotlighted newcomers like the Association, the Fifth Dimension, and the Mamas and the Papas. Frank Werber was less focused and less reachable week by week. Still, I felt I'd been adapting. I'd been playing tambourine; I'd been opening to blues.

We arrived at the rehearsal house just as John Stewart was leaving. George Yanok—the Trio's road manager, now on salary at Trident—was with him, his alter-ego, the jokester; the two were always on. John said hello on the front walk, and I asked him how the new Kingston Trio album was doing.

He winced as if I'd snapped him into an unwelcome reality. "Well, it'll be a good demo for my songs." His voice suggested anything but excitement.

Pete said something earnest like, "I'm sure it will do great like all the others have."

But as we headed inside the house, I heard John tell George, in a tone somewhere between a wisecrack and a pat on the head: "Those guys are quite a pair, aren't they? Like the Bobbsey Twins."

★ ★ ★

Whatever the rest of We Five and the Kingston Trio experienced, of course, it was Mike who carried the heaviest burden. It was Mike who'd had to compose those unused Coke commercials, any one of which could have provided the musical basis for a new song. It was Mike whom Bob and John pushed to adopt a sharper and funkier groove; it was Mike whom Frank Werber had pushed to bring back the genre-busting eclecticism he thought was responsible for our first success.

Mike's lyrics now barricaded themselves more deeply into righteous solitude, the back pages of his songbook turning as naked, literal, and confessional as Brian Wilson's and John Lennon's:

> What's going on?
> What makes me think that I see where I've been wrong?
> How come I feel that I've been down too long?
> Won't someone tell me please.
>
> What's going on?
> Why am I saying things inside my head
> Things I always thought were better left unsaid
> Won't someone tell me please
> What's going on?
>
> Sometimes I wonder, I see that I have changed
> Sometimes I feel I was better as I was.
> But I feel better as I rearrange
> So I don't worry 'bout my mind and what it does.
>
> What's going on?
> Between myself and I? Gets me down
> There's gotta be some better times around
> What's going on?
> Start to feel this is where I belong
> And I haven't felt this good in so long
> What's going on? What's going on?

At the same time, he brought in more wide-ranging cover material. There was a We Fivalized version of "Our Day Will Come." For "Inchworm," a poem by Hans Christian Anderson, Mike played dulcimer as a rhythm instrument while Pete and Bev sang a lilting duet in their upper registers—all joined to the breathy flute tones of our former schoolmate, Jerry Oshita, a Japanese American who befuddled his college professors by wearing a green tamo'shanter and breaking his last name with an Irish apostrophe.

Had Donovan released "Inchworm"—I am utterly convinced—the concept would have carved a groove for others to enter. In the hands of We Five, though, it was another shelf song that seemed only to guess blindly at the shape of music's future.

The hour was late. By March '67, as Trident showed signs of faltering, Peter, Paul, and Mary released the single "I Dig Rock 'n' Roll Music," former folk standard-bearers giving notice to the world that they could rock as well or better than either of Werber's primary acts. And their album, *1700*, proved it.

George Yanok bore much of Frank's ill temper as artist after artist in the Trident experiment to encourage creativity failed to take off. At one point, Yanok said, he was ordered to take the tapes of the Trio's live performance in Lake Tahoe and, with no experience whatsoever, personally mix them down into a marketable record. The Trio was dying, We Five was in trouble, it was all costing money, and nothing was coming in.

At some point, in what struck me as a childish act, Pete stopped carrying his own instrument to shows. He told me he had an escape plan. He could settle down and be a sanitation worker. Have a wife, a house full of kids and a 9-to-5—no more chasing rainbows. Or just begin chasing a different sort of rainbow. He was either a decade behind the moment or a few decades ahead of it.

Meanwhile, I carried his bass.

Whether it was about Pete, or in response to the damning letter from Perenchio, we found ourselves in Frank's office one day in April for a very stoned summit. The chronology is foggy, but by now Pete had announced he was finished. We told Frank we'd recently had a rehearsal where Mike played bass so we could work on the folk-blues standard "I Know You Rider," the first time I could remember rehearsing without Pete since he'd joined the group, and I'd felt very uncomfortable and strange.

Beverly's reaction: "Pete didn't resign; he was forced out. And if Pete's out, I'm out."

"No Bev, no band," Werber said, as ultimatum. "Unless." He looked at me. "Unless Jerry stays on and brings Debbie on as lead singer."

In a trance of bravado, pot-induced paranoia, and naiveté, I thought: *Why do I need the baggage of all the others, if Frank is willing to record Debbie and me?*

In this way, barely a year after the birth of folk-rock, the group whose song was going to synergize the vanguard of a new generation and of Frank Werber's "San Francisco sound" had privately disbanded.

★ ★ ★

We had only some college dates left to play. But the later schedulings would not survive the fallout of the first one, at Utah State on May 6.

As with the Baylor Beauties debacle, We Five arguably should never have flown to this tiny Mormon college. Far too much had changed in the months since the first album was released.

But the locals, who normally only saw acts like "Up with People," were excited at the prospect of our arrival. There was a healthy edge of audience intrigue within the margins of safety that the promoters thought we inhabited.

As we set up our instruments, a student glee club went through final run-throughs of the bombastic Broadway dance number "Another Opening, Another Show" to precede our concert. An odd warm-up, but at least it implied an upbeat tone. We'd been informed that the concert was a twenty-year tradition memorializing a plane crash, and although the first gatherings were somber, they'd eventually encompassed popular music—so as best I could tell, reading the trend, our presence meant it was now a celebration. Here were student performers, after all, in topcoats and tails.

But the front rows were filled with anyone who was anyone in the state of Utah—read: leaders of the Mormon Church. And within our first couple of numbers, the school liaison relayed a request through the backstage curtain for us to turn down our volume.

At first I was confused. It was the nose too close to my eyes to see, though I get it now: we'd taken the stage integrated, electrified, and kicking off a memorial with songs like "There Stands the Door" and "You Let a Love Burn Out," both proto-psychedelic, both vocally on edge. Unstated, in other words, in the request to *turn down the volume*, somewhere in the daisy chain of messaging that began in the front rows and was relayed through parted curtains to Bob, and then from Bob to me, and lastly from me to Mike, was: Where's "Tonight"? Where's "Somewhere Beyond the Sea"? We were doing a Fillmore show in Southern Utah.

Mike's first response, a la Mike, was a bandleader's joke. "They're saying we're a little loud?" He brushed the hair out of his eyes. "Well, listen *softer*."

We were shouting out the increasingly symbolic, and ever anguished "What's Going On?" to this packed auditorium—when the amps simply went mute. They'd silenced the speakers, mid-song. They did what was done to Bob Dylan at Newport. We looked back and forth at each other as the reality of the words we sang unfolded around us: what *was* going on?

Still professional, still witty, always trying to charm, Mike chatted, apologized to the audience for the sound failure—whereupon, again, the message came through the curtain, to Bob, to me, to Mike, to turn down our volume. But as in a game of telephone, we added new levels of annoyance to each repetition.

"What's that?" Mike said to the microphone after tipping his ear to me. "There's leaders of the church here? And we're too loud!?"

A head poked through the curtain one last time. "Play your hit and get off."

With no miked vocals, we delivered the last live performance of "You Were On My Mind" by the original band.

Afterward, as the auditorium filed out in absolute silence, no one approached us. It was going to be the silent treatment then. We changed clothes. We packed our instruments. We carried our own amps to the bus outside the auditorium. And all along the way a gauntlet of students watched us—saying nothing.

A brave student did step forth near the end of the line. "I just want to say we were ordered not to talk to you. We were really surprised they even let you come, and we're really sorry they're doing this to you. Don't hold it against everybody."

We had separate takes afterward on the disaster. Bob's was that the world just didn't "get it." Mike's was that we'd been condemned to a time capsule, typecast too early to outgrow a mold that no longer fit. Mine lay between that and Phyllis Diller, back when she'd scolded Bev about professionalism on the nightclub circuit. I wouldn't have let us go to Utah, but neither would I have fanned the flames like Mike. This, I thought, was the kind of outcome you got when you did whatever you felt like, without forethought.

We got on the bus, and I don't remember going on to Iowa City or Ottowa, Kansas. The collective mood was, *maybe it's better this way*. We'd already agreed to split up anyway. Times were changing. Dylan got it right.

★ ★ ★

Random memories stay with me. Driving from a concert date in Wisconsin to St. Paul. It had been a warm October day and we wore short sleeves. The evening cooled, so we raised the windows and Beverly fired up a joint, coating the car with smoke as we sank in for a two-hour drive into the darkness. Less than an hour in, I started to become entranced by the bugs in the headlights, more of them by the second, both a beautiful and strange enough whirl that I woke up Pete and Bev to watch the show. But my fascination decayed to fear in the telling when we saw the bugs get thicker still. A cloud, nearly opaque. Someone suggested that we stop, but not knowing what kind of insects we might be dealing with, I tensed and pushed on toward St. Paul, trying grimly now to figure out why the bugs left no evidence of a collision against the windshield as the speedometer climbed. The numbers grew to swarm levels. I reached to crack open the wind wing, and Beverly panicked, "NO! God, Jerry! We don't know what they are. What if they get in the car?" But to stay as we were was to remain quite literally in darkness. I was nervous but that only made the right choice clearer. I took a chance and put a single finger in the stream of the air. No bugs came in the car, but my finger returned wet. I started laughing and said, "Pete, roll down your window." He stuck his hand out too and began to laugh with me as we discovered that the temperature had dropped about 30 degrees from when we'd left, and it was snowing.

We had seen snowfall before—we weren't completely sun-baked in California—but never when we didn't expect it. As the panic passed, we tipped just as hard to the other extreme, laughing till our eyes watered—though of course not as sure of our sanity as we'd have been if we weren't so stoned.

So many things, looking back, expose how vulnerable we were right then: that we were so far from home; that for all we understood we were watching the Apocalypse; that pushing a single finger out of a car window could seem like an act of gigantic courage; that snowfall to some stoned kids from California was in some ways no less weird than a universe that might rain bugs. That our laughter, like almost everything else in 1966–1967, was both a facet of, and a break from, how incredibly lost our generation suddenly was.

★ ★ ★

And I remember the whole band the way it was while our experiment held together.

A fascinating audio clip was shared with me recently by DJ and rock-music historian Mike Callahan. It was recorded before that McCormick Place concert in Chicago, and in it, you can hear Mike Stewart, not yet twenty-one, speaking ever so eloquently about the band, its collective vision, and how he saw it fitting in to the world of pop music.

Michael's voice in this interview is casual, sophisticated, like that of a slightly more scholastic Mick Jagger. ("You're a happy-sounding group," the interviewer remarks. "Are you commercial?" "Well," says Mike, "we've sold a lot of records, so I guess that makes us commercial. But we do other things— lots of classically influenced or serious music that probably isn't a single. You can't fool teenagers, and they know what they want. But our album has really good music on it so we hope that people will like it. It's sold about 200,000 copies, so I guess some people do.")

With hindsight, I know that virtually every word was considered for effect. And that consideration took place in only the barest interval between when the question was asked and when he began to answer. Part of this ability came from Mike's skill as an observer, part from his debating experience in school, part from the comedic timing he'd developed on stage, but all of it was inseparable from who he was. He knew what he wanted to express, and that music was the way to express it, and just as he had tried out different personnel and instruments to build We Five in the first place, the process of trying, rejecting, or building on things was eternal, and he was *happy*, as long as his progress was something the industry seemed to care about.

Since the first time he'd come to my house with a banjo and a songbook, Mike had been unnaturally driven; as our popularity crested, I saw, for a short time, his desperation replaced by the awareness of his element. He was comfortable in his skin, unconcerned what his brother might be doing. And so that radio interview with Mike on the eve of the Dick Clark Caravan is, for me, a paradox suspended in time. Famous, he was briefly himself.

Bob was the musician's musician: adept at playing anything called for on a guitar. Or a sitar. Or an organ. He was always visualizing and practicing and fitting new things into his mental library. Music was the singular focus of his life, and he expected no less from anyone else; if complacency was a trap I could sometimes fall into, it was nothing Bob could understand or abide. I suspect that this may help explain why he would later find chemicals harder to kick than I did: they seemed to extend the hours available for the quest.

We knew that Pete was the humanitarian of the group, but not that his sensitivity to others in need would become the later focus of his life. In the spirit of both John and Bobby Kennedy, I think he always tried to visualize a better world than he saw ("For the rest of my life, I've been looking for dry noses"). Yet through it all, and in a strange way inseparably, he was called to music. He loved everything about the string bass: the way it felt to embrace as it leaned; the way you could draw out richness with a bow, or pluck with your fingers, or slap like a drum. Whatever the electric bass had in common with the acoustic, not everything you do on an acoustic sounds good on an electric. More important, the electric techniques were still figuring themselves out. With no training at the crossroads of electrification, and with no shortage of unsolicited opinions, he was divided. In response, he began to study—but with a symphony player. That deepened his understanding of theory and technique. But it didn't endear him to a rock band, post-1965.

John Chambers had an internal ear that was one part BS detector and one part compass set to his own true north. And regardless of what he was feeling, when he spoke, you got the ungarbled word: open, honest, and direct. He wasn't interested in anything he considered irrelevant, and it mattered to him that We Five be relevant. Almost immediately, he found a home in the San Francisco rock and blues scenes, playing with the Elvin Bishop Band, Big Joe Turner, Big Mama Thornton, and the Loading Zone.

Bev Bivens was the girl next door who, struck by a bit of stage lighting, became an icon of a transitional cultural moment. She was one of us, and yet not. The only female in a band of strong-willed guys, she learned how to create and protect her own space. They say Sinatra was like that when doing bus tours with the big bands: he loved the camaraderie but never lost sight of his duty to grow.

Recently, Bev shared an insight I'd never considered. Unlike the hundreds of performances she had done with We Five, the only visual of Light Sound Dimension was the light show. The musicians performed their explorations behind an opaque screen, invisible to the audience. Beverly Bivens had been the visual and aural focal point of a very powerful performing entity, in the charmed shindigs and hootenannies of 1965–1966, when everything seemed within music's communal grasp.

Years later, she realized the loss. Behind a screen, cut off from that vital interaction, Beverly told me, "What I missed was the audience."

I am not alone in wondering what kind of star Bev Bivens would have been had she followed the path of Sinatra—or Janis Joplin, or Linda Ronstadt—and stepped out from We Five and that screen to perform on her own. After 1968, she would not sing publicly for more than forty years.

PART THREE

I can never go home again
Never really find my town
I can see things aren't like they used to be
No need in my hanging 'round

—"I Can Never Go Home Again,"
words and music by John Stewart, used by permission

· *14* ·

The Sorcerer's Apprentice

I'd been in elementary school the last time my future wasn't linked to Mike Stewart's—a fact I didn't really process in that stoned summit meeting at Frank's office where the band agreed to part ways. Now that the awareness sank in, it was hard to tell if what I was feeling was exhilaration or just terror, like the blackness of the night on that Army ship to Japan when I was in ninth grade—because, really, the self who would have learned to make my way alone in the world was still that young. And that time around, Mike met me at Los Angeles International Airport with my guitar.

I still had Debbie, and I saw an opening with Pete Fullerton, who failed to get the day job he applied for. When you start at the top like I did at seventeen, you don't give up success without a fight.

Calling ourselves the Tricycle, and chasing the folk-textured sound of Simon and Garfunkel and Peter, Paul and Mary, we got booked in the intimate upstairs bar of a place called the Ark in Sausalito. It was a few docks from the old houseboat where we first heard "You Were On My Mind" playing on every Bay Area station, a trippy bar with a trippy poster of the show done in the Bill Graham acid-rock style. The fact that we were playing acoustic guitar and string bass wasn't a problem at first. Until the downstairs band plugged in—a power trio with four SUNN amplifier cabinets (Cream had just broken through in England). Then the room would shake like a train was coming through it.

Around August '68, Frank Werber called us to his primary house on DeSilva Island—now joined by landfill to Strawberry Point, right across the shallow bay from our old houseboat. We brought our new demo with us, because we'd always taken everything we did to Frank Werber before. The scenery on the car ride was astonishing, transitioning from freeway to redwood forest to a redwood house, nestled among the trees, that had a view of Alcatraz, the Bay Bridge, and the city if you stood in one spot and pivoted.

Vegetables grew outside, and there were extra lights strung between the cornrows—I gave no thought to that at first.

Debbie and I knocked, heard a muffled "just a minute" from within. Eventually Frank opened the door—in the nude. A woman, also unclothed, rose from a bed in an upstairs loft and disappeared into a bathroom.

"We don't wear clothes much unless there's company," he explained. "Let me get something on."

When he came back he had on pajama bottoms and a loose-fitting white shirt, making him look very East Indian. His beard was salt and pepper and his skin was deeply tanned. A glass wall the height of the two-story structure encased the blueness of the bay, and the conversation began small and very courteous.

"Well," I said. "We've wanted to thank you for letting us use the studio and record."

"Uh-huh. I'm told you're doing some really good stuff. How's that tenor guitar working out?"

"Perfect. Thank you—do you need it back? Or can I keep using it?"

"No, no—I certainly don't need it. You keep it, and keep right on using it."

"Well, as it happens, I used it on a Mason Williams song, and it really added some punch to the rhythm. Want to hear it? We brought an acetate."

"Sure," Frank said. "Let's hear it."

He took the demo disk and placed it on the turntable. We heard the needle touch down and sound surge forth from two enormous speaker clusters suspended from the ceiling. It was even better quality than the studio had, and the big sounds we'd recorded touched all the walls and filled the room. There was Mason Williams's "All the Time," and the Ron Davies composition "Somewhere," both using electric leads and sharp punches of brass to augment the string bass and acoustic rhythm. There was a bossa nova version of "Soon It's Gonna Rain" (with our old guardian angel Jerry Granelli on drums). I thought it all sounded really amazing on the big speakers. But while Frank looked impressed on some level, I picked up the sense that something was wrong. There were no attaboys, so I pressed on to the question.

"What do you think?" I asked.

"Well, I think you guys are doing great," he began cheerfully. "I'm sure something will happen for you."

That seemed like an odd phrasing. I hadn't been prepared for what it meant. He must have read the surprise on my face.

"How do you keep up with the music business?" he sighed, as if thinking out loud. "I don't even know where it's going anymore."

We tried to tell Frank that was the whole point: music was free to go anywhere now. I asked if he'd heard "Hey Jude," the Beatles' newest release. How the three-minute fade-out was longer than whole songs used to be.

"Oh, yes. I've heard it." And he fetched a copy of the 45 to place on the turntable. In fact, as it began to play, I realized something about it sounded different from any 45 I'd ever heard.

"It sounds like—stereo," I said. "On a *single?*"

"That's because it *is*," Frank said, and then repeated himself: "*How do I keep up with that?*"

"You just—you know, you keep writing and practicing and recording and doing your best."

But he must not have wanted a pep talk, because he headed mine off. "I can't do this anymore."

"What do you mean?"

"I'm done with the music business. The Kingston Trio had their run. We Five is over. Bringing new artists up to speed is hard work, and I just don't want to do this anymore."

Not even I had anything to say now. Then Frank broke the dead air. "You guys are good and you should have a shot. I'm giving you a letter of introduction to Perenchio in L.A. I'll give you acetates. Knock on some doors—go see Jerry Moss at A&M. I'm finished."

Just like that, we were on our way out, past the cornrows with the leafy stalks and the long strings of lights—the sight of which Frank gazed upon proudly.

"It's a shame you have to do this to make a living," he added.

★ ★ ★

It would be another eight months before we knew what he was growing in those cornrows.

His arrest for trading in drugs was all over the news in L.A. He beat a federal court case, but Marin County authorities tried him separately for possession and cultivation, and for that he served six months in jail. The *San Francisco Chronicle* described the saga as a circus: sheriff's officers lugging sea bags full of pot into the courtroom, Tommy Smothers bringing the roof down by testifying that "before he started smoking pot, Frank was a real asshole," and Werber's attorneys putting forth a religious freedom defense, in the form of a spiritual connection to marijuana that went back to the Holocaust. "Celebrities marched in and out of the courtroom," said the paper, "as a fan club of young women in miniskirts rooted for Mr. Werber, who, participants said, smoked pot a few times during the breaks."[1]

★ ★ ★

"I guess we'll be moving back to L.A.," Debbie said in the car, as we drove into North Beach to get the acetates of our work. There was neither excitement nor regret in her voice. "I sure won't miss it here. I was a blonde when we got married, but I don't even know what color you call this."

In the Trident building, Hank McGill cut demos of our new stuff, but he drew the line when I asked for an extra song not on Frank's list. It was called "Past Askin'," something Bob and I had written for the original group's last, unreleased album.

Even a phone call to Frank didn't clinch the favor.

"Jerry," he said, adopting the tone of a frustrated parent. "*Don't push people so hard.*"

★ ★ ★

It wasn't the 1970s just yet, but in Los Angeles you could feel them in the air. Chic drugs were becoming a jet-setter's in-joke. Performing at Seal Beach's Rouge et Noir (and postponing our trip to A&M, because I wanted to see what other connections were out there first), I popped two Contac capsules for a cold, paying for it with a case of dry mouth to go with my sniffles. Backstage, I tried to explain my condition to Hoyt Axton, who'd been a hero of mine ever since he wrote the Kingston Trio's 1962 classic "Greenback Dollar"—and he just winked. "*Oh, sure. I smoked some of that 'medicine' on the way to the club!*"

In Pomona, where we took an apartment in a quadruplex, our musician status worked its double-edged power. Our back-fence neighbors, like almost everyone else in suburban L.A., talked up their connections to the folk-rock scene: they had a brother or cousin who'd played in the Sunshine Company, or was their roadie, or some such thing. They were like a lot of new twenty-somethings, trying to find their way and have some fun. When they bought a house on the town's north end, by the foot of the Ganesha Hills—the same neighborhood Mike lived in back in grade school, the place where his dad kept a stable of trotters—they phoned to say, "Hey, we're having a little housewarming; c'mon over!" So we did, and the first clue something was amiss was the absence of any other guests in the living room.

We conversed about a little of this and a little of that, until the husband leaned forward and said, "So, we're curious—you're musicians, you're ahead of the curve. Are you into swinging?"

Debbie wore a look as if she were thinking. *Swing . . . sets? In the back-yard? Jazz dancing?*

I was thinking, *Oh my God.*

It was just that sort of assumption that kept Debbie half-soured about the music business: She hated being identified with any mindset just because she sang. Whether it was about getting drunk, stoned, or laid wasn't the point—she never quite knew whether she was supposed to witness to them about her love of Jesus, or leave. So we made a very embarrassed exit.

After turning down an invitation from Epic Records to do an album of Broadway show tunes—we needed to get hipper, said Peter—we could put off A&M no longer. At their La Brea offices, which had been Charlie Chaplin's stucco home and studio in the 1910s, Jerry Moss chatted with us about We Five's good old days, asked amiably about Frank, praised the demos—and then smoothly shifted the subject to Beverly: "Do you talk? Do you think she'd be interested in doing some recording?" He got her phone number from me before passing us off to Gil Friesen.

Friesen, too, raved about the demos, but frowned at the name of Tri-cycle. "It's so hard to start over," he said, "and everyone thinks so highly of We Five. . . ."

A thoughtful pause.

"Who owns the name now? Could you get it? Because if we could re-launch you as We Five, it would sure take down the risk level."

As we said our goodbyes, Friesen smiled, "So—do you stay in touch with Beverly?"

★ ★ ★

Back in Northern California, Pete, Debbie, and I made the rounds of the old bandmates to secure rights to the We Five name, in exchange for which each of them would receive a share of royalties on the next album. Mike signed the release in his kitchen while we watched him ruin a fried egg, be-cause he didn't know to oil the pan. Bob signed with a cigarette poking from his guitar strings; John Chambers shrugged and said, "Why not?" Bev, as was becoming her habit, postponed a decision pending a talk with her husband. None of us even realized that A&M had left out giving anyone the traditional signing bonus.

Then we returned south, got the grand studio tour, and I felt both the energy of the place and the pressure. Ever since "You Were On My Mind" had been A&M's first non-instrumental hit, the label had been on a tear. The Tijuana Brass took off like no instrumental group since the big band era; Julius Wechter and the Baja Marimba Band joined them on the charts and on the concert circuit; Sergio Mendes's pop-jazz combo morphed into Brazil '66, with twin female voices and a seductive, show-stealing rhythm section. The Sandpipers, launched to fill the mainstream bin vacated by We Five, were getting so much airplay for their foreign-language vocal round, "Guantanamera," that DJs and musicians were both equally sick of hearing it.

In the marketing suites, we found one of the reasons—Don Graham was heading up promotion. He gave us a hearty greeting, then segued into his usual nervous PR chatter. "It's like a candy store here! There's more material and talent than I can keep up with! I had to hire help!"

Then young Bob Garcia, who would later head PR, came into the room with a test pressing of the Tijuana Brass's first vocal release—"This Guy's in Love with You," written by the hit-making duo of Burt Bacharach and Hal David—and Graham pivoted so quickly from our warm welcome I got whiplash. I recalled his long-ago solution to the crisis of David Ruffin being replaced in the Temptations: "Get me some glasses! All anybody knows is the lead singer wears glasses."

Now I felt expendable, to say the least. Being signed in a spirit of why not, and having become, in the space of two years, yesterday's news, we were competing with some of the top recording acts in the world—and on the same label. We Five was no longer the gifted child.

But I rolled up my sleeves. What would Frank Werber have done? For a place to play and rehearse, like the band used to have in Mill Valley, I took a lease with an option to buy on an old Pomona farmhouse—an assertion of my roots—in a huge grove with a barn and outbuildings in various states of decay. The place had not been occupied in years, but it still contained some furniture, coated with dirt and cobwebs. I felt like Omar Sharif taking the guest house in *Dr. Zhivago*.

In a little while, two bedrooms, a kitchen, living room, and bathroom were livable enough for the drummer and pianist to move in. Most of the decorations and furnishings that were salvaged or brought in were classic hippie and thrift-store finds. And at night it felt like a haunted mansion, with dark hallways and a back stairway leading nowhere.

The neighborhood was multiethnic now, like the Haight had been, though not urban or creative in any way. It was just a buffer zone—a place where people aren't rejected for what their house looks like or what they drive or what brand of guitar they play. Until General Dynamics moved its aerospace plant there in the early '50s to make sidewinder missiles, bringing workers like my dad along with them, Pomona (which means "goddess of fruit") was a peaceful San Gabriel Valley agricultural community. Frank Zappa's Mothers of Invention, because they lived in the general area, had been playing in a Pomona bar called the Broadside when they got discovered.

For me, what it felt like was *free*—no attacks from the neighborhood, no camaraderie either.

I'd made no attempt to soundproof the rehearsal room, so curious neighbors heard us and quickly figured out we were somebody. But we weren't playing "Satisfaction" or the Doors; we were singing "Mountain Greenery." In retrospect, some may have wondered how on earth we ever found a song like "You Were On My Mind" and got it on the radio. Our drummer was a good arranger, but so new we had to buy him a set of drums.

That is how we were as we began work on *The Return of We Five*. I was determined; I meant business. At one rehearsal, when an A&M engineer brought out a vial of dope, I partook, but it did nothing for me (it may have been bad grass). It just wasn't part of my life anymore.

I was hoping to do a conceptual mix like Frank Werber had endorsed on our first album, where you'd hear a whole side of an album as a unit. And I was going to do it by the numbers. Get me a Broadway standard like Mike used to find. Get me a soft jazz ballad, a hip new rock tune. "I got this—don't tell me where I'm wrong." In that way, in 1968, we released *The Return of We Five* with what I thought was a winning formula.

★ ★ ★

The problem was that my formula was empty math. The culture had been there, seen that. Singer-songwriters were now composing better love songs than Broadway. Reviews said: *A nice sampler, but who cares?* And where we tried to do an innovative track, radio stations complained it didn't sound like We Five.

In 1965, a block of Kingston Trio–era record buyers had been drawn by an iconic song to the folk-rock idiom. In 1968, that audience was splintering. When our second, more probing, rock-flavored album had taken too long to come out, the rock camp moved on to the Jefferson Airplane and the Doors; the folkies, who'd loved the pretty-sweet romantics of our first album, took the next evolutionary step—to Spanky and Our Gang, the Association, the Mamas and the Papas, John Denver. At any moment, the river that had run from the Kingston Trio to Joan Baez and Richie Havens would arrive at country, at Crosby, Stills, Nash, and Young, at Linda Ronstadt, James Taylor, Jackson Browne, and the Eagles.

The new rock festivals reflected these changes. We'd already missed the bus by not getting to play at Monterey. (Since Werber rejected signing John Phillips, whose idea the festival was, there was no way we could hope to be invited, even if we were still touring. Phillips wrote Scott McKenzie's hit "San Francisco [Be Sure to Wear Flowers in Your Hair]" essentially as an advertisement for the festival.) We attended an Orange County Festival that was similar (the Chambers Brothers played the audience as much as their hit song, hitting a cowbell in slow motion as the crowd chanted "Time!" for a quarter of an hour)—but we wouldn't have been the kind of act that audiences came for. Nor would I learn about Woodstock, a continent away, until after it happened. Like the whole idea of communes, it wasn't who I was or where I was heading: naked wet people getting stoned and having sex behind the bushes, if they hid at all. We wouldn't have been any highlight for the crowd. (The Association, I'd heard, had little connection with the audience in Monterey—they were still doing a slick show wearing suits.)

My mistakes started to multiply. To promote our new album, Freddy Dale booked us a couple of concerts in the Midwest when our lineup was in no way solid enough to do a two-hour concert. It was Debbie's first working trip without our son—there would be nothing fun about that for her. At the University of Dayton, we followed a local act that made Paul Revere and the Raiders seem stolid: the not-yet-famous Ohio Players, flaunting a rotation of lead singers—one the chick diva, another the pimp-styled soul singer with the James Brown dance moves—in a prototype of how rap and hip-hop shows would be structured forty years later. For all I understood of funkadelia, they might have stepped out of a spaceship. My worry was that we'd brought a brand-new sound system to Dayton, and the Ohio Players were doing their best to break it. They spun mikes by the cable like lassos, once in a while managing to catch them with the other hand instead of bouncing them off the floor.

They went so far past the customary thirty to forty minutes for an opening act that I told the promoter we should just play one set ourselves.

No, he said—we had a contract. Two full hours plus the second intermission.

The audience was as exhausted as the musicians. Anyone who didn't leave after the Ohio Players left the hall gave out shortly after we began to play.

I knew how to lead a group to the Hertz desk from baggage claim and pick up a check after the show, but I was not prepared to book a trip like this, let alone road-manage it. Clearly I didn't ask enough questions beforehand about expectations on the part of the booker and the audience.

That was also true of St. Olaf's, a small Lutheran college in upstate Minnesota where folk music and We Five were still pretty big. Pulling into Northfield in a Ryder truck, we felt more like the Starving Students Moving Company than rock stars. But the show began well. It could have been 1965. The audience loved the standards; they suspended their doubts on the rest. When we finished the first half of the show with "Let's Get Together," the crowd was singing along.

Then came the request for "Leaving on a Jet Plane."

A bell should have sounded in my brain. Since early afternoon, kids had been asking if we played any John Denver compositions. By the second or third time I should have asked why.

I knew John Denver had written that hit for Peter, Paul and Mary. I knew that in '65 he'd taken Chad Mitchell's place in the Chad Mitchell Trio. I also considered "Leaving on a Jet Plane" the epitome of corn. If it were about a coffee pot salesman flying to St. Louis for a week, it could have provided a plotline for a movie—violins materializing as Donald O'Connor begins to sing. Too velvety, too sincere, almost weepy, and if the singer was really so in love, why leave? Not saying when he'd be back again conjured a relationship built on what? I felt uncomfortable about that attitude, although many in my generation were opening to it.

It may be that I'd just never experienced any real agony of separation. Those times Debbie had taken me to the airport in 1965–1967, I knew I was coming back home again. Whether that was me stuffing feelings or just being a hunter-gatherer, the song wasn't speaking the same things to me that it was to millions of other people.

Or maybe I was jealous.

Maybe I didn't like that John Denver was getting to be successful, and not me. Maybe it was a little bit of all of those things.

Yet I'm sure the song resonated very deeply for Mary Travers, and the feeling came through when she sang it. It was the life she lived, always off to catch an airplane, always saying goodbye to boyfriends or husbands. She'd had both.

Something very real happens to mothers with kids who have to put them down and go away. "For Baby, for Bobby" was a key hit for Mary Travers too.

I finally said: "People have been asking us all day to play some John Denver, so get ready, 'cause here it comes." Pleased with myself, I ad-libbed an intro. "This song could have worked in the era of movie musicals. You can almost see the dancers jump out from behind the bushes."

Pete and Debbie did some silly dance steps—a schtick that got no laughs.

The song's opening strains brought some excited recognition—then, within seconds, there were audible gasps. Trying to win over an audience with arrogance, and not sharp enough musically to set ourselves apart, we served up a country parody right out of "Hee Haw"—and finished amid virtual silence.

When we closed with "You Were On My Mind," there was only token applause—definitely no encore.

After the show, the few people who came to talk with us were still around because they had jobs to do. One fellow who'd brought a *You Were*

On My Mind album to be autographed said, "This is one of my favorite albums. I was so excited when I heard you were coming to St. Olaf." There
was a pause as he considered whether to continue. "I know that We Five is
known for doing new arrangements of well-known songs. How do audiences
generally respond to your version of 'Jet Plane'?"

"Well," I said, "something sure happened tonight. Was it something I
said?"

Almost cautiously, he asked if I knew that John Denver had attended
school there. "You know, to a lot of people, making fun of their hero—it was
probably kind of sacrilegious."

★ ★ ★

For my next indignity, there is the tale of the Beverly Hills manager. Ed
Leffler worked for an agency that was doing a good job managing mainstream-
contemporary Sinatra-type artists. You could tell right away they had something, an air of professionalism that began with the Beverly Hills address and
carried through to the staff inside. But all we had was our former name—we
couldn't perform a genuine We Five show if we wanted to. It didn't make
me feel comfortable at all.

Ed thought A&M might not be the place for us at all. "They're caught up
in making Herb a star. It's not the right place for We Five anymore. I'm going
to get you out of that contract and put you with Bones Howe."

"You mean—the engineer working with Jimmy Webb and the Fifth
Dimension?" I asked.

"Yes. But Bones is doing his own producing now. I think he can take
you where you've never been before."

That was a dramatic statement . . . but he sounded so sure of himself.
Driving home, Debbie said, "Okay. But does it make sense for us to be leaving
A&M after all we went through to get there?"

"We have to trust someone," Pete said.

Ed's vision was to create a kind of pop music that was hipper than the
Perry Como stuff from the early '60s, but not so distorted by flower-power
affectation that it lost class. Relaunch We Five and go back to the mindset
of finding exceptional songs that could be done in a new way. Use proven,
talented arrangers rather than pals, and then layer on unmatchable vocals.

We tried this. We began working on things like the "Theme from Long
Hot Summer," with a driving rock beat instead of the humid, almost inert way
it was done for the movie. We met to discuss music as an intellectual process
with people cut from Sinatra cloth, chasing this idea of bridging Sinatra and
rock. Ed would ultimately sign the Carpenters—along with Van Halen.

At our next visit to Ed's office, he casually mentioned finally having "got you out of the A&M contract. Now we can get something done!"

We held our breath—particularly after our *next* meeting when he broke the news that Bones was too busy to take on the project. "But that's OK. We'll find somebody better who can do arranging, too."

"Like a Jimmy Webb?" I asked.

"Yes! Exactly! But not him. Someone with both feet on the ground. Jimmy's a great writer and arranger, but he's got some issues."

"He's doing okay for the Fifth Dimension," I said.

Weeks passed, and Ed got harder to reach. He seemed to be out of the office quite a lot. When we finally landed a meeting in his office, he was apologetic. "I've been sick, and it's something I've never experienced before. I've got gout!"

We had no idea what that meant, other than the fact that it seemed to strike kings and people who lived on rich diets. We only knew the clock was ticking, and no record deal.

It was Pete who spoke up. "Well I can only imagine how hard that is, and we're really sorry you're dealing with that. But how long does it last? Who takes over when you're missing work? Do we have a new label or producer yet?"

Ed slumped behind the big desk. "You're right. It's not fair to you. If you want out of our contract so you can look for someone else, I'll make the arrangements."

A light Santa Ana wind was blowing outside, and it was one of those days in L.A. when you could see mountains etched on the horizon a hundred miles to the east, and Catalina Island looming thirty miles south. We drove back to Pomona, the traffic moving with an ease and swiftness remarkable even for 1969.

"I wonder if people are so distracted by the incredible weather they've stopped tailgating the car in front of them," I said.

"Maybe it's a sign," volunteered Pete. "Things are going to clear up for us. We're gonna take off like the traffic."

I wasn't so sure.

★ ★ ★

Mike Stewart was chasing no such delusions. He was busy moving forward.

Beginning as resident vocal arranger and idea man at Columbus Tower, he landed in another cutting-edge Trident combo, the Justice League, later known as West, who recorded two albums for Epic. (Both were produced by

Bob Johnston, who'd already put his mark on Dylan's *Highway 61 Revisited* and Simon and Garfunkel's *Sounds of Silence* and would soon move on to produce Johnny Cash and Leonard Cohen.) By the time the second West album was near finished, Mike's ideas for making things happen in the studio had caught the ear of Jackie Mills, a big-band drummer turned Bobby Sherman/Davy Jones producer who offered Mike the opportunity to learn the art.

Not wanting to start with a nameless band—and maybe to resolve some unfinished personal business—he phoned us, and we began work on the *Catch the Wind* album: a foretaste of country rock that got far more favorable reviews than the *Return* album. It felt like the genesis years of the original group. We were taking studio players who could do anything and letting their styles synergize in the studio, on the spot. Mike brought in songs (like Don Gibson's country classic "Oh Lonesome Me," which he put into aggressive rock mode); we brought in songs (like Donovan's "Catch the Wind," and Dylan's "Tomorrow Is a Long Time," which we did as an R&B ballad in 12/8 time, and the Beatles' "Here Comes the Sun," which we did with a horn section). It was a cohesive, play-the-whole-record album instead of a sampler. Debbie, Pete, and I sang in the vocal isolation booth while bass, horns, and definitive jazz-R&B drummer Elvin Jones all laid down rhythms live in studio.

For me at least, that began a golden interval in our lifelong friendship. We were doing stuff the way We Five used to, and we were becoming fun friends again. Mike had gone from crashing in our Pomona apartment to renting a room in the house next door, which belonged to a dogcatcher named Fred and his wife, Colleen. His mad sense of humor returned to our lives. On Thanksgiving Day, he secretly called police claiming a wild turkey was loose in the yard. Within seconds, the house phone rang, summoning Fred to an animal-control emergency. At headquarters, a dispatcher handed Fred his own address—and Fred knew he'd been had.

The funniest part, hearing it recounted at dinner, was when Mike had phoned in the description of the bird. "How big is it?" police asked him. "Oh, I don't know, about twenty pounds—it would probably take about two hours to cook." As Debbie and I laughed hearing it for the first time, Colleen was on the floor. Even Fred had to begin laughing—they weren't going to let it go.

One night, Debbie improvised a pretty table, placing a tall candle in a bud vase. I sniped, "That's not a candleholder, Debbie."

Mike glared at me. "What's that on top of it?"

"A candle," I told him.

"Then it's a candleholder," he said, winking at Debbie.

The beauty of having Mike come stay with Debbie and me was that it gave us a chance, maybe for the first time, to be friends without being rivals. For he'd also found love. A smart, outgoing non-musician who'd known

Werber in San Francisco, Kate had that knack for finding common ground and conversation with anyone: she'd ask a couple of questions, learn what you're about, and engage. Moreover, she was Mike's intellectual equal. When Debbie and I met Kate, she dropped in seamlessly. Rarely had I met anyone so comfortable in her own skin. I kept looking at the two of them and thinking: *Wow. It really is possible to clear the table and start fresh.*

The only tension between me and Mike now, it seemed, was musical. He was hiring session musicians. When I wasn't the best guy for a job, my desire to participate could argue against Mike's perfectionism. He was tactful about this. He'd learned that coach's skill of getting a player to do what was needed and not feel bad when they weren't allowed to contribute. Like lots of folkies, I was still unlearning decades of folk guitar where you got to strum as much as you liked, however you liked. And it was certainly hard to argue that I should be holding a guitar in Mike's sessions when future Rock and Roll Hall of Famer James Burton, the Master of the Telecaster, was available.

Mike also taught me the danger of getting used to playing in bars and clubs. You acquired a repertoire of stunts that made fans go home believing they'd had a good time, when a lot of those tricks sounded trite if you put them on a record. In the studio, you had to sing larger than life—something Debbie considered warily, because if she outdid herself on a record, she'd have to match it every night live. On this subject, Mike was uncompromising. He was making a record. Your bar gigs were not his problem.

Once, when Mike was in studio as a member of West, Jackie Mills pronounced a song of theirs too perfect. "I want you to loosen up. Let some spontaneity in." In the middle of the next take, according to Mike, Mills walked in and kicked over a pedestal ashtray. The band kept playing—in the days of editing tape, you always kept going until someone said, "Stop"—and when they were done, Mills explained his point: that an unconscious part of you kept playing even if distracted. Therefore, don't fear distraction—let your mind go to a next level of exploration.

That lesson meant enough to Mike that he felt the need to share it. Plan for what you want, but always build in the chance for spontaneity. For Mike, that was the whole point of music, the creative spark, the charge.

After he'd gotten really good players into the studio, and got them playing off each other instead of stepping on each other, he'd go back to his cave with this universe of moments—licks, grooves, miracles, and accidents captured on twenty-four tracks—pick what he liked, and create a symphony. A guitar sets up a flute, which sets up a piano. A drum draws in a voice, which draws in guitars and harmonies.

I don't know if Mike would have called "You Were On My Mind" his masterpiece, because years later his son, Jamie, would tell me his dad never talked about what he'd done, only what he was going to do next. He was determined to stay open, ready to create. You could set up a plan, but the rest was more like a jigsaw puzzle. Only less exact, because there were multiple outcomes, rather than just one, that could work brilliantly within the overall frame.

Soon he was known for breathing life into sterility, hearing the promise in incompletion that other people couldn't recognize. He would produce anything for money, and he made good money producing demos for songwriters. But he struck gold when, at the perfect moment, he started to work with an unknown singer-songwriter named Billy Joel.

Joel had done nothing to speak of at the dawn of the '70s. He'd been working in a hotel piano bar in Universal City under the name "Bill Martin," waiting out his contract to a record company that didn't know what to do with him. But Mike did. Joel expressed musical ideas on the fly; and Mike saw at once how to fill the form with musicians and arrangements. Joel later said Mike was the first person to understand what he was all about and succeed in recording it.

They met because Mike was doing independent work for Family Productions—the company Joel signed with when he got his name back, but before he kissed off L.A. and hooked up with Phil Ramone. In this interlude, Mike produced what would become two landmark albums of the 1970s: *Piano Man* and *Streetlife Serenade*.

In later years, when Billy Joel's life got busy and crazy and he couldn't find time to write songs, Mike warned him sternly not to let it happen.

It was a subject he knew something about.

★ ★ ★

Mike's next breakthrough came after 20th Century Fox made him its unofficial Savior of Lost Projects, by everyone from wannabe bands to stars just past their heyday, like Tom Jones. In some cases, it was material left behind by defunct bands, records that had no hope of ever catching fire—I can't name the groups, but it was the sorest of subjects for Mike. He was getting trapped in a kind of musical Peter Principle, producing benefits for other people but without long-term residuals for himself, because none of those projects would be hits. So he looked to the future. Foreseeing how synthesizers and computers would change the way music was made, Mike Stewart quietly bought a Commodore 64—and began writing what would be the first program to manage music like a word processor.

Once more, he'd anticipated the vanguard. Once more I did not.

We'd been trying to help each other at this point. I introduced him to an investor I knew, and he introduced Debbie and me to music publishers in L.A. But my case proved mostly futile, because the music world continued to splinter. The Ohio Players and Billy Joel were just a foretaste of the diversity that would soon dominate Hollywood: disco, glam, funk, novelty, arena rock, singer-songwriter pop, soft-rock. True folk music was now a historical sidebar.

So was the idealism of the time we came of age in. A lot of things that felt auspicious about the world at the outset of the folk-rock adventure were becoming unrecognizable. There was politics. When Bobby Kennedy ran for the Democratic presidential nomination in 1968, I allowed myself to be swept up in a tide of resurgent hope. I attended one of his stump speeches at the mall in downtown Pomona (the adoring crowd offered him a sombrero, which he playfully refused to wear until elected). Fourteen days later, I watched on TV as he gave his "on to Chicago" speech before taking the fateful walk into the kitchen of the Ambassador Hotel. Debbie had gone to bed just seconds earlier, thrilled that Bobby Kennedy had won.

The connection I felt to this campaign—partly because of John Stewart's devotion to the Kennedys in the heyday of folk—was one that, frankly, I had not allowed myself to entertain since the earlier assassination in the autumn of '63.

That was a sickening memory on several levels. I'd been released from school to Thanksgiving week at my parents', but once there, I learned they'd been invited to a party that night with some business friends—worse, they needed me to sing. I said it felt inappropriate under the circumstances even to gather with business friends, let alone throw a party. But the hosts had a young son who played drums, and I was expected to be his musical big brother for the evening.

So I made an inward decision. If they insisted I perform, I'd turn it into a statement. The Cumberland Three's *Civil War Almanac* album contained a traditional song called "Hallowed Ground," and I practiced along with the record, trying to get familiar enough to sing without crying:

O stranger tread lightly, 'tis holy ground here.
In death's cold embrace, a soldier sleepeth there
It's the grave of a hero, 'neath the grass-covered sod,
His spirit's in heaven, at home with his God.

When we got there, the hosts introduced me to their young son, who I hoped would be an ally. But all he wanted was to play music with someone who'd been in bands, and to find out if I could keep up with him on drums. (He was disappointed on two fronts—I didn't want to, and I could.)

Then the moment came when I was asked to sing.

I played my song, did my job, and the room went stunningly quiet. They did not ask me to sing anything else.

At least my father had shown horror at the assassination, although he was never a Kennedy man. Others in the room, with thinly veiled satisfaction, had kept insisting the Kennedys were a bad lot, that the country might be better off without the president.

When Bobby Kennedy died, all that came back: the recognition that such irrational hate could and still did exist over politics in America. Just when I'd allowed myself to be inspired once more—disillusion.

If John Kennedy dared us to ask what we could do for our country, and Robert Kennedy dared us to see not the world as it is but as it could be, the combination of their deaths, along with M. L. King's, seemed to wipe out any last resistance to the "Me First" 1970s. You could see the fallout all around you. There was the disintegration of our next-door neighbors' marriage, when faced with the burden of their son's terminal multiple sclerosis. Indeed, a whole rash of divorces in our circle followed, and they haunted me. I wrote a series of songs about it all, one of which ran, "All our friends are changing partners/Will we be next to play?"

"What's your point?" Debbie asked, suspiciously.

For my own part, I'd never learned to be a father. In We Five's early years, I'd lived like a visitor in my own house. Now I watched football while Debbie and Chris went to church.

We still toured, but it made Debbie physically ill. Doctors had to order her to eat.

Our son Chris knew his grandparents better than me. In their care, he cried for hours after Debbie phoned home. To feel less lonely, he played records by We Five.

★ ★ ★

As the '70s unspooled, husbands like Sonny Bono and Ike Turner and Ian Tyson were suddenly being eclipsed by the wives they'd tried to manage.

I remember having watched Sonny make fun of Cher's pregnancy on-stage ("We know what *you've* been doing"), which seemed the ultimate bad taste—now, within a few years, she was matching him insult for insult, and becoming a musical force as soloist. Meanwhile, Sylvia Tyson, once a vocal instrument to her songwriter husband, was becoming a megastar in Canada.

Sometimes, people heard more potential in Debbie's voice than in our collaborative material. On that basis, we were introduced to a producer inconveniently named Michael Jackson. He'd been holding a disillusioned-wife song called "Cabin Fever" for the suddenly unavailable Kim Carnes (whose bedroom rasp would make "Bette Davis Eyes" one of the most stylish debuts of the 1980s).

Jackson found the gospel urgency of Debbie's voice nothing like Kim Carnes's and yet equally original, possibly an emotional equal to the song. So A&M signed us for a new three-song deal—literally the first advance I'd been handed since the dollar bill that Werber stapled to contracts for Mike Stewart and me at Capitol Records.

All the pieces were in place: Mike Utley on organ, Leland Sklar on bass, Jim Gordon on drums, David Paich on piano, and on lead guitar Andrew Gold, who'd been busy helping shape the California mellow-rock sound with his howling riffs on Linda Ronstadt's "You're No Good" (he suggested a similar line here, played on two slightly out-of-tune Stratocasters).

In retrospect, "Cabin Fever" might have been our open door. A star as big as Barbra Streisand wound up doing it—one of a crop of new songs, from "Hotel California" to "The Pretender," that now spoke to millions of our peers about the cost of youthful choices.

But there was a concern. This was clearly a chick solo, but we'd signed as a duo. In an awkward compromise, the A side of the single was released under Debbie Burgan, but I insisted Side B should remain "The Burgans." A potential problem, because A&M had just picked up the husband-and-wife team Captain and Tennille, joining the Carpenters, who were concerned about A&M becoming the label of boy/girl duets, or so it was rumored. All I know is that if I hadn't insisted on being "The Burgans" instead of Debbie Burgan, there wouldn't have been an issue.

Instead, A&M withdrew the record, giving us an unconditional release and offering to sell us the tapes for $25,000. I asked Jackson about pursuing it, and he said he didn't have the funds.

Every innuendo I'd ever made about Svengali husbands—from Fred Marshall to Ike Turner—now implicated me.

• *15* •

Jackpot, Nevada

$\mathscr{A}$ nine-to-five life was looming, but it took me most of the '70s to wind up there. First stooping to almost every kind of musical mediocrity.

We were in the "still beats working" period that John Stewart told me about, playing clubs and casinos on the road and hoping for our next big chance, when what we were really looking for was another shot at the chance that closed in 1967.

It was the best and worst of times, musically—the era of canned improvisation (anyone with a guitar or piano and a four-track reel-to-reel recorder could turn a song into a demo), but also of artists singing their own material, with a new unvarnished honesty (Tin Pan Alley composers like Carole King coming out from behind the song sheet). Through it all, the chase for the next derivative hit infected the industry at every level, and one commercial compromise at a time you could lose sight of why you played, in the struggle to keep playing.

We followed the onslaught of boomers to Las Vegas. When Elvis started to perform again, he hired the best studio players in Los Angeles, many of whom had played on our albums, and took to the casino showrooms. After that, We Five and everyone else felt it was okay to go.

We hated every minute. The only casino I ever really liked was Harrah's, and I liked it mostly because it was in Lake Tahoe.

Backstage one night, Debbie and I watched as the stage manager counted down the last few minutes to Perry Como's show. Perry walked over and, I guess mistaking Debbie for a pretty stagehand, took the gum out of his mouth and dropped it in her palm.

We were still young—barely thirty—which by counterculture standards meant aging (except the counterculture had aged, too). In the casino showrooms, strange cousins were smushed together in the nation's search for a common denominator. A poignant figure was Sammy Davis Jr., almost superhumanly trying to bridge cultural categories. He sat near us in the Harrah's audience while Pat Collins, the Hip Hypnotist, put our pianist, Ray, under a trance. Collins first convinced subjects they had a bird on their shoulder, then asked for the bird's name—to which Ray unaccountably replied, "Tricky Dicky" (the opposition's epithet for President Nixon). Sammy Davis was navigating the '70s as a black Jewish Republican who'd stood by the embattled president, and the audience gasped in anxious concern. With all eyes upon him, Sammy started slapping the table, letting loose an unbridled, vocal laugh. Collins milked some suspense, swallowing hard before asking her follow-up question: "And what kind of bird *is* Tricky Dicky?"

To which Ray matter-of-factly said, "A Right Wing Bullshitter."

At this, Sammy did what Sammy Davis Jr. would do—he literally stiffened up, asphyxiating with laughter, before rolling from his chair onto the floor. The audience clapped, laughed, and howled, and the show went on.

In other instances, he slid into black street jive. One day, I'd gone skiing, and as part of his schtick, Sammy said snow sure was beautiful, but (heavy dialect), "We folks learned something a long time ago: That shit is cold!"

The hip take was that Davis was simply a phony, especially when he seized up in that wheezing laugh: a personality in crisis who would go anywhere, say anything, to be accepted. But I also felt that he was trying to deal gracefully with the boxes that divided all of us. He was a poster boy for This Doesn't Make Sense.

We had feelings for Jerry Van Dyke—who, like Mike Stewart, yearned to emerge from the shadow of a colossally talented brother. In his routine, he joked about having to audition for the younger brother's part on the *Dick Van Dyke Show*, only it wasn't a joke. He could be hilarious, whipping a toy horse to the theme song of "Rawhide," but he was also a frustrated musician who loved to sing and play the banjo. Almost every night he performed a song that spoke volumes about his personal demons: "Right or Left at Oak Street," the tale of a regular guy driving to work who faces a daily decision between turning right toward the factory or turning left to run away. Debbie and I were struck by the melancholy and pain, complicated by an awful lot of alcohol. By the late '90s, he seemed to have landed well, nominated for four consecutive Emmys for his supporting role on the ABC sitcom *Coach*. But the '70s were clearly a desperate time. We'd sit with him in the casino coffee shop between shows, hoping that an hour spent substituting coffee would magically make a difference.

One day Gary Lewis introduced himself—Jerry Lewis's son, whose band, the Playboys, had seven top ten hits in 1965–1966: another danceable echo of the British Invasion ultimately left behind by psychedelia. He seemed nice enough, but he looked to be intoxicated, and it was hard to break away when he kept rambling about the music, the times, and the experiences that we shared in common. When I found out he wasn't there to perform, I assumed he was visiting with the Monkees' Mickey Dolenz and Davy Jones—but when they left town, and Paul Revere and the Raiders took their spot on the marquee, Gary was still hanging on. Things went from sad to awkward when he wanted to know if he could borrow a guitar and jam. It seems he didn't have his own guitar, and I rather rudely suggested—because all I really cared about by this point was being paid to play my gigs—that maybe he should ask his dad.

I knew I'd struck a nerve when he didn't lash back, but simply admitted that calling his dad wasn't possible, because they didn't communicate.

The last time I spoke to Gary Lewis, he'd been stumbling around backstage during our show. It shouldn't have surprised me (though I'm sure the audience didn't expect it) when he suddenly swung from the wings into the lights, clutching the back curtain to keep from falling. I found out later that night that Harrah's had put him on a plane to L.A. I hope his story ended as well as Jerry Van Dyke's.

★ ★ ★

By now our agent was more for artistic purity than I was. Howard King was a trumpet player who'd started out playing jazz clubs in New York. But when he found himself in California with family responsibilities, he literally had his horn mounted in a picture frame to prevent him from picking it up. When I told him that I didn't want to maintain the We Five touring group anymore, he continued to book Debbie and me as a duet without complaint—even though our paydays barely generated income for him, let alone profit. He constantly encouraged me to work harder at songwriting and improving the act.

In 1976, he called to tell me we'd been booked to play at the Disneyland Hotel, but that the job required a trio. When I reminded him that we were a duo, Howard reached his breaking point.

"So be a trio!"

I said we didn't have a third person who knew our material.

"It doesn't matter if it's a bass player, a drummer, or a piccolo player," he said. "Put a chair on stage and have someone sit in it."

Howard didn't go so far as to say, *I'm killing myself for you!* But he was upset. He had tried both things: to get us to be great, or to get us to make money. Either way, the absurdity of me pleading for artistic integrity at the

Disneyland Hotel—when all I really wanted was to get paid without having to change—was painfully exposed.

Not wanting to be the further cause of people's disintegrating hopes, I did what Howard told me. I approached a bass player I'd heard backing up former First Edition singer Kin Vassey at the Ice House. Instantly, Tholow Chan was playing and singing like he'd been with us for years. In fact, he became a friend—as real and wise as any I'd ever had. But two years later, at age thirty-eight, he brought us the kind of news that was becoming increasingly familiar in the late 1970s.

He was under pressure from his dad to settle down, and a major bank had just launched a plan to recruit manager trainees who'd had Broad Life Experiences. To Tholow's Chinese-American family, whose grandmother had bound lotus-blossom feet, musician was not a real job. Indeed, the realization that millions of boomers who'd survived the 1960s might suddenly be ripe to rejoin the Establishment was taking root all across the corporate sector. Find employees desperate for stability after a decade's exhausting upheavals.

"Come home, America!" George McGovern wailed from the podium at the Democratic Convention.

Tholow thought no serious bank would hire him. He had also failed to anticipate the rising importance of race. If an employer could hire an ethnic minority without having to hire black, Tholow Chan went to the head of the class.

Thus, in 1978, the three of us sat in the car and hugged our goodbyes. "It seemed safe when I filled in the application!" he laughed through tears. "I told them I had an AA in music, processed film for Technicolor, and played bass with the Back Porch Majority."

All kinds of people our age were toiling in the straight world again, drinking the edge off in lounges and casinos now featuring bands whose records we used to buy. The trend to electronic music created with synthesizers and sequencers had taken a toll on live music venues. Bars and hotels that used to book bands now used soloists or duos with a drum machine. Even live studio drummers built tape loops that could play an unrelenting beat for ten minutes without a hint of fluctuation in the groove. Ten-minute EPs kept people on dance floors working up a thirst, a boon for the bar business—a lighted dance floor and a DJ with a touch of personality were the only requirements to keep single women in the building. The guy who made a living singing pop songs to tracks he created at home became a familiar type. All he carried to work was an electric guitar and a computer.

The whole thing was a meteor threatening extinction to my musical species. If you didn't differentiate or adapt, you went the way of the dinosaurs. Or you kidded yourself you were still having fun.

★ ★ ★

Given Debbie's aversion toward touring, of course, I now barely had a partner, let alone a trio. As the '80s dawned, we played a casino in Elko, Nevada: the Diamonds had played Elko, too, and so did the Four Preps. We did our gig, then went to our rented room across from the city park (the hotel had given us a room, but it had drainage problems—we only dressed there, holding our noses). Two other husband-wife acts performed in that casino—one who brought their kids with them from gig to gig, like transients, another sixty-somethings who played polka and western swing.

"I hope that's not me in my sixties," Debbie said, wistfully. We were tired, winding down, splitting a Yoplait yogurt and an apple from a convenience market.

"You hope what's not you?"

"Playing in Elko to a bunch of well-meaning drunks who're trying to live vicariously."

I considered that. "I guess the years get away from you. At some point, a week in Elko becomes the norm."

"I mean, they're good and all," she went on. "But they're not Les Paul and Mary Ford playing Carnegie Hall. This could be the high point of their tour."

"It's worse than that," I said. "They told me they live here." In fact, the husband told me he wanted out.

A sadness filled Debbie's usually cheerful voice. "You know—I hate Chris having to be an only child. If we had a little girl, I could dress her up and play with her hair. Do you ever think about that?"

"Dressing her up and playing with her hair?" I joked, trying for charming.

She wasn't in the mood for that.

"No," I added finally, "but I know it's important to you."

"I've been taking the pill for so long, I might not even be able to. I sure would like to stop taking them."

I was letting some dead air hang in case the topic might change. From our window I could see the Native Americans still playing softball in the park, their nightly release. Pretty much till one in the morning they'd be at it. I knew people like them back home, who did what they did for a living, then played softball for four or five hours and forgot about the day. Some got it out of their system on the field; others sat in the stands looking beaten. I thought of that couple with kids, leading a transient life, and that older couple. Even if what they did every night paid better than Del Taco, it was still as tedious as a music job could be.

Grace Slick famously said rockers shouldn't be on stage in their forties. She would have had to reinvent herself to continue. At first blush, I'd thought that old couple had beaten the game—that this beat working for a living. But the guy wanted out.

We had just seen the movie *Same Time Next Year*, about a couple—forget that they're adulterous—meeting once a year on the Mendocino Coast. The pure emotionalism of Marvin Hamlisch's Academy Award–winning song— "The Last Time I Felt Like This (I Was Falling in Love)"—had me feeling just that sentimental about Debbie. I wished I had a song that captured that. I was trying to write one:

> The very first time I kissed you as strangers, we changed
> And after that, we laughed many times, as together we came. . . .
> Can we go back over?
> Has it been too long?

Songwriting itself might offer a way out of this stalemate. But we were never natural writing partners—Debbie tended to hear a thing in her head as finished; I changed things over and over. And with my guitar and her twang, all the material we had was heading toward country.

I played that card now. I said we could move to Nashville.

"Nope," Debbie said. Her tone wasn't hostile; it was the expression of pure truth. "California doesn't snow, there's no hurricanes, and there aren't so many bugs that you choke on 'em when you go outside. If you go to Nashville, you go without me."

I had the feeling you get when you try to take a shortcut in your car and the street dead-ends.

★ ★ ★

It was a few months later at a bar in Pasadena, near home, when Debbie started getting sick on stage. Literally running off between songs to throw up. Driving home in the cold and dark, I hypothesized other causes, but Debbie was already feathering the cradle. "You know, it's not good to be in smoky environments—when you're pregnant."

"How can you be sure?"

"I don't know how to explain it," she said.

We left the freeway and turned in to the deserted parking lot of a Thrifty Drug store along Route 66 in Azusa to buy a pregnancy test kit. The store was beside the drive-in movie theater where I'd kick-started my '56 Chevy one night before we were married. It was also behind one of the original McDonalds' hamburger stands, actual arches at each end of the building, and not part of any '50s revival: it looked weathered and passé behind the incongruous, corporatized badge of *over xx million sold*. My youth was ending, right here.

In the empty Thrifty aisles searching for the test kit, it was like watching one movie while the soundtrack for another one was playing. I was still holding out for a negative result, but Debbie was eyeing and chatting about all the baby stuff. "I gave away most of the diapers when Chris stopped using them. Maybe we should use Pampers."

Back home I stared at my stage clothes on the bed while Debbie took the test, twice. Both sticks turned an affirmative blue.

"What are we gonna do?" I finally asked.

"I'm gonna have a baby, and you're gonna find a way to make money that doesn't involve me traveling."

"Isn't that kind of final?"

She looked at me and it all poured out. The hopes she'd put on hold. This was real, and it was a long time coming. "It's your turn," she said. "You're smart, and I'll bet you can do just about anything you put your mind to."

Unable to visualize any job for the teenager I felt like, I let myself lie on the bed and cry.

"You know what? You should get a job at a golf course," an interviewer for a steel company was telling me a few days later, as I began the hunt. "You're a friendly guy; you can tell stories about the days in music, play golf, and get paid for it!"

Right.

★ ★ ★

The final shows booked before the birth of our second child, Jeremy, were in Jackpot, Nevada, less a "town" than two casinos. One featured a large sterile banquet room with all the charm of a school cafeteria; ours, called the Horseshu, was done in early chuckwagon. The knotty pine walls had brass candleholders, branding irons, and wagon wheels for decorations. Our bass player, Paul Foti—who as much as any musician who ever lived got into the business to meet chicks—stopped mingling during breaks because any woman he spoke to could set off two or three cowboys who thought she was with them. If you weren't playing a song the crowd wanted to hear, you felt threatened till you did—like the Blues Brothers switching to "Rawhide," but without the benefit of a chicken-wire screen to catch airborne objects.

In a farewell concert set up near home, I mentioned the rustic charm of Jackpot, when Paul (who'd almost never said anything on stage) took the microphone like a dying man's last act. "I've been a lot of places, and if there's someone here from Jackpot, I'm sorry, but I really don't like your town."

We ended with Delaney and Bonnie Bramlett's classic singalong, "I've Got a Never Ending Love for You," and turned the page to see what love would bring.

★ ★ ★

And when the page turned, I'd woken up to the 1980s: a family man and father working for an international tycoon who inhaled, with gusto, the angst of the men whose companies he bought. It felt like entering the den of evil.

Yugoslavian chemist Milan Panic—who later challenged Slobodan Milosevic for the presidency of Serbia—was a classic self-made man, building ICN Pharmaceuticals over time by buying other companies, capitalizing on their brands, then selling off remaining assets. In a boardroom with a giant mahogany table surrounded by fifteen or twenty high-back leather chairs, product managers like me couldn't get close to the table without sliding forward like three-year-olds on the hard front lip of the chair; if I sat back, my body dropped so low I couldn't see the work in front of me, and everyone saw only my head.

With a management style as feudal as the table, Panic got the results he wanted, but never by teamwork. It was every player for himself. One day, the founder of a recently purchased company visited the meeting from his facility in Arizona, where he'd promised his employees the company would continue as it was. He beamed as Panic listed the products being added to our catalog. When Panic got to the part about transferring production to California, however, the new VP's expression began to change. "But you're making me feel like I sold out all my workers!" the victim pleaded.

Panic's bushy eyebrows shot up and he replied, with Jack Nicholson glee, "Oh, but you DID!"

My own turn in the crosshairs came when I'd been told to develop a marketing plan that didn't call for relationship-selling to doctors. Panic wanted a pure telemarketing operation. When I didn't give him what he wanted, I was finished. But beforehand, a good-guy executive who I suspect might have been an angel suggested I take advantage of the corporation's continuing-education fund to get a degree, and eighteen months later I returned to the University of San Francisco, where I'd once driven away in a pea-green bomb, to walk the aisle at St. Ignatius Institute in a cap and gown.

★ ★ ★

Then I had time on my hands. To play guitar at Debbie's church. To be the happy father of three kids. (Fulfilling Debbie's lifelong dream, we now had a daughter, Jessica.) To start having lunch with a coworker who knew about my Catholic upbringing and recent graduation from a Jesuit university, so we would chat about my childhood faith. Sometimes scanning the radio dial in traffic, I'd hear music that sounded almost good, almost familiar, and yet not. So I'd let it play through to see who it was. Sometimes, to my surprise, it would be a Christian station, and I would recoil, because I had heard too many of them steal hit songs, pirate the feel, and write God lyrics for them. Some still do. My dad had once told me I should do Christian music, but I didn't think it was moral to make money selling Christianity as music.

Of course, if that were true, Mozart and Handel owed somebody an apology. You could add Jimmy Webb, Kris Kristofferson, and Bob Dylan to that list.

I never really apologized to my dad, but pretty soon I got involved in creating music for our church, and I could tell that he took some joy from seeing that. It started to verge on an accidental calling. A woman named Pam Cone (now a Ph.D. in Nursing at Azusa Pacific University) began directing the church choir. She'd been born in Haiti when her parents were missionaries and percussive voodoo rhythms were the sound of danger. Threats to her parents, like in some Hollywood movie, had come in the form of native drums pounding relentlessly just out of view. It took many discussions for Pam to regard musicians separately from her fear of what their sounds meant. A distance many of my generation had to travel to get from "Sing Along with Mitch" to the Rolling Stones.

I learned how to sight-read music, sometimes even playing it expressively. Then, putting the shoe on the other foot, I taught some of the pianists how to play without notation. Once that door opened, some started writing. A Haitian piano prodigy lived with the Cones while going to school, where he was first in his class in piano and voice. Together we began to play notes, then chords, then melodies, with the ease of playing catch. When Debbie and Pam were present, lyrics would spring from the air and songs would take shape.

During the latter '80s, we wrote dozens of songs and children's choruses that brought life to the little congregation at our church.

· *16* ·

Long Time Gone

It shouldn't have surprised me that the rest of We Five took completely different paths through those same years, which were turning into decades every time I looked in the mirror. And as time went by I would sometimes think about how our paths were practically a blueprint for all the futures that sprang from that single moment of folk-rock convergence.

To trace the flowering of West Coast blues, just follow Bob Jones. At the time of our breakup, he and John Chambers started setting up space in a barn in Petaluma: it was Bob's long-awaited introduction to all those Bay Area blues and jazz players John had grown up with. The session players that formed around them—most of them black, the rest colorblind like Bob—first became the Mystic Knights of the Sea, an inside joke winking at the secret club to which all of Amos and Andy's friends belonged. Next came the Tits and Ass Blues Band, better targeting the San Francisco audience. It was "kind of the equivalent of naming your band 'Free Beer,'" quipped sax player Ron Stallings—himself a collaborator with Jerry Garcia, Jesse Colin Young, Tom Fogerty, and Elvin Bishop, and later a fixture in the horn section of Huey Lewis and the News. (Stallings also co-wrote, with Bob, the R&B power ballad "Come and Sit Down Beside Me" on We Five's *Catch the Wind* LP.)

Seeing bands now formed based on how they'd gel, both live and in studio, John and Bob were seeking a playground where the music reigned supreme and no drugs were off limits. The dream was to break free of all inhibitions, to go above and beyond, and to perform with enough fearlessness to say, "If I can think it, I can play it." The only time they got to do that in We Five was when we were warming up, jamming with the curtain down.

Through Stallings, Bob found his way into perpetual blues-band lineups, playing drums. He'd always loved drums but never played them seriously until bandmates said he played with a rhythm guitarist's awareness—always in the pocket, urging them forward with fills that announced what was coming with a cymbal splash or a shot on the snare. He landed on two albums with Harvey Mandel (another Garcia/Bishop/John Mayall alumnus whose third gig ever was to play with Canned Heat at Woodstock). I even saw Chuck Berry press Bob into service at the Whisky a Go Go. By the late '60s, he'd formed Southern Comfort, composed of session men from Blues Hall of Famers Mike Bloomfield and Nick Gravenites, and signed with Columbia. That affiliation led to his first record deal and a hillside cottage in Fairfax, CA.

Roughly during this period he met Bloomfield himself, with whom he went on to record five albums. He also did two albums with Alice Stuart in the early '70s, and two with Brewer and Shipley (who had a hit with Gravenites' composition "One Toke Over the Line").

Along with John Chambers, Bob was the closest any of us would come to being an essential San Francisco musician. He had the deal with Columbia; he had the band. Everything he'd shared backstage at the Safari Room about wanting to be in an integrated blues band in the vanguard of social change, turned out to come true. The music, the lifestyle, the sociology—it was always all one thing to Bob.

But there were drugs.

His habits could make relating with him so colorful that after a point I stopped trying. Once, when I'd finished touring per se, although still saying yes to special requests, our drummer with the last touring band asked if I could put some players together and do a fairgrounds concert in Clear Lake, CA. Lots of We Five fans in the Bay Area would come for the weekend if we agreed to play. A rich friend of his was the promoter, so the money was good, and maybe we could even get Bob or Mike Stewart to join us.

Mike wasn't available, but Bob was thrilled—provided we could get together and practice first. So we rehearsed in the garage complex behind the promoter's house, which was in the hills outside of Lakeport with a spectacular view of the lake and countryside. The rehearsal room was one of eleven fully finished garages that held a collection of Porsches, Jaguars, Bentleys, and collectable roadsters. At least it seemed a safe bet we'd be paid.

One problem was that Bob wanted us to learn something new he'd written, and he had a precise vision of how it should go: just like in the past, we "couldn't find the groove." Then he decided the accommodations at the motel weren't going to work for him; he was used to rock-star privacy. He wanted an extra room for the kids, even though the whole town was booked for the weekend.

As the rehearsal wore on, Bob's complaints finally got to our host, who asked us to leave. It was the day of the show, and we were running pretty late, with Bob seeming more and more disoriented. We'd probably wasted an extra two hours at rehearsal seeking a level of perfection we didn't really need. En route to the motel to change clothes, Dennis Wood, our drummer, dashed into a supermarket for a soda and a box of Q-tips. Suddenly, Bob wandered in behind him, announcing that he couldn't remember what he needed to buy, but if he went into the store it would probably come to him. Dennis returned with his soft drinks and started cleaning his ears with one of the Q-tips while Bob was inside. Five more minutes went by. Then ten. Then twenty.

When Bob finally came back to the van, he opened his shopping bag to show us his own, Jumbo box of Q-tips.

"That looks like enough to get you through the weekend," I said.

"Yeah," he said with no trace of irony. "I saw Dennis get some, and I thought how you never know when you're going to need them. So I bought a really big box."

On stage, he wore a suit with the waist taken in about three inches and held with a giant safety pin; his old guitar amplifier had to be coaxed to life because it hadn't been played much in his years as a drummer. With strategic hand slaps to the side of the cabinet, we managed to launch into our tunes, including the song we'd learned that afternoon. But now it felt like there was a ten-minute repeat of the line "Better a broken heart than one without love." We hadn't agreed on an ending, so it kept going around and around, until it seemed so petered out I just stopped.

Apologizing for what he called the Dionne Warwick ending—a clone of her interminable hook line with the Spinners on "I Never Knew Love Before, Then Came You"—Bob finally bore down to playing the old We Five tunes. We even shared some big hugs between numbers. But when the opportunity for an encore came, he put down his guitar and went to an extra set of drums to play along with Dennis. It was impulsive, childlike, and funny, but scary for me. There was nothing predictable about it.

Since it was just a one-time reunion, I wasn't going to confront him about anything. But the next morning I did ask him to breakfast. When he opened the door, I discovered that the kids, their mother, and Bob were all, a la Frank Werber, home nudists. No one covered up; no one cared. They declined breakfast, and we said our goodbyes.

Maybe two decades later, Mike Stewart told me he'd caught up with Bob in the San Fernando Valley and found him making some pretty creative sounds while also working in computers, like Mike himself. "We even tried to make some music together," Mike said, "but his approach to whatever we were doing was just too intense. Or maybe I was just too set in my own ways."

In 2004 Debbie and I made plans to join friends for a holiday in Maui. Having heard Bob and his Finnish wife were back on his beloved island to care for his aging father, I called to see if he had any inside info on a good place to stay. It was not anything like the voice I'd heard the last time we spoke in Clear Lake.

"What kind of Hawaiian hospitality would I be showing if I let you stay in a hotel? You'll stay at my house. Donah would love to meet you and we can catch up."

Tan, trim, smiling, he met us at the airport with a big hug as he placed fresh leis around our necks. He took instant ownership of "anything that might have happened before I eliminated chemicals from my life," and in the car, as our apprehensions dissolved, the story of his new life spooled forth.

"When I realized all my friends were dying, I asked myself, What's the common element? The only answer was chemicals." Now free of not only street and prescription drugs but even alcohol, he realized he'd probably lost some brain cells. But he had clarity again, and he could appreciate the simple pleasure of living in a tropical paradise, bodysurfing and playing in clubs. He was hosting a weekly radio show and recording a blues album with talented local musicians, and when his mother died, he and his Finnish wife had decided to restore the family house as a bed and breakfast.

One night, Debbie and I joined Bob on stage. Unlike us, he hadn't spent years doing rote performances of our hit song on the bar circuit, and his exuberance infected Debbie and me, which in turn infected the room. Once more in our lives together, we got to experience the magic that happens when "You Were On My Mind" is played by people who actually recorded it.

Bob reciprocated a couple of years later at the University of San Francisco for its 150th Anniversary Celebration, trading off brilliantly on lead guitar and drums with my son Chris. He couldn't have been nicer, more friendly, more in the moment, each of us playing off and responding to one another. The truth was, I'd liked so much about Bob, despite and even because of his intensity, that I could only wonder at all we and others had missed of him during the bad years.

★ ★ ★

I'd lost track of John Chambers early on. I know he wasted little time coming into his own (if that's how you describe someone who played with John Coltrane in his mid-teens).

We Five had been a career move for John, his ex-wife told me recently: he'd enjoyed playing the songs he enjoyed, and he rose to professionalism on the others. But toward the end, as he saw Big Brother and the Jefferson Airplane taking off, he burned to be a part of that harder-edged scene.

During We Five's breakup, he was living with Penny and their daughter, Miya, on Haight Street (a flat to which I once had to drive from Mill Valley and drop off a vial of psychic relaxers to ease him and Penny—and possibly others—down from a bad acid trip). After joining Bob in the Mystic Knights of the Sea, he went on to a group called the Loading Zone, and finally joined the Elvin Bishop Band in '69.

I saw them do a Bill Graham Fillmore East concert on TV—frontmen leaping and clapping to incite the audience, Jo Baker tearing the roof off of a lead vocal, the integrated SF soul scene in full effect—and John playing drums. He was a study in concentrated effort: eyes closed and mouth open, bottom lip drawn in over his lower teeth, his head bouncing almost randomly to the overlapping rhythms. Like his teacher, Jerry Granelli, he perched more than sat on the drum throne, left shoulder stationary like a jazzman's with the stick balanced across his palm and fingers above the snare for quick strikes with a flick of the wrist . . . while his right shoulder twisted forward as he moved from hi-hat to ride cymbal, thrusting like a fencer in the *en guard* position, lunging and jabbing in perfect time with his feet on the kick drum and hi-hat pedals dancing furiously to the beat. His sound was a flurry, with barrages of toms between the beats. No energy wasted. And none unspent.

When it was over, as the band members filed offstage, John did a very John thing. He loomed toward the camera, looked straight into it, and mugged (maybe in reference to how both audience and performers were letting it all hang out), "That big eye sure will make you feel funny!"

And then he was gone.

The details of his death in the mid-1980s remain murky to me. I'd heard that the immediate cause was a blow to the head, which raised all kinds of unpleasant questions. When I phoned Penny recently, she reminded me how John's youth in the Fillmore district had led him to seek stimulation and solace in drugs. To this day, Penny says, she suffers flashbacks from the trips he demanded she take. In Petaluma, the girlfriend of another musician had rebelled—not just against the drugs, but the communal lifestyle and free love—and told Penny, "You need to get out of here and get your daughter out of here too." Her life got better when they parted. A successful business-person for thirty years, Penny says she never thinks about those days unless she's asked.

For years, if I thought about John Chambers at all, it had been with mixed feelings. I'd learned a lot about the world by peeking through the window of his experience. But I struggled with the fact that his presence fatally changed the musical balance of the band, just as surely as psychedelics and rock changed the San Francisco sound. I don't think Pete or Bev or Mike ever thought, *Let's get a flat in the Haight and make music all the time. Eat, sleep, and smoke this life, twenty-four hours a day.* But John and Bob Jones did have that mentality. John Chambers had begun to isolate Pete Fullerton, saying we needed "a bass player who plays *bass*"—by which he meant *rhythm and blues.* And when Frank Werber called us "We Six" in his angry letter, it was a veiled shot at the possibility that John would undermine the group's founding vision.

But when I saw him on TV that time, I saw him in his element. I can remind myself today, by watching him play with the Elvin Bishop Band on YouTube, that he was happy, and that he was really good.

★ ★ ★

Pete Fullerton's journey was a very strange one. Having failed in his ambition to be a happy garbage man in San Rafael, he wound up working for Lockheed, and thought he was doing well until some of his coworkers took him aside and asked him why he didn't just calm down a little bit. "We've got an hour to sweep this floor," they said, "and you're doing it in ten minutes. You're making the rest of us look bad."

So he backed off. But as with my father, who'd said something similar about General Dynamics, the cynicism of the modern workplace didn't feel right.

At a local Catholic church he met a man named Gordon Stewart, who, in 1967, had sent a truck full of clothes and toys to a charity in the Arizona desert that served the Native American population. Gordon's daughter had called it "the Truck of Love." Volunteering to help, Pete found himself picking up donated food, clothes, furniture, and such from all over the Bay Area. When the truck was full, he'd be given an address in Arizona or New Mexico or wherever Gordon sent him. It was work that he felt he not only could but also ought to do.

Soon he left Lockheed and began helping full-time, his wife, Sue, filling in the extra income by returning to work as a nurse. Then, when Stewart retired, Peter and Sue took over the ministry.

Periodically, when traveling through Southern California, he'd stop by. And we discovered that he still sang like an angel—although he'd had to relearn guitar after a skillsaw accident. (It shortened several fingers with such "surgical precision," Pete said, that the stubs actually formed a straight line.) Now the proceeds of his CDs went to fund the Truck of Love.

So possessed was Pete to empathize with being homeless that at one point he struck out to experience it, sleeping under trees throughout the country and taking odd jobs. He got hired to drive a truck filled with household contents to a black farmer in the deep South who, in the sort of racial anger that many early dreams of equality had devolved to, drove him miles from anywhere in a downpour, dumped him, and dared him to trudge his way back to town. "Follow the river," the farmer sneered.

When Pete turned up a day later, he looked so filthy and devastated that locals didn't believe his ID was his own. He'd actually realized his vision of losing himself. It took him months to arrive back west, often foraging out of dumpsters. By the time he reached California, he was malnourished and almost blind from an eye infection.

In 1998, building a roof with a charity in Mexico, he fell, landing in a tree that grew out from the side of a cliff, which is where he hung while Sue went for help. When finally they got him to a hospital, his badly broken leg had to be amputated.

The last time Debbie and I saw them, they were packing to go to South Carolina, where a huge group of homeless were living in a forest.

★ ★ ★

All this time, requests for We Five reunions still floated in. But trying to regather our trails, and the music's trails, would have been like shoveling smoke in the air.

In '93, I found myself walking the floor at the National Association of Music Merchandisers show in Anaheim, thinking of Mike Stewart. Wondering if I might find him.

I'd visited him in the '80s that time when he tortured me in handball. He had a big house in Northridge, and a big black new Firebird sporting a hood chicken, and those breakthroughs of his on the Commodore 64 had proved to be a glimpse into the future. Bothered that so many programmed parts on a synthesizer were aesthetically useless on a record, because they lacked the human ebb and flow of playing live, he wrote a program that made musical notation as easy as word processing. Then he applied himself to bridge the gap between MIDI time code and human groove.

That was how he'd come up with the now-essential "Human Clock": a device that lets MIDI-controlled instruments be led by the swing of the band, instead of the other way around. Anyone who could tap out time now took the place of the MIDI code generator, and the sequences followed along. I saw a stage version used at an Association concert to bring in full orchestrations on synthesizers driven by the drummer's kick drum.

From there, he went to work for Digidesign—a company that was replacing tape-mixing consoles with digital ones, using computer-screen images of tape-deck controls to replace wired hardware. He helped invent Session 8, the digital recording software that emulates a tape deck and studio control board: a predecessor to Pro Tools, now the industry standard.

He wrote crazy-brilliant articles for technical magazines, all with his unmistakable humor. In one, called "The Feel Factor," he graphed into soulful gradations the milliseconds between music played on top of the beat and music played behind it—far left was "Day job," far right was "Get some sleep."

The exhibit floor at the NAMM show out-freaked any carnival midway, bringing together everything from Steinway pianos in velvet-carpeted parlors to banjo craftsmen with ripped jeans sitting on cracker barrels, the commercial offspring of all the revolutions of half a century. Dealers and barkers hawked the latest instruments and amps, flogged and twirled by some of the top players in the world. I walked past Rick Neilsen of Cheap Trick, past autograph seekers waiting for Michael Anthony of Van Halen; past a booth of mellow harps drowned out by the crash of drums and fuzz guitars from a few aisles over. I expected some relief at the Digidesign booth. How noisy could software be?

Answer: as loud as the demo recordings they played through gargantuan monitor speakers.

Reeling from the noise, I flagged a young woman's attention and told her I was looking for an old friend, but her natural reaction was: "It's a big company." I told her he'd worked on Session 8, which didn't help either. As a last resort, I mentioned Mike Stewart, which pretty much stopped time. I'd uttered the name of a titan.

"If you mean Michael, I know he's here," she said with a sudden air of urgent respect, "but he's probably in a meeting and could be anywhere. Can I tell him your name?"

★ ★ ★

He'd been thin as a rail his entire life, but the man who approached me now was clearly rounding out into his late forties. A dress shirt and sport coat didn't conceal his fledgling spare tire, although a beard and full head of hair—as much hair as I'd lost!—still conveyed the spirit of the artist. He looked really happy as he almost sang, "Mister Burgan. What brings you here?"

"Oh, a friend got me a pass, so I came to see what's new. It looks like things are good here! And you're eating well!" The jab may have been accurate, but we weren't in our old groove anymore. "I only meant it was a surprise to see you looking . . . so healthy," I explained.

He softened, then jabbed back: "And you—still selling drugs. *Got any?*"

In a quiet meeting room, he told me how the leap from music to music software wasn't really a leap. He'd always been obsessed with creative freedom, and in dreaming up software, the only limits were in your mind. The real trick in leading music people to the computer age, Mike said, was getting rid of the learning curve for all those engineers and producers who'd been using analog since the 1940s. Since Mike had created hits the analog way, too, the company trusted him to build the bridge and make it intuitive. They wanted Session 8 to look and work the same way as a studio soundboard with knobs, switches, and faders. The only difference would be using a mouse to move them.

"Makes sense to me," I volunteered.

"Me too," he said. "And I seem to be getting by with it."

What we didn't discuss much—and would not, till years later—was the work of the past. He seemed categorically finished with all that. If I pressed him, he just sounded chagrined that he had no enduring financial reward to show for it. He'd made timeless hit records and software that was soon making millions of dollars for other people—twice in one lifetime helping to inch music across a threshold to the next revolution.

★ ★ ★

It was Beverly Bivens, and her vanishing act, that the world asked about most, and for many years I almost never thought about her on my own, partly because of that.

Typically I'd be standing there with my wife hearing someone rave about how historically irreplaceable Bev Bivens was, so getting past that moment was the immediate thing for me. The "Debbie's great but she's not Beverly" line was a no-win comparison—as if it could ever be fair to compare a lyric soprano to an alto. Was Michael Jordan better than Wilt Chamberlain?

At the same time, that discomfort never got in the way of my fondness for Beverly as bandmate, singer, and friend. Part of my annoyance was that the awkwardness of talking about her threatened to hijack my memories of a wonderful past.

There are certain people whose special presence onstage is simply part of them, defying translation. Just as surely as we couldn't write repartee for Beverly onstage, her dark humor in the most exasperating times had salvaged everyone else's. Her style wasn't Gracie Allen's or Lucille Ball's— but Mary Tyler Moore might come close, as written on the old "Dick Van Dyke Show": furious and mild at once. If Mike made people laugh with a punch line, Bev made it okay to laugh without having to know why, and you laughed harder if you were in pain. Every time that Coke executive's name got mentioned, it became Beverly's cue to append "—the Asshole," as if attaching his professional title. The time we sang "When the Saints Go Marching In," with my friend Bill Crutchfield burbling out bass notes, she couldn't stop laughing because it was so not us. Laughing without malice, yet with no loss of edge. Like the song that her voice made famous, her presence inexpressibly made some joys more delightful and a certain kind of sadness survivable.

But then she seemed to become guarded, distant, a nervous negotiator. When Pony Canyon put out the digitized CD version of our first album in Japan, I bought one for each member of the group and sent it to them. Though I hoped it would bring a note from Beverly, I didn't really expect one. And none came.

I phoned her at her Berkeley home in the '90s when "You Were On My Mind" had been proposed as a Burger King commercial. I was past any pretense of artistic purity, and the proposition was simple: we'd all split our share of $100,000. "So we get money for not doing anything?" Beverly said. "I'm in." The new practicality was poignant. There was nothing like age and lack of money to temper our positions.

Another time, I needed the group to authorize me to negotiate on all of our behalf if we got other Burger King–type calls. Everyone agreed—maybe grateful not to have to deal with such crud—except Beverly, who brought a lawyer and wrote in special terms.

It would be after the millennium when I finally saw her in person. A request had come from PBS to reunite the band's living members on air. They'd been using our album for years as a giveaway on their special, "The Folk Years," without ever asking us to perform. But then, they'd been told Bev didn't perform anymore. Now, for whatever reason, they were asking.

Warning them there was virtually no chance, I found a free afternoon on a business trip to Fremont and phoned Bev to propose a visit. She sounded slightly guarded even about that. I offered to come to her house, but she suggested a sandwich place instead. I had the intuition she didn't fully trust me and that oddly, at the same time, it wasn't personal.

Still the voice was hers. Older, lower, and smokier, but Beverly Bivens.

All I knew was that she and Fred Marshall had parted years earlier, in 1978, and that by now he was dead. Mike had seen her, and Peter had seen her, and both had told me that they felt neither pushed away nor reunited with her: she was herself, she had a life, and history wasn't part of it. Mike, who'd gotten her to sing while he strummed, told me that she might sound good singing in a church choir, but he feared she may have lost the magic voice. Others wondered openly about drugs and alcohol.

And she was trying to get her Victorian house restored in order to rent out half of it, and struggling with all that entailed, and she didn't sound like she was winning the battle. You could tell it was hard on her, a source of great frustration. Eventually she would lose the house.

The café sat at the end of an open shopping complex on a quaint tree-lined Berkeley drag with a train station at one end and all the city streets splayed from running into it, and I waited at the entrance not knowing what we were going to do. I had no idea what she'd look like, nor she me. So there was some guesswork as I saw people coming and going, wondering if any could be her.

When she arrived, there was that confused instant, on both our parts. New friends who hold our album cover can't figure out which one I am when I'm standing right in front of them. Or they think Debbie must be Bev. As I considered who I was looking at, I was thinking of how people see me: this isn't who I knew at twenty-one years old, and neither am I.

She looked decades older, of course. The nifty continental chic had been replaced with a clean post-hippie look, gypsy but with dark earth tones, burnt umber and tan. Her hair was fading but she was still trim, tiny, and generally comfortable in her shoes: she knew who she was, and it wasn't the teenager on the cover of an album. She did mention that physically, she was facing challenges. She'd been to the dentist that day hoping to extend the functional life of her teeth. It was just one of any number of conversation starters for those of us nearing sixty. Anyway, it got us talking.

Eventually, as cautiously as I could (I literally pictured Frank Werber saying *Jerry, you're a good guy, but DON'T PUSH*), I passed along the PBS offer. "You know, I get queries all the time, asking if the group plays. Do you ever think about it?"

With only a courteous trace of sympathy, she said, "I'm afraid that's another life. I don't do that. Anyway, I have to concentrate on the house."

Don't push, Jerry.

So I didn't. She'd said it essentially twice now: she wasn't interested. I was happier to let her know I could be a friend, and that I wouldn't bite.

Instead we filled in the missing years. She told me how when Fred got sick and found himself with no one to care for him, she did. She brought me up to date about her kids, at least one of whom followed his parents into music (jazz saxophonist Joshi Marshall has played with Pharoah Sanders and Benny Green). Now there were multiple grandkids she loved having around.

But Beverly had always been private. She never quite named whatever heartbreaks she'd had to mend.

Grasping for a topic to align the present with the past, I brought up that night forty years earlier when we'd run over the bobcat in Bev's car. Something about that memory never left me. There'd been the blackness of the night, with the earth so dark we couldn't find our toes, but stars bright enough to light the day, in the middle of that long swath of California belonging to the memory of Spanish guitars and Kingston Trio songs—and we ourselves were crossing over from being unknown children to suddenly famous guests on Hollywood Palace, exactly midpoint in the 1960s. It was practically a checkpoint in my life. We had both wanted so badly, each in our own way, to know what to do. I was the rational person, but secretly overwhelmed, reasoning that there was no point hunting for the possible corpse of an animal that lay God knew how far away in the blackness—while Beverly was the feeling one, desperate to be sure we'd done our best, dreaming that some other outcome must be possible.

What she really wanted me to know today was that she'd let go of it, that it was settled in her mind. If anything, we'd switched roles.

"There was nothing else we could have done, Jerry," she assured me now. "It would have been crazy."

· *17* ·

Wounds Not Bound

I was at another pharmaceutical desk job farther up the ladder contemplating which product to switch from prescription to over-the-counter the day my phone rang and a voice on the other end said, "Guess who this is. Think San Francisco. . . . Think recording studio."

"Hank McGill?"

"No!" he laughed, a bit annoyed. "It's Frank Werber!"

I don't even remember if he gave a reason for his call, but at some point in the conversation I recognized that it was a chance, who knew whether the last, to make clear that I'd valued my time with Frank. I told him that whatever my frustrations, so much of what shaped me, about music and "show business" and the changing world, had been absorbed through just being exposed to Frank Werber.

"Gee," he remarked, almost surprised. "A lot of people don't think very much of me."

On hanging up, I thought, *What a shame.* The guy I heard on the phone sounded friendly, happy, like somebody's grandfather. If he lived closer, I'd have gone to see him. I'd have brought a fly rod.

It would have been easy to resent Werber for a whole host of disappointments. I remembered him at the Hollywood Bowl—the supermanager who'd built the Kingston Trio empire and allowed them to make the transition after they lost the brains and founder, Dave Guard, and everyone was predicting they were dead meat. He'd always been in control, even beginning to repeat the process with We Five. Then it all went awry. One could embrace Bob Jones's theory, that there'd simply been a tectonic shift in the culture, unleashing a tsunami over which Frank had no control. But in many ways Werber

185

was the master manipulator of events who brought that on us, who refused to listen to anything but his own genius.

Or was it something else? I wonder whether, after all those years of drug use, Werber's brain just started to process life in an altered way. "He treated grass like cigarettes, and acid like grass," his daughter Chala says. It left him a nice, mellow person, but it buried forever the whiz-kid supermanager who'd shaped destinies. Success of that sort just didn't matter to him anymore. While others were still grousing about all the things Werber had done to them, he'd let every bit of it go.

The next time we spoke by phone, he'd had a stroke, and conversation was limited. And no one called in 2007 to tell me he'd died. By then, Chala believes, he'd completely shed his business self and was comfortable in his new skin. There'd been a plan to live out his life as a restaurateur in the rebuilt Trident—the '60s jazz club in Sausalito that he turned into a psychedelic health food restaurant with rockstar patrons and braless waitresses. But when he lost the restaurant in the tide of his legal expenses, he'd lost the last of his empire.

According to Werber's friend and business associate Hans Johansen, Werber then embarked on a five-year, spiritually tinged quest for the perfect location where he could live his life in harmony with the world around him, rather than trying to manipulate it. He settled at last on "Flying Heart Ranch" in the mountains of southern New Mexico (Teddy Roosevelt once used it as a hunting lodge): a pine forest with hot springs at the confluence of several strands of the Gila River, just barely within the United States.

And died an ostensibly happy man.

★ ★ ★

Other than that last phone call, my most profound encounter with the memory of Frank Werber involved a strange experience I had in the early '70s.

The band was surviving a week of shows at the Miyako Hotel in San Francisco, with the *Chronicle* complaining that We Five was a shell of itself, and a group of drunken Aussie sailors requesting "You Were On My Mind" for the third time in one night, until Debbie told them twice was enough. ("*Wall*, I guess that's it, then—isn't it, mate!" replied the ringleader.) Eager to get some daylight before leaving the Bay Area, we squeezed in a round of golf in Mill Valley. Mt. Tamalpais to the west provided a scenic backdrop behind hills topped with houses of the rich. It was where Lisa Law photographed us singing into broomsticks by Frank Werber's swimming pool, back when he'd put us through show-business boot camp. The golf course was tree-lined and hilly, with so many balls disappearing into the gulleys that when Terry Rangno lost one in the bushes, he needed it back.

"Remember, the trees are your friends," Dennis joked as Terry plunged into a dome of foliage. "You can kick or throw it farther than you can hit it!" But suddenly, Terry reemerged with something in his hand.

"Look at this," he said.

It was a battered 45 with an A&M label. A chipped, warped copy of We Five's last charted single: "Get Together."

For years after, I liked to imagine how the record landed in the bushes of that golf course. The house had been built by Werber's father, and I know Frank lived there on and off throughout the '60s. I could easily picture Werber teetering on his balcony, flinging records into the ravine. Maybe an apocalyptic farewell to his musical ambitions, maybe just a party out of bounds. But the truth was, the house was too far away for that. More likely, anyone who was part of the Trident team, one of the We Five road managers, or Bob Jones, or Randy Cierley-Sterling, all of whom had lived within a mile of each other— or perhaps even Mike Stewart, who'd been known to play such games—had been on that nine-hole course, pre-Frisbee golf, flinging a now-worthless surplus record. In any case, the proximity of the neighborhood was too big a clue to be coincidence.

The record's flip side was "Cast Your Fate to the Wind."

★ ★ ★

Back when Debbie and I used to spend twenty-four hours a day together—from 1967 to 1981, roughly—our connection had been so close it was ESP. Driving at night together lost in thought, I'd think of a line from a song, when suddenly, out of Debbie's mouth would come the next line . . . *in the right key*. Others would marvel, but we would just laugh. We took it for granted.

But when we started spending our days apart, that Twilight Zone closeness faded, and we were challenged to reinvent ourselves too.

I knew I was still relatively lucky. I was trading my time for money; my wife and kids got to fill their days how they wanted; and was that such a bad trade, as American lives tended to go? No. But frustrated by over an hour on the freeway breathing brain-fogging exhaust fumes, I'd often get off and take streets just to keep moving. One afternoon within blocks of my house on Sierra Madre I sped past Grand Avenue, and when the car slowed in front of me I whipped the wheel to pass him on his left—just as he himself decided to turn left. I floored the accelerator and hurtled ahead, managing to dodge a collision, but when I got home, I was quaking, no longer rational. Now it was family time.

I'd stagger in, and evidence of a busy wife and kids was everywhere. Debbie was never a cleaner—she and I both hated housework and were very comfortable letting maid service clean the hotel rooms, though we never had one follow us home. But as I walked through the house, still waiting for the exhaust poisoning and road rage to dissipate, I wondered if anyone had done anything for the twelve hours since I left. I would often arrive in the kitchen a hostile man.

Once, I sat in a chair and actually said out loud, "Maybe I should get a place closer to work."

"Calm down, Dad," Chris said. "You don't mean that." Which was true.

If it was Christmas season, she'd been making crafts for the church fair, so for months you couldn't use our dining room table, because that was her workshop. Eventually her workshop encompassed the garage. On occasions that I'd be asked to fix something and go looking for tools, I couldn't find them—or they'd be broken. It could feel like this was no longer my house and that my only purpose in life was to pay for it while not making too much trouble when I was around. I hoped everyone was happy. I wasn't.

We were not finishing each other's songs in our heads now. Where once I could come in from the studio asking for input on a song, the range of things I now considered at work had narrowed. And the topics were of no particular interest to her because she was busy raising a family. The more I craved her companionship and sharing in my aggravations, the more it felt like she would withdraw. We both wanted escape at the end of the day, but in different ways. I lacked any natural ability to make my work as interesting as the movie she'd seen on TV, or the book she was reading or the craft she'd been crafting. Nor did I have guidance on how to acquire the skill.

I saw myself becoming my dad. Knowing that most generations eventually succumb to that destiny, even though the baby boomers delayed it more creatively than maybe any generation in human history, doesn't make it any easier or make it stop. I might love and flee my father's ghost forever.

Debbie stayed by me, for the same reason she stayed when she found my drugs in San Francisco. It wasn't just love of God—that's just what helped her to remember that she loves me, warts and all. It was also because she perceived what everyone hopes that the people they hurt will perceive: that although I could be terribly hurtful, it wasn't my *nature* to be. Dealt with patiently, properly steered, there was a husband in me who really wanted to be empathetic.

What's frustrating today is that I can't help but see, sometimes because she wants me to see and sometimes when she doesn't, the face of her disappointments. And even while I know what I did over the years to bring it about, I tend to feel injured. When someone's been indulged for years, and then he's not anymore, he is not happy.

When our kids left the nest (Chris left early, Jess finished college, and Jeremy stayed at home till he was thirty), I filled the time with stuff like church obligations, fly fishing, and occasional We Five shows. But all that came easy—empathy requires conscious effort. Debbie's more naturally empathetic than me, but looking for opportunities to share in others' pain is not an attractive proposition, because it can get you hurt. The controlling part of me wants to push her to be more involved, because this woman whose patience humbled and saved me doesn't feel a calling to love a vast circle of people. Or maybe she simply did it too long on me. Because when you know what's behind that door, it's a tough room to walk into.

Of course what I really fear is her death.

There was a biopsy in the 1980s. The results could have shown anything from calcium deposits to cancer—it was calcium, and it almost always is, but you still have to look—and that was the first time in my life such a threat of separation was on the table. More specifically, a threat that wasn't linked in any way to our struggle for power in the relationship. Suddenly it wasn't, "If you go to Nashville, you go without me." This was a threat utterly beyond our control. It was the moonless night.

The mom of a kid I knew in Cub Scouts died of cancer at thirty-five. My dad had run into the widowed father and invited them to join us at the Hollywood Bowl on the same night John Stewart had his debut with the Kingston Trio. That was the memory that crashed into my brain now. That someone's mom could be vibrant and young, and then gone, all in one season. And then the kid would be shaking hands with you at the Hollywood Bowl, and staring back at you, both your mirror image and not.

How I prayed for Debbie was by begging. "Please, God, let it not be true." I walked around singing "What a Friend We Have in Jesus" constantly in my head. It's a habit Debbie shares when she's scared: singing hymns rather than quoting scripture. Because there is something special about that combination of soothing words and melody that come together so perfectly in spirituals.

Colleen and Fred, our former backyard neighbors in Pomona, were on the less lucky side of the mirror, too. First a son with terminal muscular dystrophy, next the eventual divorce. Then, although they both had good second marriages, Colleen got brain cancer and died, after which Fred's second wife passed away. Today, Fred is a good friend and banjo player in the valley who would like nothing better than to be a touring musician, but life got in the way. You can hear him in the fade-out on a Billy Joel album and a couple of We Five albums, but he never quite bridged the degrees of separation that everyone had at the outskirts of the folk-rock explosion. The people he played with played with Linda Ronstadt. He didn't get the chance.

So if there's heartbreak everywhere, but I seem to have dodged it, how can I even complain about a marriage that has scars but still aspires to love and respect?

One of my old songs, "Tattered Hand Me Downs," has some lines that seem significant today: "When it's time to turn the tables/You and I alone are able/But only if we try to change our ways." The lyric came out of my own mind and mouth in the 1970s, but it's taken me thirty years to put arms and legs on it—time is a funny thing.

The other old lyric that now feels like it was written to shout at me today is "Love someone enough to bend." Now I'd change *bend* to *break*, but it doesn't rhyme.

As we head toward fifty years of marriage, I can't say I don't miss our youthful intensity—the time when we loved the night away with every nerve on end. Gone are the kind of heart-to-hearts that took us from anger to tears to sex. It takes effort to cultivate a relationship in the aftermath of young passion. But we find ways to remind ourselves who we are to each other. Sometimes it's by watching movies. There are things we need to share that are easier to acknowledge than to just speak. *Silver Streak*, with Richard Pryor, Gene Wilder, and Jill Clayburgh, we return to again and again, because it brings our kind of humor back up to the surface: it has passion couched in double-entendres about flowers, subtexts that are both obvious and carefully unspoken—pure Debbie. Instead of silly punch lines, it just quietly reveals what we've always enjoyed about each other. It was exactly the opposite of being alone in an arena watching the Rolling Stones while she was two thousand miles away.

We watch the Lakers on TV, and we watch "American Idol" or "Voices" or "Duets" and disagree with the panels of critics. Debbie gets pissed off when the most talented person gets kicked off the show, whereas I won't even invest myself in it emotionally. I know it's shock and likability, more than talent, that rule that stage.

Alongside my fear of her death is just the fear of slow, gradual isolation. What if our spending so many hours in separate hobbies is really her desire to retreat from me? What if it's a self-fulfilling prophesy?

Toward the end of the 1960s, some people who claimed to be witches told Debbie she had a gift for reading cards. One of them crocheted her a dress that they said had magic powers, so be careful what you think when you wear it. Another read her cards. And they told her she'd have a lonely old age.

So when I heard a little girl playing in the backyard next door, the daughter of a young couple, I started pushing Debbie to make friends. One of her dreams was having grandchildren, and it's begun to look like that might not happen. You'd be so wonderful for that girl, I said. Ultimately, Debbie ventured over and chatted with the mom, but the little girl acted like a monster had walked into the yard, and that was that. What is karma, what is destiny, and how much of what happens to us is still up to *us*?

I look at Debbie today at sixty-eight, and I still see the twenty-one-year-old inside. I know she's there, because I don't feel any different either—at least not until I try to move quickly or play the banjo without warming up. And I take great delight in the fact that I can still look at her and see the person out front of the Legendaires who I fell in love with.

But I'm afraid when she looks for the man she fell in love with, she has to work at it.

★ ★ ★

The last time I laid eyes on Mike Stewart, around 2000, I told myself he was on solid footing. It was easy to be fooled, because he'd cultivated frailty since pretty much the fifth grade and wore it like a hipster, along with the skeletal physique and the glasses.

He and Kate were living in the Santa Cruz Mountains, a spot so secluded that her phone directions included a well-rehearsed warning to not even *think* about GPS, because it was useless. Exactly ten miles past some minor sign on Highway 17, Debbie and I were supposed to turn off the pavement onto a shoulder, then find a dirt road in a break between some trees and follow it uphill. Luckily it was daytime, or I could still be out there.

When we stepped out of the car, the peace of the surrounding forest was palpable, coating Mike and Kate in what looked like a permanent mellow while I unwound from the complicated drive. You could see that Adobe had been paying him a decent living. The house itself had beautifully stained redwood and miles of glass, looking out not at the ocean, like Werber's place, but at a playground of squirrels—although given the vastness all around, they could have been Ewoks on the forest moon of Endor.

The first strange note was Mike's office, which he showed me while Kate gave Debbie the grand tour. I looked everywhere for his rock star imprint and saw none. No memorabilia, no guitars, no tape decks or funky handmade art. "Maybe they keep it sparse so there's no chance of asthma," Debbie said later. There was only a computer with a large-screen setup and a phone line, over which he could telecommute to work. That seemed lucky too—if the flora outdoors touched off his asthma, he could hole up as long as he wanted, plus get up and work anytime an idea struck, day or night, which he said was absolutely necessary.

"The kids I work with, they're all smart, and fast. The best of the best. I have to take a lot of Ginko Biloba to keep up."

I cracked a smile—and as soon as I did, Mike picked up on the whole fraternity of our generation without hearing a word. It wasn't quite scoring drugs, but you heard echoes of it.

"Do you guys make that stuff? Can I get it from you?"

Pretty soon we were sorting out a lot of things from the past, separating things that had faded away from those that became timeless. I marveled at the fact that our version of "My Favorite Things," which Mike arranged, and which we sang to the injured girl in the stairwell in Chicago, was still getting played every Christmas. He took that in.

"Yeah—I was a good arranger. That still holds up."

Then we took the conversation outside, until Kate and Debbie let it be known that it was getting late and they were heading to the local craft show. We all decided Mike and I would follow along separately. So we got to talk even longer, all the way to the car, and then all the way to the fair. And I got to clear some things up with him.

It's hard to describe the rightness, combined with the oddness, of reconnecting with Mike that day. There's that loyalty to a childhood bond that gets stronger the farther you get away from it—like fate, but in reverse. We weren't brothers, but if we were, he'd have been the one with the more desperate cravings—and I was the one who at least looked stable and dependable, and seemed to get good things that I didn't even know I wanted until after I had them. Mike had a feel for the dreams of our generation, especially at that moment when we all came of age at once—I was more grounded than Mike. I always wondered if there was something I should have done to ground him more. Or if what I thought was keeping a respectful distance was really just my cluelessness over how to be a friend.

The truth was, and I went ahead and told him so, I knew Mike could have done what he did in the '60s with all kinds of different people. I was just plain thankful that, after all the hurts, he hadn't gotten rid of me. When we were at Mt. San Antonio College, he used bystanders all the time to give body to a vocal line in his head. It could feel pretty threatening. Somewhere there's a woman who sang parts of "You Were On My Mind" while Mike was working it out, and today people who've heard a fragment of that story will tell strangers it was their friend, not Beverly, whose immortal voice is on the record.

But somewhere along the line, I'd stopped worrying about it, because of my ability to know what he wanted to do and be able to do it—I satisfied many needs in his hierarchy. The price, always, was where women got involved. Usually it was something like the Susie thing, where I knew he had wanted her, and then, before his eyes, I had her. And the fact that I hadn't set out specifically to cause him pain wasn't the point. I didn't like remembering what I did. It hurt the group, and it hurt my best friend. I didn't have to say yes to Susie. If you and a best friend both want the same thing, maybe say, "You have it." Or just don't partake, because the friendship is important to you.

Of course, my line of thinking back then had been: *If I don't take Susie, he will, and then I'll be hurt—so better him than me.* But because we had to constantly work together as a group, it was always there in front of him. I was blind. I was just—there.

We were all fighting hormones, we were striving to be the best, and people make strange, not necessarily rational decisions when they're teenagers.

"I know I've never really said it," I told him in the car. "But I really regret the pain it must have caused. I'm sorry. And I've always been thankful that you continued to work with me in spite of it."

"It was hard," Mike admitted. "But we found a way. And I'm glad I did."

When we arrived at the craft fair, it was like being transported to a Golden Gate Park Love-In, perfectly preserved. The street vendors were set up with tie-dyed shirts, drug paraphernalia, macramé sculptures, and psychedelic art. Nothing had changed, in fact, but the merchants, who were now in their fifties and sixties. Mike said it was a "Brigadoon experience." There were simply people who'd decided to be hippies and never renegotiated.

Now Mike was the master of ceremonies again, taking in the scene, responding to the diversion of the moment—like his brother, whose MO was to look at the sights and see Funny, regardless of who was the target.

"Look at the guy with the love beads and the beer belly," he chuckled. "I always figured old hippies evolved—that guy just turned gray and got fat!"

★ ★ ★

Ironically, it was staying in that house that may have killed him. While all of us worried about the allergens outside, Mike developed a respiratory ailment eventually traced to a black mold inside the edifice.

I got one particularly strange call from Pete Fullerton, on whose couch Mike temporarily landed—the reasons for his homelessness were murky. But the symptoms Pete described sounded as much like Alzheimer's as anything respiratory—and of course Mike was too young for that.

Then the problem was linked to a fungus that impacted his sinuses, and after the doctors cleared it up, he moved back in with Kate. The two of them relocated to Sacramento, so Kate could take care of her mom (not to mention taking care of Mike), and I'd still hear from Mike on and off. During one of those phone conversations, hinting at how raw things must have been, and how dependent he was on Pete's help, he remarked, "You know, Peter lives on a spiritual plane that you and I are not familiar with."

In 2002, Mike sounded like he was possibly on a different plane himself. He had spoken to Debbie on the phone about wanting to visit us and record some spirituals. He sounded great, she said. So I tried to phone back the next day, but it was too early in the morning—it was hard to even get up when he hadn't had any oxygen all night long. Doctors had cleared his sinuses, but the lung damage was irreversible and he needed oxygen to function and speak normally. He asked if he could call back, and even if I couldn't see the struggle in his body language, I could literally hear it. He was really uncomfortable.

When he called back in an hour, he sounded just like Mike, but he admitted he'd had a couple of tough years. He talked about having one project left in him that, to radically oversimplify, was going to reform the whole Tower of Babel of how computer codes talk to each other. Without my getting what he was talking about, it made sense to me to say that *he* probably got it. Because that was his magic, after all, to first see the clear path that doesn't exist yet, and then work on the incongruities without quite letting them distract you. That was what had made the human clock possible—a simple concept, unearthed from all the distractions.

We were in the midst of all this when he added that what he'd *really* like to do was make one more album. This time, spirituals.

"If I can figure out how to get my oxygen tanks down to your house, can I come down and work with you?" Was it the music trying to get out of him, or was it the spiritual longing? I didn't have a clue.

I thought of the roadblocks—the logistics of getting the oxygen here, and whether I could measure up to the other people in the business he'd worked with. And the fact that I didn't have time to do this, a thought that was instantly driven out by: *I don't have time* not *to do this.*

I couldn't help but picture us strumming "Follow the Drinking Gourd" on the edge of my bed in Pomona.

"Of course," I said. "We'd love to have you come and stay as long as you like."

But he never got here. He died two days later.

· 18 ·

Funeral for a Friend

$\mathcal{T}$he L.A. Times reported that Mike Stewart, fifty-seven, former member of
the 1960s folk-rock group We Five, died in Sacramento after a long illness.
In interviews and public blogs, his son Jamie Stewart—whose own body of
work as leader of the indie band Xiu Xiu has made emotional openness and
courage practically a performance art—would later insist that his father died on
purpose, fulfilling a lifetime of ambiguous suicidal threats. In the final analysis,
I have to admit I will just never know.

But whether or not Mike chose the moment, the fact that his respiratory
problem was terminal, and that death by suffocation could have come any
night when he went to sleep, was never in question.

The news reached Debbie while I was at work: that he'd been taking
oxygen all day, then going off the oxygen in order to sleep, every night an
adventure because you couldn't be sure if he'd wake up, and this day he
hadn't. Kate was a bereavement counselor herself, never much of a candidate
for denial or false hope, so alongside all the irony of that job description, it
meant she had a pretty expert handle on what had to be done next.

The most satisfying obituary, aside from an unusually sensitive and de-
tailed piece in the London Independent, would come from our brainy former
high school classmate Leo Green, who'd anchored a network TV news affili-
ate in Little Rock while Bill Clinton was governor, then moved on, landing
at a newspaper. Billy Joel provided the vital comment that Mike was the first
person who'd ever really understood him musically and captured on tape what
he was trying to do. Indeed, Joel eventually bought out Mike's producer royalties, so the Stewarts could live.

All day, Leo kept phoning and phoning us to check facts, a writer on
a mission. Then my son Chris, his wife Jen, Debbie, and I headed north to

Sacramento, driving half the night to our hotel, the last ten miles on an empty tank.

It was a late-morning service, but we showed up even earlier to rehearse, because Kate's plan was for Debbie, me, and Peter to sing Jimmy Cliff's "I Can See Clearly Now," and then for John Stewart to join in on "Amazing Grace." The trouble was, John lived a long drive away, somewhere like Petaluma, and he was late.

After a few exchanges of "sad day, but he's in a better place," we tried to run through what we could without John Stewart. Pete had lost weight, and he got around so gracefully it didn't even dawn on me to remember he'd lost a leg, till he bumped into an end table and had to remind us why. Kate was in hurry-up-and-wait mode, probably frustrated that John wasn't there, and the small chapel was full to capacity, mostly with friends of theirs from Sacramento. It was a modest, upbeat setting, nothing like flowers and pictures crowding out every wall, but a small shrine of photos, mostly from prime time in his forties with Kate, caught my eye. There was a pastor who chatted with me, homing straight in on the same thing that always left everyone in awe of Mike, that his insights and counsel were out-of-the-box brilliant—that he had a knack for seeing a big picture that the pastor couldn't really get from anyone else in the congregation. I kept asking the pastor more and more questions, because I felt something very right and healing in the fact that Mike and Kate had found a church home he could feel good in, and that just by being who he was, he became indispensable there.

★ ★ ★

At long last, John Stewart walked in—we'd either just started without him or pulled the trigger the instant he drove up, because, for better or worse, a party with John never started without John. He was in his mid-sixties now and, to steal a line from Beverly, still tall. Having walked away from big record labels, he'd gone back to his folksy-hip comfort zone: a jacket and dress shirt with a hard-shell guitar case carried in one hand. (For the album *Gold*, with Lindsey Buckingham and Stevie Nicks, the studio tried to style him a gold-suited rock-star.) He'd found, through home recording, a way to keep writing and producing things that were as complex and refined as he wanted, and thus he'd circled back to who he really was: a poet, songwriter, and comedian playing comfortable country-folk venues. McCabe's hosted him with a band; the Coffee Gallery had him with just a bass player. Later, he would suffer a stroke and start playing alone. He ultimately died of one.

But today he had the task of eulogizing Mike, a complicated assignment that was equally interesting for what he didn't talk about: the childhood years.

At that time I could still only extrapolate the tensions that shaped and drove the Stewart family. What was clear was, at least for this day, it was extremely important to John Stewart to acknowledge that his younger brother possessed something he himself did not—that mystical ability to hear a work in all its parts and hold it in his head. It was a gift that exceeded that of the other great producers and arrangers John had known. This was meaningful. It was John admitting that the admiration, and perhaps the envy, between the Stewart brothers ran both ways.

For if John had never shown signs of being threatened by his younger brother's talent, or how it fed into the electro-folk tsunami that washed away the Kingston Trio, he'd certainly had his own frustrations—the fact that his hit composition "Daydream Believer" turned out to be, for all practical purposes, his retirement song, the fact that his incredible album *California Bloodlines*, which virtually invented the genre of Americana, never broke through to popular success. Once, I'd said to Mike, who was producing him at the time, "Don't take this the wrong way, but why doesn't he do a 'Big John' kind of story song? He doesn't have to ham it up like Lorne Green or Walter Brennan, but he's so good at it." And Mike agreed. But John hated the thought. He couldn't go there.

The John Stewart I watched speaking to the crowd today was a human, fallible figure, both frailer and humbler than the one I'd idolized as a kid. I'd heard he'd had his teeth replaced, hoping it might remove the vibrato he hated in his voice. There'd always been two things I knew John was self-conscious about: the way his ears stuck out on his first album with the Kingston Trio (after which he'd had surgery pull them closer to his head) and that tremolo in his voice (the Trio hired him mainly for banjo, comedy, and songwriting, and he knew it). Now at the funeral, and indeed for the rest of his life, every time he smiled with those new Bucky Beaver teeth, it almost lightened things for me. . . . I couldn't help but smile. Except that I couldn't divorce it from the other unforgettable sight, which was John processing, and not enjoying processing, a little brother's funeral coming before his own.

My own eulogy reminisced about everything: Mike's childhood asthma, and the Southern California smog, and the boys' choir where we met, and tuning my dad's four-string guitar like a banjo to play "Follow the Drinking Gourd" until our voices were hoarse and our fingers bled; and sitting in wonder while the Kingston Trio rehearsed; and young Mike blossoming as an arranger to produce that soundtrack for the NASA film. And then the We Five phase and the Billy Joel phase and the leap to computers and the phone call, after a season on Pete Fullerton's couch, when Mike said, "You know, Peter exists on a spiritual level with which neither you nor I will ever be familiar."

I said that it seemed Mike, in wanting to come over and record an album of spiritual songs, had come full circle to the first song he wrote as a kid.

> Last night I heard my Lord calling
> Sing out! Join in and pray
> Boat to heaven is the one I'm calling
> Don't wait for another day
> You've got to Sing Out! if you want to get to heaven
> Sing out! Join in and pray

Finally we tried to play "Amazing Grace" the way we'd rehearsed it—only John Stewart more or less took over. He co-opted the part Debbie was supposed to sing, and the rest of us did our best to fall back on professionalism and just go with it. Debbie's gospel approach was abandoned, and we followed John into more of a folk waltz, a traditional 3/4 hymn, whereas gospel favors 4/3.

"Yup!" Peter is able to laugh today. "It was like old times, actually. Like a hootenanny. 'Anyone have a guitar? Feel free to join in!'"

As for me, I'd been struggling with tears, and so my voice had no real air support. I kept thinking, *Can I just get through this and cry later?* I told myself to pretend I was back at swimming lessons as a child, gasping while the instructor said, "You've got all day to breathe!" I had all day to cry.

★ ★ ★

A lunch at Kate's house followed, and everybody was there. Mike's son by a former girlfriend was there, too, and, from the looks of things, thoroughly embraced—Kate had pointed him out at the funeral. Originally he'd tracked down Mike because he had questions about the family's medical history, and that was how they finally became acquainted.

As an inspired touch (it was Mike's request, according to Jamie Stewart), a portion of Mike's ashes had been mixed with paint in order for all of his children to create a textured painting of a rhinoceros on the wall above the mantel. I was impressed with the concept: that rather than a jar there now stands a canvas, the creative expression of feelings from the next generation he had loved into being.

★ ★ ★

Still, I went years with the uneasy feeling that I'd never really understood Mike's inner workings or all the facts surrounding his final years. It was only recently, partly through undertaking this book project, that some of the puzzle pieces I'd missed or overlooked started fitting into place. Especially ones having to do with his and John Stewart's childhood.

There was Jamie Stewart's blog about Mike's suicidal threats, with casual references to Mike having survived a horrific home life as a child. When I read that, I called Kate Stewart, and a lot of my memories started to make more sense.

I knew he'd always been hand-delivered to school by his mother, because of asthma and so on, and that she'd always seemed, while the perfect home-maker, also distant. I knew that Mike avoided his father for vague reasons, and when the two interacted, it would be "Hi, Pop"—and then out. And when we started playing together, it was always important that his dad not be around. Indeed, Mr. Stewart was intolerant of music, Kate says. "Enough with the bumpity bump on the banjo" was the general attitude. It seems significant, looking back, that Mike's banjo was kept at my house. Ostensibly it was because neighbors of theirs had complained about the noise. Only now I'm inclined to believe it was a neighbor named Dad.

Much of what Kate Stewart says aligns with Jamie's story: That Mike's father had been alcoholic and brutally violent, particularly to John. As a young boy, the abuse freaked Mike out; unlike his older (and bolder) brother, he ran away, grateful to hide at my house. Waif-like, he mastered the art of conversing with his father without ever displeasing him—a style of interaction that was pretty well refined by the time I met him. My impression, supported by Kate fifty years later, is that Mr. Stewart favored Mike and spared him his wrath, while in return Mike played his father's model son. Which seems to have driven a wedge between the family.

He had two older sisters: one living with a grandmother, the other more apt to maintain an awkward front of things being okay. What Kate reports, which seems plausible, is that Mike became an affront to his mother, in whose eyes John had been the golden child and Mike the de facto traitor. Kate says Mike told her about his mom having been victimized, too—whether overtly or by neglect, I don't know. Either way, the sisters and mom and John would have shared a common fear of Mike's father, and the irritation of Mike's escape.

If so, it makes sense that Mike learned to do what Mike did—to joke, to be brilliant, to disarm, and to flee rather than fight. Socially he used his slyness and humor to keep a permanent upper hand—and if ever that didn't work, he'd exit fast, sometimes with a shrill, almost-feminized outburst. That described his bailing from the car during our triangle with Susie: since we were all staying connected in a band, he couldn't make the agony go away—so he ran, later to return, completely composed, as if the outburst never occurred. And in my naiveté, I'd think everything was fine. Of course, everything wasn't.

When he'd landed in the psych ward in San Francisco, I'd been able to rationalize (1) that he was melodramatic and (2) that he was identifying too closely with Brian Wilson (already known in music circles, if not publicly, as a disturbed genius). It was easier for him to take after Brian than John, who seemed invulnerable, and who sometimes lorded fame and fortune over the little brother that Dad liked. I knew Mike had come to San Francisco largely to be accepted by John, and that, for whatever reasons, the magnet that brought him to the city wasn't strong enough to keep him there. He walked away from school and went back home, where his mom took care of him again—not a job she particularly relished, Kate has since disclosed. Like many mothers of the era, however, she likely couldn't show it.

Kate confirms, too, that the words "I'm going to kill myself" were not unfamiliar coming from Mike. She has even suspected he might have qualified as bipolar, something we'll never know, since he wasn't tested. We do know that when he was nice, no one could be nicer. When he was not, you didn't want to be around him.

Jamie doubts the mold-in-the-brain theory altogether. Yet Kate is utterly certain it was valid—*something* modified Mike's body to such a great degree that he could not breathe or sleep or function as he had before. And when he couldn't get enough oxygen to think clearly, he'd kept trying to find a room in the house he could function in. As for his idea of a universal computer code, Debbie just dismissed it as over her head, and Jamie did much the same. Yet when Mike spoke to me about it, it arose naturally out of discussing what we both did professionally (I was a project manager who had to design products to align two companies' needs)—it didn't sound inconceivable to me, genius that Mike was. His wife, on the other hand, worried otherwise, and was reminded of the anguished hero in *A Beautiful Mind*. She said Adobe ultimately called her to come get him from work in the middle of the day, because he was behaving irrationally. That was still a couple of years before the end.

What we do know is that Mike looked at life differently, saw things differently, perceived things differently. There is no question that he heard, in the lines of Sylvia Fricker's "You Were On My Mind," a response to pain that offered meaning to his childhood, not to mention the potential for a joyful sound that could speak to millions. This in a time when people didn't talk much about either depression or domestic abuse. (Sylvia's lyric "Got some aches/Got some pains" might now be heard in a very different vein than I'd heard it at nineteen.) Some of Mike's uniqueness was super-intellect, and some of it was an emotional and creative reaction to what he'd lived through. What I'm left to suspect is that in his final years, the dam of his psyche may have crumbled, for reasons both medical and otherwise. But even there, I console myself with hope, because I know that his trials also brought him back to his God, and to thrive in the environment of a church, where there are flaws but also forgiveness. And because his last phone call told me he'd like to make some spiritual music with my wife and me. In that respect, we hadn't arrived in very different places.

* * *

Indeed, what can be said about our particular experience that will be remembered as unique? My parents' generation had been called "the greatest" because they survived the Great Depression, won a war that saved the world for freedom, and then built a prosperous consumer nation upon their work ethic and moral standards. But one of their greatest legacies—both for good and for ill—was giving birth to the biggest generation in American history and giving even the most typical middle-class kid a future that allowed access to virtually anything money could buy. Those who were trained from an early age to function well in the school system got degrees and became professionals; others felt empowered to become merchants, craftsmen, and artists. Like generations before, we banded together as teenagers, tested the truisms of our parents, experimented with lifestyles, challenged taboos, and through it all entertained ourselves and found identities in the music of our tribe. We all had ready access to portable, affordable music and for many, it became a life soundtrack. For me, it actually set the direction of my life.

But unlike generations before, the dream of having music become your life wasn't limited to a select and gifted few. Overnight, almost anyone in my generation could imagine catching a star, becoming suddenly wealthy, doing whatever we pleased, and being set for life. In my case, that largely came true, simply by being in the right place at the right time. Growing up in a music-filled home. Meeting the Stewart brothers at an early age. Discovering the folk process, and benefitting from the imagination of new writers following paths carved by Woody Guthrie, Bob Dylan—and Sylvia Tyson. Reaping the new technology that let pop music get made and sold without a big studio or orchestra. Taking a thrill ride on tracks laid down by the Kingston Trio and their manager, Frank Werber. Sharing space with everyone from Fred Astaire to the Rolling Stones. Discovering that even the misses brought unexpected satisfactions. All this was a lucky gift, if you knew how to appreciate it.

Frank Sinatra sang to his get-it-done generation about the ups and downs of fame and fortune ("That's Life"), but I'd always found his life and "My Way" message egocentric. I never bought into the idea that life is simply about amassing booty—of any kind—or about losing it. And it ought to be clear by now that the people of my generation who staked their hopes on freedom unrooted in values paid a price I wasn't willing to pay, even though I drifted off the tracks for a number of years. I'm forever grateful for the concepts I learned from church and family that were implanted deep enough to stick, and especially for an enduring relationship with the great love of my life, Debbie—in which she often bore a disproportionate amount of the enduring.

I have regrets, but in the years left, my hope is not to create new ones.

★ ★ ★

That whole shared journey hung over a mini-reunion I got to have earlier this year with Bev Bivens and Bob Jones. I'd been trying to reach Bob for a couple of months when his wife, Donah, called with the bad news that he was fighting pancreatic cancer. I knew from prior conversations that neither he nor Donah believed there was any place in Hawaii he'd feel confident about receiving major surgery.

Ultimately his insurance granted a change of venue, so he flew to San Francisco for the operation, staying in Marin County at the Fairfax home he'd long ago purchased with his now ex-wife using Southern Comfort bonus money. The post-op plan was to build up his strength there for a few weeks before starting chemo back in Hawaii. Realizing this might be my last chance to see Bob on the mainland, I asked if I could come see him—and possibly bring Beverly with me. He said it was a wonderful idea, so I called her.

Though genuinely interested in hearing about Bob and his circumstances, there was hesitation in Bev's voice—she needed to ask Bob directly if he was okay with this. I'd arranged my schedule so as to drive within a mile of her new place as I headed north to the Richmond-San Rafael bridge, but right up to the eve of the visit, she hadn't called him. At last I asked Bob to give her a ring. She got back to me that night, and though I could feel the reservations in her voice, she told me Bob had asked her to come.

Her place was in a warehouse district between Berkeley and Richmond, very reminiscent of where Bev and Fred lived in 1967: a loft-like arrangement defined by a bare edifice with a single unmarked door, and internal quadrants divided by functional furniture instead of walls, doors, and hallways. She had tried hard to make a good life in the Victorian house, but I think it felt honestly more natural to see her living here.

Heading out, she seemed a little nervous about how she looked. "I didn't have a chance to get my hair done," she said. "Maybe I should get a hat."

I admitted that I didn't know what her normal best was supposed to look like anymore. "You look fine to me. But I do have a hat you can wear if that would feel better."

"No," she said. "Not a baseball cap—something a lady can wear."

"Well, don't get the wrong idea, but I actually bought it at a women's clothing store. It's kind of a designer Pete Seeger cap in basic black. I wear them on stage to hold down the glare on my bald head."

"It'll be too big," she said.

"It's adjustable," I countered, so she tried it on in the car.

"Okay! This might work. If I need a hat. We'll see what it's like when we get there."

After a few wrong turns, we got on the freeway headed for the bridge to San Rafael, and I flashed on the hundreds of times I'd made that drive years before, whether to voice lessons with Judy Davis or rehearsing at Bev and Fred's, that wonderful sea breeze filling the car as we gained elevation, and the bay opening up before us with the Golden Gate off in the distance. I selected a lane that would give me the best view and asked Bev if she'd ever been to Fairfax.

"Probably—but it's been years. This sure feels like old times, though. How many years has it been?" she asked, her tone not really needing an answer.

"We did a lot of miles like this. All we need is Pete and a bench seat."

It was a beautiful day with blue skies and a few soft clouds as we descended the north side of the bridge and San Quentin disappeared behind the hill and we turned toward San Rafael following the directions of the semi-seductive voice coming from the Garmin with a New Zealand accent. "Exit on to San Rah Fah El."

"Shouldn't we be going to Sir Francis Drake Boulevard?" Bev worried.

"I'm sure that would work, but the GPS calculates speed and distance, so this way is probably faster."

We got off the freeway and headed north, picking up Sir Francis Drake at last, which put us both at ease as we passed a sign telling us the town of Ross was only ten miles ahead. Memories of that very first We Five road trip flooded back. I asked Bev if she remembered the gingerbread cottage where we lived during the recording of "You Were On My Mind," everyone sleeping on the floor or chaise lounges.

"Wow. Was that up here? I don't remember anything about it."

Now the Garmin's directions kept coming about thirty yards after it was too late to turn, so I let my internal compass do its thing before finally turning off in Fairfax to head uphill on a desperately narrow road cut out of the side of the hill to afford everyone some kind of view, and it might have been almost safe if it were a one-way street, which it wasn't. I reparked the car a couple of times before Bob's ex-wife, Alice, shouted that we could leave it in the neighbor's carport as long as we were gone by 5:30.

We stepped out—Beverly contemplating the hat, then brushing her hair back with a hand as we stepped down through a vine-covered, gated porch to the front door, where Alice welcomed us in. A tight left turn into the living room gave us a view of the tree-covered hillside at one end, a chair and a guitar amplifier at the other—and Bob sitting in the middle of a couch along the wall between them, grinning through the discomfort.

Actually, for someone who'd eliminated the pancreas, spleen, and gall bladder from being a future threat to his health, he looked quite good. "Nothing like major surgery to get your weight down!" he said, pointing to his thin neck and baggy clothes. You could tell he was tired, but the adrenaline rush of seeing Beverly for the first time in decades literally lifted him off the couch, and as they hugged, I knew that if nothing else happened, the trip was worth the effort.

There was some small talk, but Bob's health was the most important thing on our minds. He told us everything about the operation, which doctors deemed a success, and about his current efforts focused on getting acclimated to life as a surgical diabetic. All this time the electric guitar was staring at me from the edge of the couch.

"Is that a borrowed guitar?" I asked him.

"Oh no. That's my anywhere, anytime guitar. I put it in a bag and carried it on the plane with me. I couldn't be away from playing. Why?"

"Well, I don't know. I brought an acoustic and the ukulele that I bought up the street from your house, in case—"

Beverly looked nervous. But without noticing her, or even waiting for me to finish, he told me to go bring them in.

By the time I'd got back inside, he'd turned on the amp and was playing some blues lines. Beverly watched quietly as I found the key and we began to riff back and forth for a few minutes. Then he paused. He fingered a chord and said, "Maybe you can help me with this. I've been trying to find the changes, but I'm not sure of the key."

Suddenly I thought I recognized the pattern he was trying to locate. It was "High Flying Bird." But I didn't blurt it out. I was conscious of the fact that Beverly did not look inclined to sing. Perhaps she feared it was a setup. Indeed, Bob started to sing the words and then asked, mid-phrase, if Beverly could help.

"I really don't sing anymore," she smiled politely. "That was another time."

I started singing a Dylan tune to take the pressure off, hoping we could revisit it later. And Bob did ask again, and we even worked out the key and figured out all the changes. But Beverly never sang.

At this point Alice came in and reminded Bob that it was time for a blood sugar test, and we got to see him go through that whole routine. It said he needed insulin, and without any of the apprehension some might have felt injecting themselves in front of an audience, he completed the process, with mechanical precision. As he went about this business, almost a charade of the drug-dealer '60s and '70s, he mentioned how hard it was for him to have to go on the post-operative pain pills. "I'd spent a lot of years getting that craving out of my system, and now they tell me I can't do without it." We all agreed that the Catch-22 was ironic.

There was kind of a natural segue to talking about a call I received from a writer working on a book about Mike Bloomfield. The blues-rock guitar legend, with whom Bob recorded five albums, had been found dead of an overdose in 1981. Now the biographer was anxious to interview Bob. We exchanged some contact info, and then Alice came in to ask if she could get a picture of us all out on the patio, which we did. But once there, you could tell that Bob was looking very tired—and so we began our departure.

The drive back was very relaxed, and we talked easily about nothing in particular, much as we had years before. I asked Bev if she'd mind stopping at a sandwich shop in Fairfax so I could meet with the head of my record company, and she agreed. Coincidentally, their sons were friends, and Joshi Marshall had even played on some recordings he had made. Had Bev ever done anything with her son? the man asked. And Bev's reply, though friendly, expressed no reaction other than "no." When we pulled up to her place, she told me with great sincerity that she really appreciated my bringing her to see Bob, and when I opened her car door preparing for goodbyes, she gave me a hug. Our hands remained clasped. She told me again that it was a wonderful day, but there was sadness in her voice, as she looked at me and added: "I should have sung 'High Flying Bird.'"[1]

· *19* ·

Folk Songs and Stories

If I'm introduced to anyone outside the music world today, it's more and more typical that the people introducing me remember vividly the first time they heard "You Were On My Mind" on the radio, and the people meeting me have never heard of it. There's some perspective for you.

Still, for an awfully long time, that transitional song and the ride it sent me on defined me to the world. Though the high-water mark I left outside of music was managing the launch of our company's equivalent to Claritin (its revenue surpassed anything generated by my music!)—to coworkers my age, I remained the in-house celebrity, the guy who'd once had a hit record.

All the more humbling, because my whole brush with the dawn of folk-rock arguably happened because the only other guitar player in our grade school didn't have a guitar, so Mike Stewart chose my house to drop by with his banjo. Not that I didn't make some very willing choices. I made a decision to leave a scholarship at the University of San Francisco and a childhood sweetheart for a chance at living the Bob Shane life. I wanted to be part of the next Kingston Trio.

I can't know whether We Five existed for some preordained reason. But it does seem that where and what we were, combined with what we did, was a complex synthesis of the sometimes unrelated motives and actions of not just five people who met, but a lot of others whose movements those five people represented. And if I were a hippie, I guess I'd call it a convergence.

Think about how much music and history spun from so compressed a beginning. The fact that my Catholic boy's school music teacher would go to New York to join the Cumberland Three with my friend's brother, John Stewart—and then, as Stewart left for the Kingston Trio, would play with the Serendipity Singers, the Highwaymen, and Harry Belafonte. Meanwhile

creating a fertile environment for his son, Tim Robbins, to become a success-
ful actor. That the Cumberland Three's Mike Settle would move on to the
New Christy Minstrels and the First Edition (before being replaced by Kin
Vassey, who would introduce me to his Back Porch Majority bandmate, my
great friend Tholow Chan). That We Five would begin in L.A. clubs like the
Troubadour with barely known groups like the Byrds, later to join them on a
Dick Clark tour playing for thousands, and that as both groups changed with
the trends, some members helping birth county rock, others updating R&B,
there would emerge the Mamas and the Papas, Spanky and Our Gang, the
Association, the Eagles, and Fleetwood Mac . . . all from the same seed that
was planted by Tom Dooley and the Kingston Trio.

Consider: Leadbelly begets Woody Guthrie who begets Pete Seeger who
begets the Weavers who beget the Kingston Trio who beget a wheel of styles
and directions: the Chad Mitchell Trio who beget both John Denver and
Roger McGuinn, who beget the Byrds, who beget the amplified Bob Dylan, a
breakthrough that spins off in myriad directions, while the basic Byrds sound is
perpetuated today by Tom Petty and a thousand other acts. The Beach Boys'
harmonics would spin off from folk music to meld rock and roll with the Four
Freshman and the Four Preps. The New York folk movement produces the
smooth folk sound of Journeymen, the relevance of Peter, Paul and Mary,
and the jug band/R&B-based Lovin' Spoonful. I can follow my own lineage
through the Journeymen, and the Modern Folk Quartet, to the pre–Mamas
and Papas' John Phillips and Scott McKenzie at the Eyes on the Stars session,
and to the Association, whose leader introduced us to Beverly Bivens, a senior
at Santa Ana High School.

The folk period in my life lasted about four years, the rocket ride for
about two years, the flameout for about two years more. And for better or
worse, because of the altitude we achieved, we fell forward for another ten
years before finally crashing down. I spoke recently about it on the phone with
Jerry Moss, cofounder of A&M Records, who rode to the top of the world
creating the largest independent record company in history, and then gave it
all up to raise race horses and win the Kentucky Derby. After all that, I feared
he might not remember me. His humility and clarity were refreshing as he
moved quickly from the blowback pitch that I should really see coming by
now ("Do you ever hear from Beverly?") to what touched me most: that he'd
been totally in touch with what was really happening, and how it was both
exciting and scary at the same time.

"We were just a small independent operation," he said, "trying to get
along and sell some records when suddenly *Taste of Honey* took off for the
Tijuana Brass at exactly the same time *You Were On My Mind* was selling.
Suddenly I had to make a decision to buy over one million records hoping I

could sell them over an eight-month period—and then they were all gone in six weeks!"

Indeed, the white-hot intensity of the Brass's and We Five's success in the summer of 1965 and early 1966 overwhelmed everything else at A&M, until they could bring in new managers in pursuit of the new music from England.

But the struggles We Five experienced during the next year, as we tried to make everybody happy while pleasing no one, had faded from his recollection by 2013. Our second album, Jerry Moss struggled to remember. And the third, try as he might—not a chance.

★ ★ ★

As folk-rock approaches its fifty-year anniversary, it's been gratifying to see that historical chroniclers from Alec Palao to NPR have rediscovered the grandeur and strange fate of Frank Werber's Trident Productions. That pre-psychedelic San Francisco experiment, people are slowly coming to recognize, marked a crucial, but uneven and often overlooked, tipping point in music history, one that may have failed to rule the world as Werber had hoped, but that certainly changed it.

There have been other happy recent developments to report. In 2009, Big Beat Records released *There Stands the Door: The Best of We Five*. And that same year, Beverly Bivens sang for the first time in forty years, at the opening of a San Francisco rock exhibit.

What makes me happiest nowadays is that I get to make music with all three of my kids—each a talented musician blending characteristics of both Debbie and me. Never taking a formal lesson, but being an intuitive observer, Chris became an excellent guitarist who has done several albums and moves in the company of people like Laurence Juber, playing acoustic finger-style guitar and searing electric with equal ease—all while pursuing a career in education, heading the art department at Glendora High School down the road from us.

Jeremy began playing guitar in family music circles with his grandpa Woody, but eventually took his parents' suggestion and got a degree, playing bass in both the symphony orchestra and jazz program at Cal State Long Beach while adding a double major in Business. As I write this, he's playing keyboards in a group following the new trend of signing to a major label (Capitol) for American distribution, while connecting with Canadian, British, and European labels for access to distribution and touring money outside the United States.

Jessica, the youngest, has many characteristics of her mother's voice, but with more comfort and flexibility in the upper register. She began miming Mariah Carey in grade school and writing songs on the piano in high school. One day in college, she asked about getting a guitar. We obliged, and within weeks she was writing songs on it.

★ ★ ★

Deciding what to do with the rest of my own life has required some taking stock. Without a Mike Stewart, I'm not one to read the tea leaves of my times and speak to millions of people. Moreover, I've learned that my years in the scene made it hard to make and keep real friends. So many artists marched to their own drummers, and fans were not friends, only fans. The whole journey also stunted my development as a father to my kids.

But clearing the table after all I've done and seen, I know there are still some songs to be written and songs to be sung.

Debbie is content to join in, too, so long as she doesn't have to take up the old life again.

★ ★ ★

Which is how I find myself standing in the corner of the Village Bookstore in Glendora, my hometown, debuting a one-man show called "Folk Songs and Stories" composed of slices of life about the music of the American past and why it mattered.

I sing little-known, far-left verses of "This Land Is Your Land," and watch the Republicans in the audience roll their eyes.

I sing "Party Doll," one foot behind the line of official innocence.

Offstage stands the bookstore owner, an aging flower girl with Emmylou Harris–style natural gray hair and cheery smile, serving cheese and wine.

With phantoms of Bob Dylan and Pete Seeger in my eyes, I think: "I can do this—and I should."

For no logical reason, a joke comes to mind that Mike used to tell on stage. It's the one about the guy who gives up everything, home, wife, job, and climbs a mountaintop in Nepal to ask a guru the meaning of life. "Life is like an orange," the guru tells him. And when the man protests (I gave up home! Wife! Job! And came to Nepal! And you tell me life is like an orange?), the guru is shaken. "Life . . . *isn't* like an orange?"

What a thing to remember, and yet somehow it seems to apply. Thank you, Mike.

Then an audience member calls out a request for "You Were On My Mind."

I consider the limitations of the room, the personnel. Finally I decide to comply by playing the old Sylvia Fricker version of the song. *Got some aches and/Got some pains and/Got some wounds to bind.*

One voice. One guitar.

Notes

CHAPTER 1—FORESHOCKS

1. This '50s folk group gave the world its first hit recording of "The Banana Boat Song." It was a traditional folk song the group created by combining two Jamaican tunes that were being sung in Greenwich Village by folksinger Bob Gibson. I loved their version, released in November of 1956, because of its rhythmic blending of vocals and acoustic guitars. It bothered me when it was eclipsed on the radio by "DayO!"—which Columbia pulled from a Harry Belafonte album called *Calypso* to take advantage of the song's success. Harry's version reached number 4 on the Billboard charts, and the album became the first LP to sell a million copies. (Only Bing Crosby's "White Christmas" and Tennessee Ernie Ford's "Sixteen Tons" had reached the same mark for singles.) It started the calypso craze, triggering numerous covers—including Stan Freberg's parody where a hip studio musician is offended by the singer's shouting. In addition to doing a pre–Kingston Trio recording of "Tom Dooley," the Tarriers were the first commercially successful group I ever recall seeing racially integrated (though I was too young and naïve to realize what it meant sociologically) with a black man, Bob Carey, performing alongside Erik Darling, Eric Weisberg, and Alan Arkin. Yes, that Alan Arkin. The Tarriers landed a scene in the movie *Calypso Heat Wave*, and he never looked back. Eric Weisberg, who took Erik Darling's place when he joined the Weavers, would later rise to prominence for playing "Dueling Banjos" in *Deliverance*.

2. The banjo had been modified to extend the neck by three frets like the one first invented by Pete Seeger to play more easily with guitars in the key of E. It was handed down to Michael when his brother John bought his first Vega long neck, the model then being popularized by Dave Guard in the Kingston Trio.

3. Based on an actual murder that took place in 1868, the song was first recorded on Victor way back in 1929 by Grayson and Whitter. It's a great example of how the folk process can migrate hand to hand, because Frank Warner, unaware of the 1929 recording, learned the song from Frank Proffitt in 1940 and passed it on to Alan Lomax, who published it in *Folk Song: USA*. The Tarriers recorded it in 1957, as did the Kingston

211

Trio, whose version sold more than six million copies and topped the U.S. Billboard Hot 100 chart in 1958. The Trio's record had only two chords, three verses, and a chorus. It is generally acknowledged as the song that triggered the commercial folk revival, and the recording has been inducted into the National Recording Registry of the Library of Congress and received a Grammy Hall of Fame Award.

4. High-fidelity recording began in Germany during World War II utilizing a Magnetophon, the pioneering reel-to-reel tape recorder developed in the 1930s, instead of traditional wire or discs. One thing this technology made possible was editing Hitler's speeches prior to broadcast. German radio also produced experimental stereo FM music broadcasts in Berlin around 1941. After John (Jack) Mullin investigated German recording technology for the Allied Forces at the end of the war, he introduced high-fidelity to the rest of the world. His work improved on the Magnetophon, and he created standards of performance still used in the recording industry today. Focusing on the film industry, Mullin gave a demonstration of his machine in Hollywood in 1947 in which live musicians played behind a curtain for a blind comparison. After hearing Mullin's recorded playback, many audio professionals could not tell the difference. Bing Crosby's technical director, Murdo MacKenzie, heard the demonstration and arranged for Mullin to meet Crosby. Bing had stopped doing live radio but realized that he could use the equipment not only to prerecord his radio shows with sound quality that matched live, but also to edit them precisely and replay them many times with no loss of quality. A test show was taped successfully, and Crosby became the first major music star to master commercial recordings on tape, as well as the first to use tape to prerecord radio broadcasts. Recognizing the importance of the technology, Crosby invested $50,000 in a local electronics firm to make the equipment. The Ampex Model 200 tape deck, developed from Mullin's modified Magnetophons, revolutionized radio broadcasting. When Crosby gave one of the first production models to musician Les Paul, it resulted in Paul's invention of multi-track recording. Still working with Mullin, Ampex went on to develop two-track stereo and then three-track recorders. "You Were On My Mind" was recorded on a three-track machine.

CHAPTER 4—THE FIRST TIME EVER

1. Doing overdubs (singing with yourself) worked fine for the Kingston Trio, because each member had his own track and it all blended nicely. If other instruments like drums and electric guitars had been played during the original recording, those sounds could "leak" into the room while overdubbing, sometimes blotting out the vocals. To solve the problem, engineers replaced the big playback speakers with headphones. That eliminated the leakage, but changed the way it felt to sing along. Later, when We Five began recording, it took me quite a while to get accustomed to hearing just my isolated voice.

2. Once, following a Fleetwood Mac concert, John Stewart approached Lindsey and observed that he had an unusual playing style for an electric guitarist in a rock band, almost like he was frailing, claw-hammer style, on a banjo. Lindsey was quick to

turn the remark around, telling John that, in fact, he owed his playing style to listening to Kingston Trio records and watching John play. Even the Beach Boys had begun their musical journey with an homage. They emulated the vocal creativity of the Four Freshman (while playing a surf beat) but took their approachability straight from the Kingston Trio—right down to the vertically striped shirts.

3. John Stewart was familiar with the true folk roots of the Almanac Singers and the Weavers. While he was in the Cumberland Three, they did a two-record concept album called *Civil War Almanac* that was comprised, one album each, of folk songs from above and below the Mason-Dixon line. His itinerant research into the way people thought at a grassroots level was the perfect foundation for his "Quiet Fight" campaign where, following Pete Seeger's example, he went from school to school doing folk music assemblies during the day while traveling with the Trio and performing concerts at night.

CHAPTER 5—IF YOU'RE GOING TO SAN FRANCISCO

1. Following our lip-synch performance of the song "Small World" on the Bob Hope show, the guitarist from the live orchestra approached Bob Jones (who'd been playing along perfectly) and asked if he knew we were doing the song in 5/4 time. When told that we'd done that by design, the musician was surprised that a bunch of kids could grasp the concept, let alone play and perform it so well.

CHAPTER 6—CONVERGENCE

1. 2007 Grammy nomination for Best Historical Album: *Love Is the Song We Sing: San Francisco Nuggets 1965–1970*, various artists, Alec Palao, compilation producer. 2010 Grammy nomination for Best Historical Album: *Where the Action Is: Los Angeles Nuggets 1965–1968*, various artists, Alec Palao, compilation co-producer. 2011 Grammy nomination for Best Album Notes on the box set, *The Music City Story: Street Corner Doo Wop, Raw R&B and Soulful Sounds from Berkeley, California 1950–75* (Ace), various artists, Alec Palao, writer.

2. The Yodeling Brakeman from Meridian, Mississippi, was born in 1897 and recorded some of the classic songs that became the foundation of modern country music before he died of tuberculosis in 1933. My uncle Gene gave me a copy of the album *Train Whistle Blues* when he saw me learning guitar, because the record store owner told him Jimmie was a classic folksinger. Thinking it was the same Rodgers who did "Honeycomb" (which I'd really liked), I was most disappointed to discover something very different indeed. The record included "T for Texas," "Mississippi Delta Blues," "My Little Old Home Down in New Orleans," "Hobo Bill's Last Ride," and "I'm in the Jailhouse Now." My dad was quick to make fun of hillbilly singers, so I'd had no exposure to this classic American music—but I recognized there was something unique about it and kept the record. It was simple but sincere—and not

the least bit hokey when you understood his background. After trying to play guitar a few times with Debbie's dad, and being unable to follow where the chord changes went, I pulled out the Jimmie Rodgers album and discovered that Woody's playing and singing flawlessly matched the style and intonation of the originals—right down to the dropped beats.

CHAPTER 7—WHEN I WOKE UP THIS MORNING

1. Now called the Sentinel Building, it is home to Francis Ford Coppola's Zoetrope Studios, whose website states that it was built in 1906 and survived the San Francisco earthquake. In later years the building went through a variety of transformations, from its initial heyday as a restaurant in the early 1900s, to a speakeasy in the 1920s, to the *hungry i* nightclub (where the infamous Lenny Bruce performed standup) in the 1950s, to a recording studio for the Kingston Trio in the '60s, and finally a recording studio/ screening room for American Zoetrope Studios in the early '70s. Naturally, Francis added his own signature to the building's long history: all of Martin Sheen's narration for the movie *Apocalypse Now* was recorded in the basement of this quirky landmark space.

2. The editing block and razor blade were standard items in every studio I ever entered until digital took over. Along with cutting out sections to modify the actual song recordings, it was also used to cut the final takes from the reel of unused material, and to put color-coded blank leaders at the beginnings and ends of songs. The block was often strapped right to the top of the recording machine for easy editing. A box of razor blades and an assortment of editing adhesive tape were always nearby to ensure clean cuts with sharp edges. You can't really hear the splice in "You Were On My Mind," but they're very often audible in records from that era if you listen for them. One that catches my ear every time it's played comes near the end of "Monday, Monday" after the tacet (musical terminology for "silent" or "do not play"). It appears that, unlike "You Were On My Mind," the Mamas and the Papas used an early take for the bulk of the song, with an ending tacked on from much later. When the voices come back in, the tempo suddenly slows and the singers' voices are slightly lower. I've often suspected that a splice was responsible for a similar drop in tempo that's audible near the end of "Michelle" on the Beatles' *Rubber Soul* album. Another botched splice tripped up the intro to "I Saw Her Standing There" on its American release. George Martin had retained Paul's full count-off ("1-2-3-4") for extra energy on the British release, but when it appeared as the American flip side to "I Want to Hold Your Hand," the record company lost the first three counts and left the fourth.

CHAPTER 8—AWE AND SHOCK

1. In his book *Turn! Turn! Turn!* (Backbeat, 2002), Richie Unterberger quotes Frank Werber as follows: "Some of the drum licks, and that solo guitar pick thing, I think, that ends it, were added post-recording by me, with their tacit approval." I'm not sure who got confused, but the incident as quoted did not happen. The scream-

ing guitar solo ending had been clearly visualized in advance by Bob Jones and is well described in this book. Jerry Granelli recognized the opportunity to help drive the message home and added the bass drum under Bob's line as he played it live. What Frank did add after the fact—and *without* our approval—were the six chords in the first verse played by Rex Larsen on a Rickenbacker.

2. Decades later I became friends with a local named Taylor Ingebretson, who told me our visit was a marker event in a very small town. He became a proto-flower child in Eureka—and literal florist—immortalized forty-five years later by the indie band the Wackers on Elektra Records in their song "White House."

CHAPTER 11—THE LONELY CROWD

1. Marianne Faithfull with David Dalton, *Faithfull: An Autobiography* (Boston: Little, Brown, 1994).

2. Debbie Reynolds, among other investors, lost money on the Scopitone idea. There either wasn't enough of a playlist, or there weren't enough bars and restaurants willing to spend the installation cost.

CHAPTER 14—THE SORCERER'S APPRENTICE

1. Peter Fimrite, "Frank Werber—Charismatic Music Agent, Entrepreneur," *San Francisco Chronicle*, June 8, 2007, B7.

CHAPTER 18—FUNERAL FOR A FRIEND

1. On July 24, 2013, at the same moment that I was typing up my description of Beverly's goodbye, my cell phone buzzed with a text message from a Facebook friend and longtime We Five fan. "Dear Jerry," it began. "My condolences on the passing of Bob Jones." Bob died on July 22, 2013, of an infection that followed successful surgery, chemotherapy, and radiation related to pancreatic cancer. His friends and family gathered for a "Celebration of Life and Music" in the house his grandfather built in Wailuku, on Maui. The program inscription reads, "E lei kau, e lei ho'oilo i ke aloha," which means "Love is worn like a wreath through the summers and the winters. Love is everlasting."

Acknowledgments

$\mathscr{P}$eople had been telling me for years to write this book while I could still remember the details—though at least one less enthusiastically said, "Must you?" Since the story could not be told without my wife, Debbie, special thanks go to her for not objecting, and eventually providing some very sharp and valued insights that breathed love into the book.

Knowing that a journalist's eye would be important, I brought the idea to Dr. James Willis, a friend, writer, and chair of the Journalism Department at Azusa Pacific University. Too busy for direct participation, he affirmed the concept and suggested I meet with fiction writer and journalist Alan Rifkin to discuss it. Alan's uncanny understanding of the song "You Were On My Mind" triggered his curiosity, but there was also an immediate personal connection. After reading what I had begun to write, he agreed to join me in the project, taking responsibility for what I considered to be the heavy lifting: massaging my memory downloads into a readable narrative that cast my story in the context of seventy million boomers coming of age in the most interesting of times.

Armed with a story to tell, along with Bennett Graff's recognition of its value as a sociological record, and Alec Palao's expertise as a music historian intimately familiar with Frank Werber's Trident experiment, we forged ahead, drawing highlights from A&M alums Jerry Moss, Joe Gannon, George Yanok, Don Graham, and Bob Garcia. But the heart of the story isn't really about events as much as it is the highs and lows of life everyone encounters. For that I must acknowledge the generous and often intimately painful memories shared by Kate Stewart, Jamie Stewart, Bob Jones, Pete Fullerton, Beverly Bivens, Donah Jones, Alice Hofer, Penny Chambers, and Chala Werber.

While this memoir is a personal reflection, some sources enhanced my understanding of the history I'd lived through in ways I did not expect. I lost days just reading. Robert Cantwell's *When We Were Good: The Folk Revival* (Harvard University Press, 1996) provides a well-considered and scholarly look at how the folk process, which had pretty much worked in an unchanged way for millennia, took on a new dynamic when back-porch performers met mass marketing and socially conscientious material became the basis for a major new music economy. His analysis helped solidify my thoughts on the changing world that Pete Seeger bequeathed to Frank Werber and my own generation. The Museum of Magnetic Sound Recording website (http://museumofmagneticsoundrecording.org/Links.html) reached the geek in me as I followed click after click to the disparate paths that recording technology took, from Edison's adventures in sound to the use of high-fidelity tape recordings of Hitler's voice over the radio to reach the masses, to the utilization of that refined technology by performers like Bing Crosby and Les Paul to achieve commercial success unimaginable without it. *Temples of Sound: Inside the Great Recording Studios*, by William Clark, Jim Cogan, and Quincy Jones (Chronicle Books, 2003), delved into the symbiosis of musical creativity, engineering imagination, and right place/right time positioning that thrived during the time when I was beginning my journey. Aligning my experiences at Capitol Records with their research helped me visualize what life was like in some of the other great studios of the time. William J. Bush's *Greenback Dollar: The Incredible Rise of the Kingston Trio* (Scarecrow, 2013) revived my memory of folk music at the moment when all the potential and diversity of the prior years reached critical mass in the form of a group of collegiate party boys who struck a nerve with the postwar generation, as Americans who'd learned to sing folk songs with Pete Seeger and Woody Guthrie began making their own music and utilizing every aspect of the recording and broadcast technology at their disposal to follow wherever the muse led them—from folk to pop to country to rock and beyond.

Life doesn't happen in a vacuum, and throughout this project I have been helped along by my amazing children, Chris, Jeremy, and Jessica, and by my siblings, the late Louise Burgan, Kathy Burgan Adams, Mary Kay Burgan, and Jeff Burgan. In addition, I have been blessed to have friends with no agenda beyond lending emotional support while I worked to get it all down. Some, like Kevin Forstner, Jack Miller, and Fred Heilbrun, went to school with Mike Stewart and me more than fifty years ago. (He was Mike when I met him, Michael later in life, and you'll see both names throughout the book.) Others I'm bound to by shared musical lineage, like Fred Thompson, Terry Kirkman, Barry McGuire, Bob Stane, PC Fields, and Karl Anderson. Still others like Mike Vaughn, David Gibbons, Terry Roland, and Hans Reifer inspired me by their writing.

I am also indebted to friends met at the intersection of music and faith: Joe and Mary Krake, Terrel and Muriel Berry, Tom and Elaine Stricklin, Jimmy and Robin Dunn, Shane and Sonia Schupbach, Dave and Pam Cone, Louima Lilite, and Vicki Taylor.

Support takes many forms, and writing this book was really driven by fans, but two couples stand out. My sister-in-law, Carol Nelson Graf (no relation to Bennett), was coming to see the Ridgerunners while I was still in high school and knew about me long before we actually met through Debbie's brother, Gary, whom she stood with at my wedding and later married. Along with Tom and Karen Tancredi, they have provided unconditional support for my musical endeavors throughout my adult life, not to mention trudging to some infamous destinations for no apparent reason beyond finding new joy in hearing us play material they know at least as well as I. God bless them.

Because the book is told in the context of my experiences as a member of We Five during the brief period when folk music morphed into rock, it doesn't dwell much on the remarkable musician friends I had the good fortune to record and work with over the years. What a band!

Michael Stewart	Ray Scantlin
Bob Jones	Terry Rangno
Beverly Bivens	Dennis Wood
Pete Fullerton	Michael Lewis
John Chambers	Tholow Chan
Frank Denson	Ron Schwartz
Rich Tilles	Rico Lozano
Mick Gillespie	Paul Foti
Jimmy Dunn	Glenn Nashida
Steve Kidda	Tom Murray
Chris Burgan	Jeremy Burgan
Jessica Burgan	

Finally I must end where this book begins: with Sylvia Tyson. Had she not heard the muse and written down her first song, my life, and this story, would have been very different.

—Jerry Burgan

★ ★ ★

This whole book belongs to Jerry Burgan, whose knowledge and photographic recall are a treasure that music history should keep mining until he's too exhausted to say more. In our smoothest moments, Jerry tilted his head back and riffed while I typed. But when it came to the sound of "You Were On My Mind" and what it felt like to hear it in 1965, I'm afraid I almost didn't let him talk.

Janet Duckworth, Christopher Ward, Claudia Bryan, and Sally Dworsky read the manuscript in draft and offered invaluable comments. Kristina Munn listened to early chapters out loud and was the first to be moved by the parallel destinies of Jerry and his friend Michael Stewart. Ed Maxin, Fred Miller, Karen Schwenkmeyer, Patrick Emmett, Steve Howard, and Ann Howard helped locate the story's hook. Jim Willis introduced Jerry to me having no idea that We Five's recording of Sylvia Tyson's song had been a mystical lifeline in my youth. My students at California State University, Long Beach, wrestle beside me with the mysteries of writing, and Nathan, Ben, and Abby give me the love and perspective to remember daily what's at stake in any story. Fifty years after the birth of folk-rock, if asked what their father has been writing about, they sing the song.

—Alan Rifkin

Index

About the Authors

William J. Burgan—known professionally as Jerry—is a musician, singer, songwriter, and musical director who has produced numerous albums, commercials, and corporate shows in the entertainment industry as co-founder and current leader of We Five, the folk-rock group whose recordings of "You Were On My Mind," "Let's Get Together," and "Cast Your Fate to the Wind" sent them to the top of the pop record charts in the mid-1960s.

During a twenty-year hiatus from the road to raise a family, he also found success developing and marketing dietary supplements and over-the-counter medications for the pharmaceutical industry.

When not performing with We Five, Jerry also teaches guitar, banjo, and ukulele; leads his church music program; and makes solo appearances as a guest speaker—telling stories of his career and performing a selection of the songs that shaped him musically. With his wife, Debbie—who also sings lead in We Five—he has three children and lives in the Southern California community of Glendora.

Alan Rifkin has been short-listed for both the PEN Center USA Award in Journalism and the Southern California Booksellers Award in Fiction. Of his fiction collection *Signal Hill* (City Lights), the *Los Angeles Times* wrote, "Hauntingly beautiful—the work of a gifted storyteller with a sharp eye but a tender heart," and *Kirkus Reviews* wrote, "Rifkin is what might have happened had Nathanael West lived on and been even more talented—exquisite." A veteran contributor to such publications as *Details*, *L.A. Weekly*, *Premiere*, the *Los Angeles Times Magazine, Black Clock*, and the *Quarterly*, he has taught magazine writing, short story, and creative nonfiction at Santa Monica College, UCLA Extension, Chapman University, and California State University, Long Beach. He is active in the homeless ministry at St. Luke's Episcopal Church in Long Beach and is the father of three children.